What people are saying about
Prisoners of the Paradigm...

"This book is a tremendous effort, well researched, coming from the heart and brain of many years of educational experience. I see this as an essential reading for all school board members across the country. An intelligent set of answers for any school board member or employee of a district who wants to truly have educational reform happen in their community and for their children. Every school district in this country should have copies enough for all the school board members, superintendents, assistant superintendents, principals, and teacher leaders."

**Nelson Thomas, Teacher and
Educational Association Leader**

"Dr. Alan Hafer's book is a significant work for school administration. It should be read by every school board member and administrator in the country."

**Sandy Christie, School District
Business Manager**

"This book reflects the reasons I selected Alan Hafer as an administrator for the first time. He (and his writing) are child centered. He really cares about all children and their ability to learn."

**Ralph Schuster, Retired Career
School Administrator**

"*Prisoners* is about the delicate relationship between the lay board and professional educator . . . a relationship that is delicately balanced only when each knows the other's responsibility. Hafer's book explores that relationship with sensitivity, and with great insight about what it means to students and education in general."

**Audrey M. Cotherman, Ed.D.,
Assistant Director-University of Wisconsin
Comprehensive Center**

PRISONERS
OF THE
PARADIGM

What School Board Members, Legislators,
and Community Leaders
Must Know to
Reform American Public Education

ALAN HAFER

FalCo Books
Boulder, CO 80302

First printing 2000

ISBN 0-9677754-4-2

LCCN 99-97754

ATTENTION CORPORATIONS, UNIVERSITIES, COLLEGES, AND PROFES-SIONAL ORGANIZATIONS: Quantity discounts are available on bulk purchases of this book for educational purposes. Special books or book excerpts can also be created to fit specific needs. For information, please contact FalCo Books, P.O. Box 21355, Boulder, CO 80308-4355, ph 303-499-8629.

Contents

Preface vii

Introduction ix

1 Time to Change 1

2 What Is Isn't and What Isn't Is 7

3 What Is It You Really Want, Anyway? 21

4 Why We Must Believe All Children Can Learn 39

5 The Paradigm in Action:
    Why Don't All Children Learn? 47

6 The Pyramid Cannot Stand Upside Down 61

7 The Cycle 71

8 Money, Equity, and Learning: Educators' Shame 91

9 Be Prepared for Your Day in Court 117

10 Superintendent Employment and First-Year Care . . 131

11 The Board Member Primer 137

12 Rules of Boardsmanship 159

13 Shared Purpose and Not Autocracy:
Empowerment and Not Democracy 167

14 End Note: Ethics and School Leadership 179

Appendices 185
References 199
Bibliography 208
Index 219

Preface

I believe that all of our children can learn. I believe that the adults in schools control the conditions of schooling. I believe that with the creation of proper conditions the overwhelming majority of America's children can achieve at the same academic levels as those students we presently consider our very brightest. I believe that the mission of public schooling is to teach all of our children and to teach them well.

The fulfillment of this mission is the responsibility of the citizens elected to school boards. Enough has been discovered about the science of the arts of teaching and learning to make this quest a reality. There are conditions of schooling that foster learning by all children and there are conditions that do not. There are practices in American schools that enable all children to learn, there are practices that harm many children, and there are practices that do neither.

We now know better than to use harmful practices and we no longer have time to be ineffective. Board leadership must be effective. This is what separates service on a school board from service in any other public office. Although many public agencies need to do what is political, school boards, when it comes to teaching and learning, must do what fosters student learning. Serving on a board of education in the future will demand courage, dedication, and perseverance. No longer may board members do only what is popular; they must do those things that create appropriate conditions for successful learning.

Our system has never before been asked to teach all children. Many school districts are not prepared to meet this burden. Many citizens and educators do not even believe that it is possible. If public education is to survive in the form we currently know, board members must lead school districts to effectiveness. In order to save public schooling, they must change it; in order to transform it, they must be willing to see what it can be and forget what they think it has been. Public education has never been what we remember, but it can become what we think it should have been.

This book is intended as a guide for board members, citizens, and community leaders to use in the fulfillment of this mission. To be successful, leaders are even going to have to change the way they perceive phenomena. If you wait to believe that the successful learning of all children is possible until after you see it, you never will. You will see it only after you believe it.

Board members need to begin acting as if the future of our society and nation, along with the ability of our future citizens to enjoy an affluent life, depends on our work today. We no longer have time to wait.

Introduction

Every day the sun rises over the snow-capped mountains to the east, casting long shadows across the valley floor; it sets over the mountains to the west as their shadows mimic those of the dawn. Every day during the school year, children hurry off to school, just like they do every place else in America. Most parents believe their schools are pretty good. "After all," they say, "our football team had a winning season and for the fourth year in a row, one of our math teachers won a national award—and there is great community support; parents just helped build a new playground for an elementary school."

The high school's dramatic arts department has a wonderful reputation; extremely talented young actors and actresses practice their stagecraft under the watchful eyes of a special teacher, a genius who produces polished thespians. A group of parents working with the business community has just raised enough money to replace the high school basketball floor, hoping that new wood might improve the recent losing record. Another group of parents is planning to meet with school board members to convince them to implement an International Baccalaureate program in the high school. The baccalaureate is a well-known course of study founded on world-class standards. "A world-class district," the parents and several teachers argue, "needs a world-class curriculum." Even without this program, however, some of the community's children are very successful and go on to attend the finest of colleges and universities.

The district has one of the highest salary schedules in the state and teachers claim to be satisfied with working conditions. They also know that they have what may be the entire country's best retirement program and that their negotiated Master Contract is the envy of all other teachers associations in the region. At the high school level, teachers hold a great deal of decision-making power. In fact, a group of department heads was commissioned years ago to operate the school, and the principal was relegated to the role of coordinator.

The district appears to be a great place. Well-behaved children, satisfied teachers, pleased parents—how could there ever be anything wrong with the system? What is wrong is that the district has a drop-out rate of more than twenty percent, the highest in the entire state—exacerbated by the fact that there are very few minorities or extremely poor people living in the district. Dropping out of school is not only condoned by the district, it appears to be supported and even mandated. The Board of Education has an official policy known as academic probation, which decrees that secondary students who fail two classes in one semester must drop out of school for a semester before re-enrolling. Students who fail three classes in one semester must drop out for an entire year. The state does not fund the education of students over nineteen, and the district will not enroll them if they reach that age before the start of the school year. There is almost no way a young person forced to sit out of school for a year can graduate.

There is an alternative school in the district that purports to signify the district's commitment to troubled youth. Perhaps! Students who are failing regular high school and would like to attend are placed on a waiting list until the teachers in the school, acting independently of the rest of the district, admit them. There are no written policies—attendance and dates of admittance are left completely to the staff. Of course, if students are out too long they probably will not graduate because of the age-nineteen rule.

The school appears to operate successfully. Students are very polite and a visitor is immediately struck by the quiet, the almost complete absence of whispering among the students, and very little talking by the teachers to their students. Pupils pick up their packets of "independent, individualized" work from teachers, return to their desks, and work hard at their assignments. Enrollees know there are very real benefits to attending the alternative school. They are allowed to step out the back door and smoke whenever the urge hits and attendance is never taken. Students graduate when they complete the required number of packets. Those who are allowed into the program usually do graduate, if they can finish their packets before they are too old to attend school. The district's very high drop-out rate does not include students in the alternative school.

Like the alternative schools in many districts, this one is held in disrepute by the teachers in the regular high school who profess that they would not be caught dead teaching in such a place because of the low level of expectations. Everyone knows, the rumor goes, that the alternative students could not pass any kind of academic exit exams—if they were required. Adolescents do not attend the school to learn academics; they are there to learn about life so that they can go out into the real world armed with a diploma.

Actually the alternative school is just one end of a continuum of academic groups for junior and senior high school students. These schools group students into advanced, honors, regular, and basic classes. Although there is some flexibility, one notices that the students in one basic class are in basic classes all day—the advanced and honors students rarely leave their groups. Different curricula with differing expectations are taught to each group—but they all receive the same diploma. This appears to be correct according to community leaders. The local newspaper, in an editorial, used the phrase "blatant banality" about the slogan all children can learn.

The district has a high tax rate due to the willingness of voters to approve high yearly mill levies caused, in part, by the state legislature's unwillingness to fund education. Each year the percentage of state funding declines and more state dollars are replaced with local taxes. On the positive side for most educators and school supporters, the state also makes very few demands on districts—accountability is something that is talked about in other places. This is a state in which the local boards are supposed to be in control. However, in this district, the building level administrators and a few powerful teachers, irrespective of their own union, have been able to capture control. The board, always elected by organized educators, usually serves as a rubber stamp—teachers and administrators have a good deal.

The Master Contract provides such complete protection that it is doubtful any educator will ever be dismissed. The last time the board tried to release a nontenured teacher the proceedings did not work out well for the district; he was out of work for a year before the board rehired him as a result of the grievance process—and awarded him back pay for the year he did not work. The board took him back because it had not followed all of the dates in the contract's time line and administrators could not prove that the teacher was offered the highest minimal level of assistance as called for by the same document.

The retirement plan is one of the most lucrative in the nation and pays off after thirty years of teaching or administration in any district in the state as long as the last one is in this district. Amazingly, the community is unaware of the advantages of the plan. Not only do citizens not know how well the plan pays, board members have completed entire terms without being told. It is a lucrative secret that helps keep administrators and teachers satisfied.

Is this good enough? Athletic teams win, the smartest students go on to great colleges and universities, the plays are always good, and students from the sixth to the twelfth grade can play in an orchestra as well as a band. Parents help elementary schools build new playgrounds and the activities of children and their teachers are covered in the local newspaper. The issue of "good enough" in this district holds all the nuances of the major issues facing American public schooling. Is it good enough for the brightest and most scholarly to do well in school and go on to attend prestigious universities while twenty-five percent drop out of school? Is satisfaction of the community the ultimate measure of schooling? If a district has satisfied, noncomplaining, well-paid teachers and administrators, does the system qualify as great?

In another school district, similar to this one, except that it is larger and the mountains are taller, a portion of the superintendent's evaluation is based on a survey of the staff. The board conducts this data gathering completely in the open—everybody knows that the superintendent needs to receive high marks from those who work in the system. In the previously discussed district, the board does the same thing, only not in a formal fashion; members just ask employees they know personally.

Both boards are concerned about whether the staff is happy or not, so the extent of their satisfaction is noted in the leader's evaluation. If the old adage that what gets measured gets done is true, the superintendent's priority becomes one of keeping the staff satisfied. In the same philosophy of giving people what they want, some states and school districts allow charter school parents and teachers to initiate the type of schooling they believe is best. These schools range from back to the basics bastions of fundamentalism to complete-child directed places with little structure. The concept seems to be that whatever a group of parents and a couple of teachers can design must be as good as or better than the schools established by mainstream educators and school board members.

Several years ago America's oldest living teacher (she had passed the century mark) was asked what made great teachers. She replied that some people are born to teach, some people should be born but never teach, and some people should never be born at all. Was she right? Is good teaching nothing more than the right blend of genes? Is it true that if parents set up schools for their children and hire only those people born to teach, all our children will learn?

Trying to find only those people with the correct genes, especially the ones that will allow them to be successful in certain types of schools, is a difficult task. For instance, one teacher in a district offered the opinion that it was time some of the parents in that district realized their kids were swimming around in the shallow end of the gene pool. In the same relatively affluent district, one teacher held in high standing voiced the opinion that her students could not score as well on standardized assessments as inner-city youth because although urban children needed good scores to escape the ghettos, her kids just wanted to stay in the area and enjoy life. Would teachers with such attitudes be considered born to teach?

The question of what is good enough in assessing the performance of our system of public schooling is perplexing. Many school districts, like the first one described, are hosted by seemingly satisfied communities because some students do well academically, some excel in the arts, and some assemble into athletic teams and beat the team from down the road in football. Some students excel in all three areas while many others do well in none. As long as the philosophy of the community is that all students cannot (and should not be expected to) perform well academically, there probably will be a great deal of public satisfaction with the system.

The trend toward charter schools and satisfaction-based evaluation of the superintendent is formalizing the concept that satisfaction should be the primary measure of school effectiveness. For years, satisfaction has been the chief standard for profitability for private businesses. People purchase cars, television sets, toasters, and golf clubs based on their own satisfaction and reports of satisfied customers by the company's marketing department. Satisfaction in the private arena is based on a combination of cost, performance, and utility. We do not expect the same performance from a $15,000 automobile as from one that costs $40,000, but we sure expect it to be comparable with or better than others in the same price range. No one would be satisfied with a two-seat sports car if a vehicle was needed to haul large, heavy rocks; again, we supposedly will turn to the model that offers the best performance in the same price range.

In our system of public schooling, however, customer satisfaction may not be the best measure of production—or of excellence. Many might judge that a school district with a satisfied voting group that has a twenty-five percent drop-out rate is not good enough, let alone excellent. We might guess that a district that decided to raise money for athletics by not purchasing computers and preparing its students for a technological world—to the delight of the voting community—might not be considered good enough.

School board members are asked many difficult questions and face a myriad of complex issues to work through. Are good teachers born or made? Is direct democracy the answer to all our educational woes? What do school board members do to build an excellent district? And what are the characteristics of excellence that should be sought? What causes learning? What level of achievement should be expected of most of our children? What type of relationship should there be between board members and the professional staff? Fortunately, we now have answers to many questions including how to evaluate schools for effectiveness, how to set up programs and schools that cause learning, and how to effectively manage a school district. There is a body of knowledge to lend science to the arts of teaching and learning. Some practices and programs work better than others and some found in almost every school district in America may do more harm than good.

There is a great difference of opinion about the answers to all of these questions. Our nation's future and the future of our children depend on the leaders of our schools answering those questions.

CHAPTER ONE

Time to Change

*We can, whenever and wherever we choose, successfully teach
all children whose schooling is of interest to us. We already
know more than we need to do that. Whether or not we do it
must finally depend on how we feel about the fact that we
haven't so far.*[1]

We will never again be the way we have been. What we have done,
we cannot do anymore; what we thought we were, we cannot be any
longer. In truth, we have never been what we thought we were and we
have never done what we thought we did. Many of our fondest memories pervade our thoughts in the same way as do those of an old man
remembering his life: As each year passes, the girls of his youth grow
prettier, and in his memories, the young man he once was grows braver
and stronger.

The problems that plague public education are among the most
discussed issues of our time. For many people, solutions are simple.
Schools should be more businesslike and educators should be more accountable and spend less money. Almost every person who has ever
attended school has an opinion—and will give it freely. Unfortunately,
most people's perceptions are based on what has never been. Myth provides an unlikely foundation for problem resolution; we have never been
what we remember we were.

For many who have labored in the rocky fields of public education,
the end of what has been is not a new beginning; it is just the end. Few
know how to cope with the contempt of critics; fewer still can envision

a bright future. Many educators struggle against the inevitable, holding on embittered until they can quietly retire. Others plead with school board members to legislate against the future, as though they could build a dike to keep out the sea of change. Educators have become extremely defensive as they listen to the incessant public criticism of their work trumpeted in the media. They are resistant to almost any change, especially since much of it is predicated on the belief that what has gone on before, what they have done in the past, has been wrong and even harmful to children.

Change is always hard. Educational change is traumatic. In private enterprise when products do not sell, companies retool. When necessary, prices are slashed until all inventory is sold. The company continues to make money. No one is harmed except those who lose their jobs. Life goes on. But teachers who accept that what they have done was wrong have to accept guilt for hundreds of lives. Even if we say they did the best they knew how at the time and we just know more today, we still pass judgment and imply that they may have harmed those they wanted to help. We can replace cars and television sets; lives are a different matter.

Our education problems are compounded by the management design of school districts. Influenced by an unshakable belief in grass roots democracy, Americans have always thought that private citizens could operate anything better than bureaucrats; consequently, local control of the schools was invented. The United States is divided into more than 14,000 school districts, ranging in size from huge organizations with thousands of employees to one-teacher schools miles from the nearest town. All the districts are governed by trustees who campaigned on a platform of wanting the best education possible for children. Unfortunately, few of them have any real idea how to achieve that end.

Every board hires certified educators to manage its schools and to teach the community's children; board members and employees usually believe their administrators and teachers are doing an excellent job. However, most of those in the schools do not believe school board members know anything about education. Therefore, the best way to improve the schools, people with certificates believe, is to leave the teachers alone to do what they do. However, a growing number of people believe the concept of governing boards should be abandoned altogether.

This belief is commonly expressed in columns such as the one that appeared in the *Denver Post* under the headline "Standard Idiocy in Jeffco" (Jefferson County, Colorado). The writer began by quoting Mark Twain: "In the first place God made Idiots. That was for Practice. Then He made school boards." The columnist ended the paragraph by writing, "Take the Jeffco board—please."[2]

Millions of pages and thousands of books and articles are published every year about the problems with our educational system, but few are directed at school boards. Those in charge have been left out of the loop; they are usually not studied as part of the problem and are never seen as part of the solution. While academicians ignore board members, many district employees would say that school boards need to be either abolished or, at the least, recalled. (And then replaced with their slate of candidates.) Citizens will usually echo that idea, accompanying their statement with demands that teachers and administrators work harder and for less money.

To trust a school board is to have faith in democracy. The notion of educating children in schools directed, managed, and financed by local communities is still in the experimental stage. Questioning whether a school board can operate institutions as large, as sophisticated, and as important as most modern school districts is the same as asking if people can really govern themselves. Education for all, by definition, must exist in an atmosphere of total equality and nondiscrimination; but many people still have doubts about the human ability to behave in such an altruistic fashion.

At the end of the twentieth century, for the first time, we have a body of knowledge about education and have developed a science of the arts of teaching and learning. We have made great strides in understanding how children learn and how to create conditions that maximize learning. Yet the only qualification for service on a school board is the ability to favorably influence a significant portion of the electorate, often by promising to throw out the malfeasant scoundrels who have been operating the schools. When an intention to clean house is combined with promises to cut costs, candidates are often unbeatable.

Genuine political power is not within most people's grasp. Few of us can work directly against the president or a governor, for example. Many of us remonstrate about the lavishness of Congress, but can do little to change the situation. We wisecrack about highway crews leaning on shovels, but all we can do is joke. School systems are different. Those who get elected gain enough power to make a difference; election to a school board is participation in the political process closest to the people. School districts are governments over which small groups can exercise control because few people vote and fewer still are informed about the election. Elections are generally about personalities; educational employees often control the outcome.

American public education has been criticized from the day the first school opened. Today, although the rhetoric is louder and the sense of urgency greater, denouncements remain the same. In fact, very little about public education has changed, including teaching and school management. Children are still caged in box-like rooms listening to teachers talk and are still sent to the office for disruptive behavior; only the clothes of the disciplinarians and the punishments have changed. Teachers have too many students, too few of whom are serious about learning and too many of whom drop out. Few students do homework. Perhaps the only significant educational change in the past fifty years has been that schools have become far more dangerous places.

Economic and political realities have transformed the world so completely that public education must change—or disappear. Three forces controlling our time mandate educational effectiveness:

1. In a global economy based on technology and information, the intellectual sophistication of the workforce has become a force of arms.

2. Dreams that children will live better and enjoy a good life are endemic in parents. For the first time, education is a path that must be followed to find that life.

3. The graying of America is real; the ratio of economic producers to retired citizens is growing smaller. Future economic prosperity depends on increased productivity and knowledge is the key to production.

Every student must be educated. As the ratio of producers to nonproducers continues to decline, it is not acceptable for 25 percent of our future workers to drop out of school while many others simply do not learn enough to become producers. One need only look around to

4

know fundamental changes must occur. In the past, public education has only taught those students who cared to learn. Schools have never been charged with educating all students. Those mentally inclined to succeed academically do; the rest quit. Americans have never believed all students could learn or cared when they did not. One purpose of schooling has been to cull those stamped unsatisfactory; only the most able have been taught.

A coalition of school employees and uninformed community members have propagated a noneducating, nonaccountable system with a denial of responsibility for learning serving as its foundation. American public education needs direction, a sense of urgency, and responsible leadership focused on the lessons we have learned about managing schools and teaching pupils.

School board members must take charge. Their first task is to learn how school districts as management organizations should function. The second is to hire school leaders who understand teaching and learning as well as the management of knowledge organizations. Third, they must ensure that districts follow the best research-based educational practices and then let their knowledgeable professionals work. Although education is neither a hard nor an exact science, there is enough evidence of what should be done to point schools in the right direction.

Time is of the essence. As days and years pass while we discuss, debate, and delay, the current system harms more children; harms them not because educators do not work hard enough but because the past has shaped a system that prevents the academic learning of all children.

CHAPTER TWO

What Is Isn't and What Isn't Is

A paradigm is a set of rules and regulations (written or unwritten) that does two things: (1) it establishes or defines boundaries; and (2) it tells you how to behave inside the boundaries to be successful.[1]

Whether you have been elected to a school board, are interested in what goes on in schools, or work in one, American public schools need your help. By trying to understand how to make schools more effective, you are starting a journey without an accurate map. To find a route, you may have to put aside many cherished beliefs. You may even have to change your patterns of thinking.

In this land of smoke and mirrors nothing is as it seems. What is isn't and what isn't is. Thinking about schooling is like answering the following riddle: What do you sleep on, sit on, and brush your teeth with? To get the right answer, ask a kindergarten student; usually no one over the age of nine ever answers it correctly. (The answer is found on the bottom of the last page of this chapter.) After you think about it for a while, analyze your attempt to formulate an answer. Perhaps you thought of a solution like *your hand.* Perhaps you are tried to identify some new instrument that can do all three activities. Give up? The answer is three different things. You couldn't come up with a solution because in your paradigm a riddle should have only one answer, not three.

We view everything from within a set of boundaries that defines our behavior. Education's paradigm is omnipresent. Everyone, especially most educators, views schooling within boundaries, according to rules set hundreds of years ago. There is an unwritten induction ceremony through which people connected with schools pass, certifying that forever all will remain the same. Educational tradition is so strong that research cannot change it; heretics who try soon feel the heat from a modern inquisition.

An axiom of a paradigm is that once inside you cannot feel its embrace. You cannot see the walls, but they box in thinking as securely as a penitentiary restricts the physical movements of convicts. Paradigm surrounds everything; we are able to view phenomena only through our perception. What we think is more important than what we see. We filter everything through what we know. One way to identify the boundaries of a paradigm is by listening to the phrases, slogans, and catchwords of the inhabitants. If you listen carefully when people discuss education, you will probably hear the following comments: "That won't work." "We already tried that." "That is not the way we do things here." "All this theory is great, but give us something practical to use in our classrooms." "All I really want to do is to be left alone to teach." "I learned how to teach when I was in college. What do I need to go to an inservice for?" "You can use research to prove anything you want." "Why do we have to change? What's wrong with what we have been doing?" "How am I going to add this new curriculum to what I already have been teaching?" "You can't measure (i.e., test) what I teach."

The list is endless. Education consists of rings of concentric paradigms, intermingling and overlapping, combining into one huge, change-resistant, mind-imprisoning system.

Consider a small city district in a rural area containing 3,000 students, most of whom have nothing in common with their contemporaries brutalized by life in inner-city America. The brightest and best in this district matriculate at colleges around the world; the alumni boast two U.S. senators, scores of political leaders, doctors, lawyers, and even some genuine Indian chiefs. After graduation, the next lower echelon attend local colleges, work in businesses, and remain in the community. Of the least academically successful, 20 percent drop out of school, most of them sentenced to a life of menial tasks.

Community leaders are happy with the sorting and selecting process that separates intellectuals from laborers. In their opinion, creating an intellectually founded caste system is an essential function of schooling. A proposal to form a system in which all children learn the required outcomes of instruction is seen as an attempt to subvert the fundamental order; it is an impossible quest—an unnecessary and unnatural change.

These perceptions have been sustained with little regard for predictions that the succeeding century will not be charitable to those with neither skills nor advanced education. Dropouts, if such forecasts come true, will be condemned to falling wages and declining lifestyles. Gloomy economic forecasts are easily understood in the context of a global economy in which goods can be manufactured in third world countries and shipped to American consumers. These are predictions that every person who has children, works in a school, or serves on a school board should heed; they may be the most prophetic remarks of the end of the twentieth century—and the beginning of the new one.

> The effective supply of unskilled workers has expanded enormously. As a consequence, wages must fall for the unskilled who live in rich countries. Quite simply, supply and demand require it. In a global economy a worker has two things to offer—skills or the willingness to work for low wages. Since products can be built anywhere, the unskilled who live in rich societies must work for the wages of the equally unskilled who live in poor societies. If they won't work for such wages, unskilled jobs simply move to poor countries.[2]

Community leaders seem to embrace this future, viewing education of children as a parable of life in the jungle: The strongest and most fit will survive. Life is not fair, they say. Some children inevitably will learn and grow economically strong; others will fail and become servants to their masters.

Although the educational class system was defended by most educators in the district we are considering, either because of apathy or the mind-numbing effects of the paradigm, administrators decided that it was no longer acceptable. They set out to build a system in which all students would meet high academic standards and there would be no failures. Working with a few enlightened teachers and a sense of urgency, they determined to accomplish five goals:

1. Raise expectations for the successful education of all students.

2. Ensure that each child was ready for kindergarten through a readiness program for preschool children.

3. End the elementary school cycle of failure by creating nongraded elementary schools.

4. Drastically reduce the high nonattendance rate.

5. Abolish the 15 to 20 percent dropout rate.

The small band understood that change had to be systemic and revolutionary; the system could not be fixed by tinkering. An early child care center congruent with school experiences needed to be established for those children whose parents, either because of work schedules or lifestyle, could not adequately prepare them for kindergarten. Elementary schools, the group decided, would drop the arbitrary classification of children into grades based on age and would teach them according to their developmental stage rather than where the system decided they should be. At the secondary level, teaching was to be transformed from lecturing to mentoring and facilitating; a belief in high expectations for the success of all students was to become contagious. A culture was to be created that denounced dropping out as unacceptable.

The group knew it had to proceed carefully, beginning slowly so conservative elements of the community were not completely overwhelmed. Those involved decided the first step was to modify the existing high school class schedule of seven forty-nine-minute periods. Energized by the exhortation, "If we keep doing what we've been doing, we will keep getting what we've been getting," they petitioned the Board of Education to sanction a four-period schedule. Students, according to the plan, would take four ninety-minute classes each day, completing one year's study in a semester and a semester in nine weeks.

The request, which was made publicly to the board, paraphrased Albert Shanker, president of the American Federation of Teachers. Imagine, they told their audience, that you were just hired to begin a new job. When you arrive on your first day, a director meets and guides you to a room occupied by twenty-five other workers. Someone from management spends thirty minutes explaining in a monotone what you are to do. He or she allocates twenty minutes for you to work, cautioning you that speaking with a coworker may result in dismissal. You must raise your hand for permission to discuss problems with a supervisor. When you do, you are told to figure it for yourself.

At the end of fifty minutes a bell rings and you are herded into another room in which there are twenty-five different employees and another manager. New duties unrelated to what you labored over earlier are assigned. After another thirty minutes of explanation, you have twenty minutes to work. Again, you may not talk to anyone and must raise your hand if you have a question.

At the conclusion of fifty minutes, the bell rings again. You shuffle off to yet another room filled with people you have never seen, work on assignments that have no relationship to what you have been doing, and you are not to converse with your colleagues. You do this five more times during the day and are allowed to speak only at lunch or in the rest room.

If you do not understand how to do the task at the conclusion of a period, you will not receive additional instruction. When it is time to change tasks, all do so at the same time. Poor work will be reflected in your evaluation.

Most adults would not endure one day. A company that operated in this manner would not stay in business; it could not compete. Few employees would master intricate chores while controlled by this organization. There is no supervisory responsibility over the completed product. But this is the way Americans assume high school students learn. The model worked fairly well for industrial assembly lines. It has never worked for teaching.

The educators making the presentation wanted to forge a place where teachers and students worked together with time allowed for thought and reflection. They believed it was paramount to decrease the number of classes held each day, resulting in less stress and giving students an opportunity to concentrate more specifically on work assigned by fewer teachers. Teachers, they thought, could be more effective with fewer students. By teaching three classes in a four-period schedule, instead of six in a seven-period schedule, the teachers' student load would be reduced by half. Students would have homework from only three classes instead of six and would have more time in class to work cooperatively.

The first year's results were incredible. The drop-out-rate fell dramatically. Grades rose in almost every class; students earned more As and Bs and fewer Ds and Fs. A preponderance of teachers favored the new schedule, reporting improved relationships with pupils and enhanced student effort. Most teachers believed pupils learned more, especially those traditionally at-risk. Morale of students and teachers grew higher than ever before. Mean scores on standardized tests increased an average of 5 to 7 percent.

From its inception, the strategy and accompanying rationale was assaulted by a coalition of community members and elementary school teachers who alleged students would no longer learn academic content. Emotionally overwrought, they wailed that this was an untested experiment in which their children were being used as guinea pigs. Some parents threatened to send children to school in neighboring towns; others prophesied that the number of home school students would increase dramatically.

Because the town's largest employer, a branch of an international corporation, transferred staff every three years, company officials and employees angrily charged that their children would be unable to transfer in or out of the school. Again, lack of knowledge was fundamental. They believed all other high schools in America offered the same classes on the same seven-period schedule. High school students in the eleventh grade in Louisiana, they reasoned, should be able to transfer into their school and study American history on the same page of a standard book.

During the second year of the new schedule, emotional appeals dwindled. Most parents and students reported they liked the plan. But just when all seemed to be going well, rumors began to circulate through the community like wildfires through forests. "Teachers have never had it so easy," many said. "High school teachers have quit teaching; the new schedule doesn't work but teachers won't complain. They would have to go back to work," other townspeople exclaimed. "Teachers have lost all expectations for excellence on the part of students. Our kids won't be able to go to college" was a belief that distressed many. "Students don't do any homework; it's all done in class" was an interesting charge leveled by others. "Test scores will fall and colleges won't admit our kid" more began to believe. "This schedule is just another fad like new math." Most believed it would fade after their children's education was ruined.

Issuing a comprehensive report documenting the success of the new schedule neither changed perceptions nor stopped rumors; it was the agent that caused the cancer of fear to spread. Misconceptions and prevarication were brought into the open where they increased in number and consequence. The report validated all criticisms because the paradigm can rationalize anything. "Sure the teachers love it. Everyone already knows they quit teaching and are letting the kids do what they want." "The teachers know the kids don't do their homework, but why would they say anything? If they did, the school would have to go back to the old schedule and the teachers would have to go back to work." "Of course more students are staying in school. They don't have to do anything and they can still graduate. Besides, those students should not be in school, anyway. Everyone knows that they are just lowering our standards." "This schedule is dumbing down our curriculum. Some of those kids shouldn't be able to pass. They should fail."

Studies and subsequent reports by administration and faculty had little credibility, even though the positive effect of the four-period schedule had been researched and reported nationwide. Research and logic do not penetrate the paradigm's walls. Most animadversions were fabricated and sown in fertile fields of distrust by a conspiracy of the oldest and most traditional teachers who knew that real high schools have seven class periods. Students, everyone knew, were supposed to listen in class and complete their assignments at home. Knowledge to be acquired, they believed, should be broken into bite-sized pieces and spoon-fed to freshly washed students sitting in straight rows.

True believers found welcome followers. Former students of all ages knew what schools should be like because sometime in the past they attended one. Comments from America's past were thrown around relentlessly. "It's the way it is—some students do well while others fail. What's this business of trying to have them all pass?" "Superior grades by most students can only be the result of rampant grade inflation." "Homework is to be piled on nightly. With this new schedule they're working on it in school and not taking it home." People believed real high schools were characterized by jostling, crowding youngsters moving frequently and rapidly from class to class; they could see schooling only through the vision-enhancing, corrective lenses of the paradigm's optometrists.

The new high school schedule met with such criticism that nongraded elementary schools were never attempted. The muttering in the community about that idea was just too widespread. Although absences and dropout rates in the high school fell, the new program fell far short of the goal of creating the systemic change in which all children succeeded because little was done to adjust the schooling of elementary children. They were still going to arrive at the middle school as unprepared products of assembly line education.

Lamentably, the democratically controlled American school system is dedicated to the survival of the paradigm, which explains why many modifications introduced in schools are contemptuously remembered as gimmicks and fads and are never permitted to take root and blossom into systemic improvement. As soon as alterations become visible, traditionalists mobilize to eradicate them. If there is no latitude for change, there can be no improvement. Americans know what school should be like. It should be as they remember it was when they were young, not like it really was.

Every time significant systemic change is contemplated, a coalition of those in the profession and those who once attended school hurls the weight of democracy against it. One of the great enigmas of our time is that although many Americans complain about public education, few will allow it to improve. Most remember halcyon days that never were.

Changes not embraced by the paradigm seldom survive the next school board election. The story of one school district's bid to change senior assessment for graduation is archetypal of the futility of struggling against the paradigm. It is also an example of a phenomenon of paradigms that may exist only in schools. Public education has evolved so obtusely that the paradigm of paradigms must be altered to understand the forces preventing change in schooling. Because paradigms filter out new ideas, change is normally proposed by people outside the system who do not wear the blinders of tradition and will not accept as truth what practitioners say is impossible.

In education even the paradigm of paradigms is wrong: Usually only a small number of people working within the system understand the changes that need to occur. The forces of reaction consist of a combination of those who once went to school and do not understand education and those who work in schools, still do not understand education, and do not want to change.

The school leaders who proposed the changes in the district asked the question we all ponder: What should a high school senior know and be able to do in order to graduate and how do we know they know

14

it and can do it? In response to their questions, they rewrote the graduation requirements as tests of knowledge and skills and insisted that seniors pass them to qualify for graduation. But graduation requirements within the paradigm are based on sitting and not on learning; negative polemics became histrionics. Intellectual discussions of the meaning of graduation were replaced by ardent pleadings for a return to what had been. "Go back," citizens demanded, "to real schooling." Scores of residents packed meetings to urge the board to restore the graduation requirements to what they had always been and the way it was supposed to be.

Residents, knowing what school was ordained to be, used ballot boxes to preserve the status quo. Graduation requisites and outcomes education became the focal points of the next election. Candidates inside the paradigm crushed incumbents who had shown the courage to venture outside the boundaries. Standards-based education was rescinded, tradition was re-established, and agents of change were vanquished.

In America, the custom of students sitting in class, taking paper and pencil tests, and performing at minimal levels has become sacrosanct. Requiring students to exhibit evidence of learning is assailed as preposterous. Measuring the thickness of the callous on the posterior from sitting through classes remains the primary tool for the assessment of learning.

The belief that schools should always be as they once were locks education into absurdity. What about the charge that schools are not what they once were? According to Diane Ravitch, a historian of education, the decline of publican education has been going on for a long time.

> The public schools sustained yet another blow when the College Board revealed in 1975 that scores on the Scholastic Aptitude Test (SAT), taken each year by more than a million high school seniors, had declined steadily since 1964. More than any other single factor, the public's concern abut the score declines touched off loud calls for instruction in "the basics" of reading, writing and arithmetic.[3]

Lower test scores are representative of the total learning of a student and not just the result of one year of study. If tests taken by high school seniors began falling in 1964, it is evident that the parents and grandparents of today's children did not do so well in school either. Those who suggest we return to practices of the past fail to realize those practices did not work.

The decline in test scores announced in the mid-1970s shocked the nation; condemnations increased in fury until the National Commission on Excellence in Education announced in 1983 that "the educational foundations of our society are presently being eroded by a rising tide of mediocrity that threatens our very future as a Nation and a people."[4] For some reason, the fact that more than half of earlier generations of young Americans in this century opted not to complete high school was never mentioned. Public education has never successfully educated all the students who arrived at schoolhouse doors. Yet we continue to remember a past that never was.

Is there a solution? Can education change? The answer is yes, presuming that representative democracy is viable and that we care enough to cause it to happen. Because school boards command education they must serve as the catalysts of change. Without board leadership based on knowledge rather than myth, public education will remain mired in a search for a past that never was.

Pro active school board members need to understand what their critics are saying. John E. Chubb and Terry M. Moe, writing in *Politics, Markets, and America's Schools*, propose removing schools from the control of lay boards and from the political process. They lead the reader to assume that responsible board leadership is an oxymoron. Bruce Maclaury, president of the Brookings Institution, wrote in the foreword that the authors "argue that government has not solved the education problem because government is the problem."[5] Elected representatives of the people cannot, they believe, improve education because their election is the root of the problem.

The condemnation is not of school boards as entities, but of the influence of the democratic process that empowers them.

While we too would like to be optimistic about the prospects for better schools, we think the reforms adopted thus far are destined to fail. Our reason, when all is said and done, is that they simply do not get at the underlying causes of the problem—which have little to do, at least directly, with graduation requirements or teacher certification or any of the other obvious characteristics of schools and their personnel that have so occupied reformers. It is our view that the most fundamental causes are far less obvious, given the way schools are commonly understood, and far less susceptible to change. They are, in fact, the very institutions that are supposed to be solving the problem: the institutions of direct democratic control.[6]

Chubb and Moe see the system as dominated by a fortified, resolute bureaucracy subordinate to the vagaries of political decision making. School districts cannot improve instruction for that would mean doing what is right—instead of what is politically necessary. Bureaucrats work to maintain their standard of living while school board members first think of how to be reelected or how to make sure their faction stays in control; unions exist to ensure their own survival. The situation is the same on state and national levels; persuasive agents are merely larger and more powerful. Enormous sums are spent to sway legislators. Statutes that affect education are political, influenced more by the efforts of lobbyists than the needs of children.

The truth is undeniable. Proof can be found in every school in America. Board members and legislators need to listen to teachers and administrators gossip and complain. Most can relate a myriad of anecdotes chronicling the trespass of politics into teaching and learning. Faculty room conversations often describe the audacity of political machinations and the frequency of political settlements to dilemmas that affect schooling.

Politics are so prevalent in schools that the true measure of a decision is whether it survives the next board election. Superintendents are judged competent if they survive the popular vote. Because they are the only educators who never gain tenure, most make decisions that will allow them to remain employed. Head football coaches have a chance. They are retained or terminated around their record; superintendents are fired by political antagonists, as teachers might be if tenure did not protect them from small town politics, even in big cities.

The general public is not even the most powerful group that influences public schooling. Educators are constituents of powerful associations (unions) that lobby at national and state levels and extend networks of control into local politics.

The most powerful political groups by far are those with vested interests in the current institutional system: teacher's unions and myriad associations of principals, school boards, superintendents, administrators, and professionals—not to mention education schools, book publishers, testing services, and many other beneficiaries of the institutional status quo.

These groups are opposed to institutional change, or at least any such change that is truly fundamental. Current arrangements put them in charge of the system, and their jobs, revenues, and economic security depend on keeping the basic governance structure pretty much as it is. They do struggle among themselves for power. Most obviously, teachers, as the perennial bureaucratic underlings, are constantly striving to enhance their authority and status.[7]

The quest for power has divided educators into warring camps. Teachers have always denounced school boards and administrators for scurrilous behavior, accusing them of making arbitrary and capricious decisions with neither teacher participation nor input. Listening to teacher rhetoric, one would think school districts maintain personnel procedures first written by the robber barons of the nineteenth century. Administrators and board members counter that teachers work for three reasons: June, July, and August. The problem with teachers, they say, is that they are only part-time workers. According to angry teachers, administrators don't work at all. Unfortunately, the general public has listened to, and believed, both sides.

Public education is controlled by those who amass the greatest number of votes. Our children's schooling is directed on national and state levels by partisan politics and politicians. We may believe in local control, but Washington, D.C., is home to the major players. Influencing those who make decisions about education is big business. Within several years of the publication of the *Nation at Risk* report in 1983, six major educational organizations built multimillion-dollar national headquarters in and around the nation's capital.[8]

Just as national groups attempt to control education through lobbying and membership networks, special interest and employee groups attempt to influence local boards at every step. Groups that are on the losing side in any major decision, at any level, usually mount organized opposition campaigns at the next election. Behind it all, controlling, directing, and emotionalizing in displays of anger, tears, and anguish is the power of the paradigm. It is strong enough to deny logic and to eradicate knowledge.

Political machinations pervade public education. Some Americans even assume the possible existence of a gigantic conspiracy involving virtually every public school administrator and board member. Fear of computerized demographic information collected by schools combined with a cataclysmic governmental transformation leads to the warning that "schools will, in fact, be able to help government inflict a kind of computerized slavery on every man, woman, and child in America."[9]

Only members of school boards can change the paradigm that paralyzes schools. They must learn enough to understand that public education is about teaching and learning and that the efficient and effective operation of a school district is possible. Boards of education must support learning instead of politics; they need to take leadership in their communities to smash the power of the paradigm.

If school boards cannot help Americans understand how school systems should work, if they do not make decisions that enhance learning and teaching, public education will continue to flounder. Board members need to begin by asking and finding the answer to two old quandaries. What should students learn before they graduate from high school and how do we know they learned it?

(Answer: A bed, a chair, and a toothbrush.)

CHAPTER THREE

What Is It You Really Want, Anyway?

We are convinced, that you mean to do us Good by your Proposal; and we thank you heartily. But you, who are wise must know that different Nations have different Conceptions of things and you will therefore not take it amiss, if our Ideas of this kind of Education happen not to be the same as yours. We have had some Experience of it. Several of our young People were formerly brought up at the Colleges of the Northern Provinces: they were instructed in all your Sciences; but, when they came back to us, they were bad Runners, ignorant of every means of living in the wood...neither fit for Hunters, Warriors, nor Counselors, they were totally good for nothing.[1]

Several years ago an outwardly innocent small story appeared in newspapers across the country. Parents in a small Midwestern town angrily demanded that the Board of Education implement a weight-training program in the curricula of the high school because they were tired of the manhandling their young athletes regularly received on the football field. The board members responded quickly to public opinion and weight training became an authorized course.

The October 5, 1994, issue of *Education Week* proclaimed that a program for Massachusetts high schools was among ten winners of the Ford Foundation's annual competition for innovative state and local government initiatives.

21

The Student Conflict Resolution Experts program was established by Attorney General Scott Harshbarger of Massachusetts to train students to defuse violent or potentially violent disputes. Launched as a pilot project in two schools, it has expanded to 20 schools in 10 cities.[2]

The same issue carried an article about school districts adopting policies to protect the rights of homosexual students. "Anti-harassment policies," according to the paper, "are often followed by calls for changes in the curriculum."[3]

Public schooling, criticized since its origination, has been under intensified attack since the National Commission on Excellence in Education compared the system with foreign sabotage: "If an unfriendly foreign power had attempted to impose on America the mediocre educational performance that exists today, we might well have viewed it as an act of war."[4] Accusations of an inept nationwide system are raised because of perennial low scores on standardized examinations (no matter what the scores are, the perception exists that they are not high enough) and dismal performances on tests that show American students are consistently outscored by pupils in other countries. Unfortunately, neither weight lifting, violence diffusion skills, nor classes in the rights of homosexuals are appraised by these assessments.

American curricula are laden with anti drug programs, sex education courses, and classes about healthy lifestyles and vocational pursuits, none of which are considered by developers of norm-referenced tests. Classes in driver's education, shopping, marital relationships, welding, and cooking in microwave ovens are found in most secondary schools. But none of these courses count if the standard for which schools are held responsible is a product of academic testing.

The ultimate dilemma in American public education, the genesis of all others, is simply that no one really knows what schooling is supposed to accomplish. It is not just a question of what content should be taught. The issue is much broader. Americans have not yet decided for what purpose public education exists and until purpose is agreed on, correcting the system remains impossible. Without an agreed-on end there can be no measure of success; there can be no progress because there is no goal.

The inability to allot a specific purpose to schooling is a relatively recent phenomenon. Native North American cultures were marvelous examples of the original purpose of education. Through songs and sto-ries, elders taught tribal history, religion, culture, customs, beliefs, fears, and hopes. When they taught their progeny how to track deer, grow corn, catch salmon, and drive buffalo over cliffs, they were teaching them to be productive citizens. They assured the continuance of their culture by molding its future members. Primitive residents of ancient Europe educated their offspring in the same manner. Through immer-sion in local culture, children grew into productive members of society who, in turn, would transfer learning to future generations.

Difficulty in determining the purpose of schooling seems to have grown along with civilization. As mankind became more enlightened, the purpose of learning became more obtuse. Issues predominant in modern American public education were first identified thousands of years ago and have continued throughout history. Controversies that surfaced in Grecian city-states have never been answered; contentions endure to this day. Successive civilizations carried on while discovering new areas of disagreement; newly identified dilemmas have just been added to previous quarrels. Most of the issues that create controversy today created it before. The criticisms of education that consume our energy and time have been devouring educators' energy and time for centuries.

Today, we are plagued by the questions raised by earlier societies while we accept none of their answers. Is the purpose of schooling to transmit culture and traditions to the young, forming them into pro-ductive and patriotic citizens? Should schools teach only academic knowledge without influencing values? Is the answer a combination? Should we teach knowledge and values? Do schools exist merely to pro-vide workers for our nation's economy? Is the purpose of education a combination of all of these or is it something else? Why do we do what we do? Why do we teach children what is taught in schools?

Somewhere in the answers to these questions is the solution to an-other puzzle. Were antiwar protesters during the Vietnam War products of a good or a poor education? If schools are to create loyal citizens invested with a belief that their country is always right, then educators surely failed. If schools exist to teach independent thought, analysis, and free will, teachers across America were wonderfully successful.

Throughout the ages, purpose in schooling has been as varied as cultures and teachers. The original professional educators, Sophists, were

23

peripatetic teachers with a utilitarian curricula. Harbingers of those who believe education is to provide grist for economic mills, they instructed their charges how to prosper in Grecian economics and society. Socrates, the first of the famous Greek pedagogues, believed that a true education cultivated principled citizens and held moral excellence to be superior to technical or vocational training. Using the power of education to shape the future by molding the young was his ultimate goal.[5] He believed education was for the development of thought, not knowledge.[6] Unfortunately, Socrates was put to death for corrupting youth as well as for impiety to the Gods, charges that may sound familiar to many modern educators.

Plato identified one of the purposes of education that still characterizes schooling in modern America. He believed in a cerebral and scholarly education tasked to sort and select students into three groups: The most erudite were to become philosopher kings; those of strong will (instead of intellect) would serve as warriors; the least able would be workers. He postulated that because children learn most of their parents' prejudices and vices, they should be raised in state nurseries.

Aristotle labored to create schools in which teachers would have expert knowledge and be skilled in its transmission.

> Like most of the Greek theorists, Aristotle made a distinction between liberal education and vocational training. Aristotle saw the liberal arts as a liberating factor, enlarging and expanding one's choices. Occupational and vocational training in trade, commerce, and farming were servile pursuits that interfered with intellectual pursuits.[7]

By this time, most of the arguments about the purpose of education had been clarified. Ancient Greeks pondered whether education should be vocational or academic; some perceived it a mechanism for sorting and selecting, others as an agency to mold citizens for society. Although we do not force people with contradictory ideas to drink poison, arguments over these issues continue to arouse great passion.

Perhaps none of the issues is more debated today than Plato's belief that students should be separated by ability and provided differentiated curricula.

> But the democratic promise of equal educational opportunity, half fulfilled, is worse than a promise broken. It is an ideal be-

24

trayed. Equality of educational opportunity is not, in fact, provided if it means no more than taking all the children into the public schools for the same number of hours, days, and years. If once there they are divided into the sheep and the goats, into those destined solely for toil and those destined for economic and political leadership and for quality of life. . . Schooling must have for all a quality that can be best defined, positively, by saying that it must be general and liberal; and negatively, by saying that it must be non-specialized and non-vocational.[8]

Many Americans, however, persist in the belief that sorting and selecting is a necessary part of schooling. Phyllis Schlafly of the American Eagle Forum warns that if we do not segregate students into groups from the most to the least able, every student's education will suffer.

Rather than enabling children to reach their full intellectual potential as individuals, outcome-based education, as an egalitarian process, holds the entire class to the same level of learning. When every child is required to attain the same outcomes, the outcomes must be dumbed down to a level everyone can master.[9]

The controversy over the efficacy of vocational instruction is also still raging. It seems predestined to become a dominant political issue as America enters the next century.

Among all the changes that will sweep our schools in the 1990s, none is more inevitable than the coming renaissance of job training as an alternative to the standard high-school curriculum. Ten years from now, any state that has not built a modern vocational-educational program will be scrambling to catch up with its more foresighted neighbors.[10]

The author of a widely read book with a current school reform project based on his work made an equally good case when he wrote that job training is not a part of education literacy; in fact, he claimed it does not make students ready for the modern world of work: "a practical drawback of such narrow training is that it does not prepare anyone for technological change."[11]

The paradigm of education uses all of the contradictions of divergent educational philosophies to its advantage. The belief that the system is not working and the consequent persistent arguments about purpose

maintains the status quo. As long as there is no agreement about purpose, everything must stay the same.

The notion that education should mold children for the perpetua-
tion of culture has dominated thinking about the purpose of education
for centuries. The "common school" in France, the Netherlands, and
the United States "was to be a society-shaping institution, the most
powerful possible means of forming the attitudes, loyalties, and beliefs
of the next generation."[12] Thus, formal schooling in America did not
begin with the confusion over purpose that characterizes the modern
era. Puritans were eager to have their children learn to read in order to
search the Bible for God's word. The opening of the famous *New England Primer* sent a very strong message to young readers: "Heaven to
find, The Bible mind." Surely, "In Adam's Fall, We Sinned all" has a
more powerful message than "See Spot jump."

Early Americans wanted to use public education to produce residents of high moral character who would support their society and
institutions. Massachusetts established the Board of Education in 1837
for the governance of common, or elementary, schools. Horace Mann,
appointed secretary of the Board in 1838, wanted to better the human
condition.

> Our school system is designed to promote the development and
> growth of the understanding, to cultivate upright and exemplary
> habits and manners, to quicken the vision of conscience in its
> discrimination between right and wrong, and to inculcate the
> perfect morality of the gospel; while it reverently forbears to
> prescribe by law, the belief which men shall profess respecting
> their Maker.[13]

The United States of Horace Mann's time was a sparsely inhabited
magnet for Europeans who desired a fresh start and a better life. Immigrants were pouring into the country as the foundations of our
educational system were being laid. One utilitarian purpose, along with
creating improved conditions for all men as desired by Mann, was the
Americanization and assimilation of people who came from other places,
invested with a diversity of beliefs, customs, and traditions. Residents
of Massachusetts and other states looked around and saw their way of
life threatened by an un-American mob. A system of
government-controlled public education was needed to teach loyalty

to the new American way. Foreigners descending on American shores needed to be assimilated into the mainstream. The mayor of Boston noted a purpose of schooling:

> By education and moral means, to place our free institutions on such a basis that those who come after us, the descendants both of the foreign and American citizens may be free and independent.[14]

As the purpose of education became one of shaping citizens, another problem that plagues our modern system could be identified. Distrust of public education and the motives of school boards troubled even Mann's administration. One group called for the abandonment of the Massachusetts Board of Education because it was afraid too much power had been placed into the hands of a few.

> The majority of our Committee do not specify a single instance, so far as we can recollect, in which the Board of Education have attempted to control, or in any way to interfere with, the rights of towns or school districts. They seem to be in great fear of imaginary evils; but are not able to produce a single fact to justify their apprehensions. It is the alleged tendencies of the Board, to which they object. There is a possibility, they think, of its doing wrong; of its usurping powers which would endanger freedom of thought.[15]

America's system of public schooling is difficult to change because its problems are ancient. They have been with us, growing in intensity, since the opening of the first schoolhouse door. Little is new! Poorly disciplined children and problems caused by parents who would not cooperate with teachers troubled even Massachusetts common schools.

Defining the purpose of education became considerably harder when courts approved tax levies for the support of secondary schools late in the nineteenth century. No longer was education focused only on elementary school children. High schools were constructed, and young Americans gradually began to attend them. At the turn of the century about 10 percent of those eligible were in school; 50 percent attended by 1930 and 93 percent by 1980.[16] The population tripled between 1870 and 1940, while the aggregate of secondary school students increased from 80,000 to 7,000,000—almost ninety times.[17]

Once again the arrival of large numbers of unassimilated immigrants and their struggle to raise the socioeconomic standing of their children impacted schools. The influx of students from foreign cultures and divergent socioeconomic strata ignited the great educational debate that rages today. The spark was provided by the question, What should be taught to these great numbers of youngsters? All of a sudden (when juxtaposed against the long history of education) schools were expected to enroll and educate everyone who showed up at the door.

Public education had never before been expected to provide secondary schooling for everyone who wished to attend. The schools, unprepared for this role, were asked to do something that had never been attempted before. In retrospect, they were unsuccessful; most of the Americans who fought in the Second World War were not high school graduates. In the 1940s, for every 1,000 children who entered fifth grade only 455 graduated from high school and only 160 of those entered college.[18]

The low commencement rate was certainly not because Americans had not spent time and energy analyzing reasons for holding school. In 1893, the National Education Association assembled the Committee of Ten to arrange an appropriate course of study for secondary students. Their philosophy was characterized by the belief that a man who digs a ditch should be able to quote Shakespeare and hum Mozart; according to their reasoning, all pupils ought to be academically prepared regardless of whether they went on to college.

Every subject which is taught at all in a secondary school should be taught in the same way and to the same extent to every pupil so long as he pursues it, no matter what the possible destination of the pupil may be, or at what point his education is to cease.[19]

Endorsing four years of high school and four different curricula known as Classical, Latin-Scientific, Modern Language, and English, the committee prescribed subjects in Latin, Greek, English, German, French, Spanish, algebra, geometry, trigonometry, astronomy, meteorology, botany, zoology, physiology, geology, physical geography, physics, chemistry, and history.[20] The course was set for American children to receive an academic education through the study of recognized disciplines. Of course since seventy-six of the one hundred who worked on

28

the report were either college presidents, college professors, or head-masters of private schools, collegiate domination should have been expected.[21]

Twenty-five years later, the metamorphosis of the National Education Association seemed complete with its publication of the Cardinal Principles of Secondary Education. The principles (what schooling should consist of) were (1) Health, (2) Command of Fundamental Processes, (3) Worthy Home Membership, (4) Vocation, (5) Citizenship, (6) Worthy Use of Leisure, and (7) Ethical Character.[22] The association's principles became synonymous with progressive education. "Its writers fought educational elitism, sought to discredit older notions of discipline and training 'faculties of the mind,' and rallied around the new field of educational science."[23]

Progressive education, an early-twentieth-century educational development, repudiated by the public almost since its inception, spread rapidly before the Second World War. Its disciples held the teaching of conventional subjects in low regard. The purpose of education, they proselytized, was to prepare young people for a successful life; therefore, rigidly structured academics were unnecessary. The influence of progressives remains so strong today that we must understand them to make any sense of modern practices. An explanation of what progressive educators rejected describes what many people believe is still discarded by modern teachers and administrators:

> Among the features of traditional schooling that progressive education rejected were: the belief that the primary purpose of the school was to improve intellectual functioning; emphasis on the cultural heritage and on learning derived from books; the teaching of the traditional subjects (like history, English, science, and mathematics) as such; the teaching of content dictated by the internal logic of the material; adherence to a daily schedule with specific subject matter allotted specific periods of time; evaluation of the school program by tests of the mastery of subject matter; competition among students for grades and other extrinsic rewards; traditional policies of promotion and failure; reliance on textbooks; the use of rote memorization or drill as a teaching method; the domination of the classroom by the teacher, either as a source of planning or as a disciplinarian; corporal punishment.[24]

Progressive practices swept the country, accumulating staunch advocates such as those in Hackensack, New Jersey, who reported with satisfaction that they had triumphantly reduced enrollment in college preparatory courses by a large percentage.[25]

From 1925 to 1957 (the year Sputnik was launched), many educators embraced a philosophy that was anti-academic and directed toward teaching for life, a movement expressed in extreme with the founding of contemporary vocational education. The famed Prosser Resolution, volunteered at a conference facilitated by the U.S. Office of Education, set the program on its way.

> It is the belief of this conference that, with the aid of this report in final form, the vocational school of a community will be able better to prepare 20 percent of the youth of secondary school age for entrance on desirable skilled occupations; and that the high school will continue to prepare another 20 percent for entrance to college. We do not believe that the remaining 60 percent of our youth of secondary school age will receive the life adjustment training they need to which they are entitled as American citizens—unless and until the administrators of public education with the assistance of the vocational education leaders formulate a similar program for the group.[26]

Thus, American educators announced that they were not up to the chore of providing an academic education for all who entered high school. In fact, they saw no purpose in the quest for a high-level academic education. Almost sixty percent of young people needed neither preparation for college nor sustained vocational education. They needed life adjustment education, which meant that...

> ...far greater attention be given than in the past to the development of ideals, interests, attitudes, understandings, concepts, and habits rather than to the relatively exclusive monopoly of attention by the acquisition of information, certain to be ephemeral with respect to retention and of limited utility in making life adjustment.[27]

Young people needed guidance and learning about citizenship, home and family life, use of leisure, health, tools of learning, work experience, and occupational adjustment.

The objective of American education, in the perception of its leaders, was skewed overwhelmingly toward life skills and occupations. Academic subject matter was held in little regard by many licensed educators who could find no justification for courses of study based on irrelevant topics such as math, science, history, and literature. Present-day comments about the sad state of education are similar to the invectives hurled at the system after the war. Educators, in the public's notion, were (and are) misguided social reformers involved in a conspiracy dedicated to subverting the nation by failing to educate its youth.

Contemporary public education is adrift in a sea of confusion without a prevailing philosophy. Determination of the purpose of education is relegated to independent school districts where most decisions are made by pragmatic board members for political reasons. Most pedagogical routines are copied from those developed centuries ago. Teaching has changed very little since the first teacher began talking to students. Like their predecessors from the Great Depression, many teachers still insist that most children cannot successfully conclude an academic course of study.

Louder than ever before, with the drum-beating of the media and politicians seeking publicity opportunities, today's public schools are censured for the failure of students to master academic subjects. This is merely the paradigm's insidious ability to conjure up a time when education was successful, when all children learned to read, write, cipher, and know everything about science, history, literature, geography, and everything else—a time when all children learned and grew into healthy and wise adults. The great tragedy is that those halcyon days never existed.

Americans shall never be satisfied with, or gain dominion over, public education until its mission is known. A series of organizational axioms is pertinent to this predicament: "What gets measured gets done." "What gets evaluated gets done." "What gets rewarded gets done." "What gets paid for gets done." Americans just need to decide what they want done.

In a talk in his hometown of Powell, Wyoming, W. Edwards Deming, the architect of Total Quality Management and the famous management method he originated, recited a parable about purpose that should be heeded by all school board members. Deming, seated at a table, asked his audience to imagine that someone had just asked him to clean that table. With those instructions, he said that he would not know how to do the job; he needed to know why. Was it so people could eat on it? If so, he said, the table was fine as it was. Was it needed for surgery? That was different. Now he would have to scrub all of it, including the bottom, sides, legs, and floor around it with a strong detergent and sterilizing agents. Perhaps he would even have to clean the walls. Then the table would be prepared for surgery. If you do not tell someone the purpose of their work, then, except by chance, they will not do it correctly.

> In the American style of management, when something goes wrong the response is to look around for someone to blame or to punish or to search for something to "fix" rather than to look to the system as a whole for improvement. The 85–15 Rule holds that 85 percent of what is wrong is with the system, and only 15 percent with the individual person or thing.[28]

American school board members need to look at the whole system rather than concentrating on the parts. An architect would never design a building without knowing the function the structure would serve. Certainly, a commercial building would be quite different in design from a house. How could an automotive company begin to produce a machine that sits on four wheels for transport without knowing the market and specific uses of the vehicle? Yet American teachers enter classrooms day after day without understanding what product they are expected to produce. Even when we use the term "product" to mean the learning acquired by the student, we do not know what the result should be. Are our schools to be happy places where some students are expected to learn and others are just expected to enjoy the experience? Is the major purpose of secondary schools entertainment in the form of concerts, activities, and athletics? Is the purpose to supply a certain number of doctors, lawyers, and engineers while producing a host of blue-collar workers? Or is the task to ensure that all students learn at high standards? Perhaps the task is to educate youngsters to carry on the traditions of this country both patriotically and emotionally. School boards must look to the flawed system; they must figure out what schools are supposed to do and hold them responsible to do it. If the purpose of education were agreed on, research toward those ends would be embraced; teachers and school systems would begin doing what was expected.

Barbara W. Tuchman, in *The March of Folly: From Troy to Vietnam*, illustrated how governments have persistently carried out policies that did not work. Her opening passages appear to have been written to describe American public education.

> A phenomenon noticeable throughout history regardless of place or period is the pursuit by governments of policies contrary to their own interests. Mankind, it seems, makes a poorer performance of government than of almost any other human activity.[29]

To qualify as folly a policy must meet three criteria. It must have been perceived as counterproductive in its own time, a feasible alternative course of action must have been available, and it must be the policy of a group and not an individual ruler. Woodenheaded is defined as "assessing a situation in terms of preconceived fixed notions while ignoring or rejecting any contrary signs."[30] Sadly, American public education as it is practiced without purpose and, consequently, without a valid measure of quality, is folly; to perpetuate the current system is woodenheaded.

We have learned from the history of public education that we have learned nothing from history. Most reproaches of public education are only modern extensions of ancient controversies. Most things we protest have been objected to before.

> Others complained about poor discipline in progressive schools; about poor mastery of the fundamentals; about the failure to teach respect for hard, sustained effort; about the absences of any common standards or values in schools; about the tendency to adopt the latest fads from child study experts; about the use of children as guinea pigs; about children who were so well "socialized" that they lacked the ability to play alone; about the sacrifice of individuality to group-conformity; about the experts' contemptuous attitudes toward parents; about parents' dependency on expert opinions; about the introduction of psychological ratings and personality inventories in place of report cards and grades; about the education profession's impenetrable patois, which was unintelligible to laymen.[31]

A portrait of the condition of American public education in the new century? No! It is a description of American public education during the decade before World War II. It is time for a nationwide movement to transform education based on a common purpose.

There is a great difference between education and all other industries or services in terms of purpose and accountability. Customer satisfaction cannot be an acceptable goal for education because satisfaction to most people is defined within the paradigm. For example, a high drop-out rate consistent with a lack of success by some students denotes to some Americans the maintenance of high standards. Some parents may accept low scores and lower levels of learning simply because they believe that their child may not be as bright as others. For education to successfully teach all students, the purpose of schooling must be found outside the paradigm.

> The crisis in confidence in public schools so evident today draws much of its irrational quality from the exaggerated hopes that we have cherished over the past century and a half. We have expected that our schools would banish crime and social divisions, that they would make our children better than we have ever been. Horace Mann and others promised us that, and we believed them.[32]

During the early part of the twentieth century, a metamorphosis from the Committee of Ten to the Cardinal Principles may have been under way. Progressives might have been pondering pedagogy, but the state of Wyoming had decided very clearly what students needed to know, including why country life was good.

Eighth Grade Examinations
November, 1915

Agriculture
1. Define agriculture and four divisions of the subject.
2. Give five advantages of living in the country.
3. Define rotation of crops and give three reasons why farmers should practice it.
4. Name five plant enemies and tell how to get rid of each.
5. Give the best ways of conserving the moisture in the soil.
6. Name five weeds and give the best way to destroy them.
7. Name five breeds of cattle and give a short description of each.
8. Name and describe three kinds of horses and two kinds of hogs.

9. Name five trees found in Wyoming and give the uses of each.
10. Give five kinds of birds and five kinds of other wild animals found in this state and tell whether each is beneficial or harmful to man.

Arithmetic
1. (a) Write in figures the number: Five hundred billion, forty-one million, forty-one thousand, forty-five.

   (b) Write in words the number: 306408502005.
2. Divide the product of 15625 and 25 by their quotient.
3. 135.05 divided by .037 equals?
4. Find the cost of carpeting two rooms, one 12 x 16, and the other 15 x 18, with carpet 1 yd. wide @ $1.25 per yard.
5. Bought of R. Partlow, Sundance, Wyoming:

   24 lbs. Rice @ 6 ½ c

   20 lbs. Sugar @ 6 ½ c

   18 bars Soap @ 6 c

   8 pkgs. Starch @ 7 c

   Find the amount of this bill.
6. If I live 1 ½ miles from the school house, how far will I walk during a 7 months term, if I attend every day of school?
7. How many barrels of flour at $4.75 per barrel must be given for 3T. 5 cwt. of coal at $6.50 per ton?
8. A farmer sold 782 bushels of wheat @ 78 ½ c per bushel

   534 bushels of oats @ 33 ½ c per bushel

   428 bushels of potatoes @ 75 c per bushel

   How much did he receive in all?
9. What is the amount of $392.00 for 5 years, 7 mos. 24 days at 6%?
10. A man bought 5 loads of wood, each load 7 ft. long, 3 ½ ft. wide, and 5 feet high. What did it cost at $3.75 per cord?

Geography
1. Name the states and their capitals.
2. Name and locate the five largest cities in the United States.
3. Give three productions of each section of the United States.
4. Define peninsula, isthmus, strait, archipelago, and promontory.
5. Name the different possessions of the United States.
6. Which do you consider the most necessary to the development of a country, its cities or its farms? Why?

35

7. Name the countries involved in the present European war and tell on which side each is fighting.
8. Name the principal countries of Europe and give their capitals.

Grammar
(Penmanship will be based on this paper)

1. Name and give an example of the eight parts of speech.
2. Write a declarative sentence, an interrogative sentence, and an imperative sentence.
3. Write a simple sentence, a complex sentence, and a compound sentence.
4. Diagram or analyze the following sentence: I like to go to school when the weather is fine.
5-8. Write a description of your home, telling the things you like about it and the thingsyou would like to improve. Describe the improvements you would like to make.

Orthography

numerous	islands	against	crates	valuable
beneath	perhaps	orphan	duet	foreign
coral	lies	ankle	currants	presence
druggist	value	wrist	to-morrow	reindeer
business	skeletons	calico	raspberries	region
window	dreaming	shoulder	diamonds	military
really	various	eighth	precious	bananas
growth	suffice	explanation	ascend	bouquet
ivory	dandelions	bruise	receive	February
decided	cambric	drizzling	chief	Wednesday

Physiology and Hygiene

1. Define hygiene and give two reasons why we should study it.
2. Name the different kinds of teeth and give the uses of each.
3. What organs are contained in the chest, and what is the use of each?
4. Describe the progress of a mouthful of food, from the time it enters the mouth until the nutritious portion is absorbed into the blood.
5. Describe the circulation of the blood, from the time it leaves the heart until it returns to it.
6. Describe the nervous impulses that take place when we touch something hot, for instance, and give the names of the organs through which they pass.

7. How often should we bathe? Why? How often should we wash our teeth? Why?
8. How can you tell when an artery is cut? What should you do?
9. What would you do if one had swallowed poison?
10. How would you revive a drowning person?

Reading

1–40 Write a short sketch on the life of Longfellow, at least 100 words, giving the place and date of his birth, the date of his death, some of the schools he attended, the positions he held, and list five of the poems he wrote.

41–100 Write the story of Hiawatha, at least 150 words, giving the principal events, the chief characters, and telling what we may learn from the story.

U.S. History

1. Name four Spanish, three French, and three English explorers and tell what part of the New World each explored.
2. Give the names of the thirteen original colonies and tell who settled each.
3. Give the years included in the Revolutionary War and three causes of that war.
4. Name 10 presidents before the Civil War and give one event in the administration of each.
5. Give the causes of the Civil War and the dates of its beginning and close.
6. Give the results of the Civil War.
7. Give the names of the leading political parties since Washington's time, and tell something of the doctrine of each.
8. Name 10 generals in the Civil War and tell on which side each fought.
9. Name 10 presidents since the Civil War and give one event in the administration of each.
10. Give the name of the present President. Give one event in this administration and tell whether you think he should be re-elected, giving your reasons.

Wyoming Civics

1. Give the date of Wyoming's admission as a state and name four annexations, or purchases, from which its territory was formed.
2. What progressive law, or right, was first adopted by this state?
3. Name the three departments of government and tell what each department does.

4. What are the two branches of the legislature called, how often does it meet, and on what years?

5. Give the name of the present governor and give four of his powers, or duties.

6. Define naturalization, arbitration, pardon, and veto.

7. Who elects the teachers in this county, when is the annual school meeting held, what does the school age include, and when is the compulsory school age?

8. What is a civil case and a criminal case? Name three kinds of courts.

9. Give the name of the state superintendent, give some of her duties, and name three kinds of schools. Give the names of all the county officers and give one duty of each.

CHAPTER FOUR

Why We Must Believe All Children Can Learn

In this view of him, as Man Thinking, the theory of his office is contained. Him Nature solicits with all her placid, all her monitory pictures; him the past instructs; him the future invites. Is not, indeed, every man a student, and do not all things exist for the student's behoof? And, finally is not the true scholar the only true master?[1]

Genetics or environment? Nature or nurture? Genes or parental aspirations? Family, race, culture, heritage, or the shallow end of the genetic pool? Why do some children succeed in school while others fare so poorly? Has nature preordained some people to be smarter than others? Should schools sort and select students on the basis of intellect, preparing the most able as professionals and leaders, the rest as servants and workers? Did God or nature intend that there be vast differences in ability to learn?

Imagine that two babies are born at precisely the same moment. One is delivered in an ultra-modern, climate-controlled, music-filled birth room in a wealthy American suburb. Both parents are professionals, have a house full of books and computers, and travel throughout the world; they are anxious to share these advantages with their child.

The other infant arrives amid deprivation and poverty in one of the worst slums of a poor third world country. Birth occurs in a tin and cardboard hovel occupied by four siblings and the parents, all of whom are illiterate. The father ekes out a meager subsistence, seizing any job available. No one in the family has ever ventured beyond the walls of the slum; if they had a book they would burn the pages in the daily cooking fire.

In your imagination, exchange the babies: Place the child of the ghetto in the arms of the American mother and the new suburbanite on the mat beside the mother who knows only poverty and despair. Think ahead eighteen years: Which child is ready for graduation from high school, excited about football games and prom while preparing for college and a professional career? And which is dressed in rags, trudging through the daily struggle for survival in a world of poverty?

Our presumption is that both infants will be successfully assimilated into the culture in which they were deposited. Infants are born, we believe, with only intellectual potential; development of intellect is a result of environment. We believe that either child will do as well (or as poorly) where they are raised as would the other. Our belief is based on the notion that intervention, the introduction of stimuli to promote intellectual maturation along with good nutrition and healthful care will enhance intellectual capability.

When we say that all children can learn, we propose that every student (with the exception of those handicapped by physiology) can acquire the essential knowledge and skills comprising scholastic curricula. Almost all students can learn what is expected—and they can learn it well. Most importantly, they can learn at higher levels than we currently demand of the elite.

> What any person in the world can learn, almost all persons can learn if provided with appropriate prior and current conditions of learning.... It applies most clearly to the middle 95 percent of the population.[2]

Is this merely a theory—an unproven liberal harangue from education's radical fringe? It is not. There is more than enough evidence to support a conclusion that we may successfully educate all children.

> We can, whenever and wherever we choose, successfully teach all children whose schooling is of interest to us. We already know more than we need to do that. Whether or not we do it must finally depend on how we feel about the fact that we haven't so far.[3]

Benjamin Bloom found in 1981, two years before the original *At-Risk* report, that in classrooms in which mastery learning is used almost all students reach the same final criterion of achievement (usually at the A or B+ level) as approximately the top 20 percent of the class under conventional group instruction. Researchers found that slower learners were able to learn equally complex and abstract ideas as their quicker friends and that they could apply such learning to new problems. A further finding that they retained the ideas equally well is important for the administration of standardized tests.

> There is growing evidence that much of what we have termed individual differences in school learning is the effect of particular school conditions rather than of basic differences in the capabilities of our students.[4]

> Most students become very similar with regard to learning ability, rate of learning, and motivation for further learning when provided with favorable learning conditions.[5]

Bloom, effective schools researchers, and other scholars have clearly shown that the conditions of schooling, which are controlled by adults, influence student learning. This great news should be welcomed by everyone: It is possible to successfully teach every student.

Unfortunately, most Americans and most educators, under the influence of the paradigm do not believe this statement. Worse, the belief system necessary for success is not even welcome in many schools. Successful learning, many believe, is determined by family variables including genetically derived intelligence, socioeconomic status, and attitude toward formal education. According to this group, the experience of schooling will have little positive effect if the student does not have the proper lineage.

The belief in intelligence as a number, measurable in humans to judge the smart from the rest is not, as most assume, an absolutely proven factor in determining success; indeed, its presence as a single essence is doubted by many. Alfred Binet, the father of IQ who in 1904 was asked to determine which school children needed special help by the French minister of education, "did not want to jump from the fact that some people seem to behave more intelligently than others to the presumption that there was one essence, a single mental resource."[6]

He feared it would offer educators the excuse to ignore the plight
of poorly performing students on the grounds that they lacked
the intelligence to do better. It also might give educators grounds
for dismissing under motivation and behavior problems as symp-
toms of low intelligence.[7]

We continue to discover that ability is driven by more than IQ
scores—and that utilizing IQ as a single essence to determine ability is
to do a great disservice to human beings. According to Daniel Goleman,
author of *Emotional Intelligence*, the ability of a four-year-old to delay
gratification in the choice of one cookie immediately or two in twenty
minutes is a better predictor of school success than intelligence scores
and the measured characteristic of optimism in college freshmen is a
more accurate predictor of collegiate academic success than SAT or
ACT scores.[8]

The belief that not all children can learn with a high rate of success is an example of the influence of culture on science and the power
of the paradigm to manipulate teaching and learning. Throughout history, most people were not recipients of an academic education; only
the upper classes were granted formal schooling. The belief system that
controls educational process in many schools is a derivative of the feu-
dal class system. The idea of offering common school education is less
than 160 years old; the notion of secondary schooling for all adolescents has existed for only several generations.

American secondary schools were founded for a variety of reasons.
Immigrants and poor families believed that their children would prosper if they were educated. Capitalists and organized labor wanted to
improve the quality of workers, and patriots wished to protect the American way of life through cultural indoctrination. The answer to all these
divergent purposes was the comprehensive high school: an institution
that offered something for everyone—based on ability to learn. In the
same building, future engineers, doctors, lawyers, and professors would
attend one level of classes while those destined for a life of labor would
attend classes at a lower level. Some would be taught to dig ditches;
others to engineer great structures. Subsequently, junior high schools
were created as life's sampler, offering a range of experiences so that
children of disparate abilities, assisted by school counselors, would know
which track to select in high school.

The land of the free conceived a system of sorting and selecting, of tracking and ability-grouping, based on the belief that not all children could learn. American public education dictates its pupils' futures more surely than the formal selection processes of Europe and Japan, for American schools select subliminally, managing classroom experiences to convince susceptible children that they are not smart enough to learn. The land of capitalism and competition begins teaching children at an early age that not all can compete. The school of hard knocks begins in kindergarten.

Tracking, grouping, and the esteem-assailing characteristics of comprehensive high schools were initially justified by the theories of social Darwinists who believe that people cannot escape their environment.

It followed that ethnic minorities and the poor were seen as being responsible for their terrible living conditions, as inherently "less fit" and at a lower evolutionary stage than Anglo-Protestants. Their lives of squalor and seeming depravity could be traced to developmental deficiencies that were biologically determined, not to the social conditions in which they were immersed. They simply lacked the internal resources necessary to make better lives for themselves.[9]

The American system of segregating students on the premise of perceived aptitude is an extension of ethnocentric abstractions of nineteenth-century pseudo scientists. American high schools have never been expected to instruct every child. They were conceived and survive as agencies to sort children into the occupational and social roles they will fulfill as adults.

One of the most famous reports on American schooling, published in 1966, supported this idea; it announced that the pursuit of a system in which all children learn was, indeed, futile. This study was so shattering that the conclusions should have been the object of national attention, overshadowing any other domestic crisis. But no one seemed to be listening. Congress had commissioned Professor James Coleman to prepare an equal opportunity survey in response to the passage of the Civil Rights Act. His inferences should have fallen across the land with the force of counterrevolution—for his findings from the paradigm condemned the poor to poverty and the children of the uneducated to ignorance. The problem was not that his findings were not true, but

that they were, and are, a report of the paradigm's influence on schooling. Instead of forcing people to examine the problem, the study allowed
those governed by the paradigm to use the results to justify their behavior—and beliefs. Instead of a call to change education, the report was a
signal that changing education was useless.

> Schools bring little influence to bear on a child's achievement
> that is independent of his background and general social con-
> text; this very lack of an independent effect means that the
> inequalities imposed on children by their home, neighborhood
> and peer environment are carried along to become the inequali-
> ties with which they confront adult life at the end of school. For
> equality of educational opportunity must imply a strong effect
> of schools that is independent of the child's immediate social
> environment, and that strong independent effect is not present
> in American schools.[10]

Some practitioners, laboring in the fields of education at a time
when they were respected greatly and paid little, simply shrugged and
agreed. At last, someone told them what they already knew. No matter
how hard they worked, how diligently they prepared, a lot of kids just
were not going to get it. The integrity of educators was secure. Those
who could learn did; the rest failed. Accountability for learning was
directed only at children and families. Teachers could not be expected
to overcome their students' beginnings.

> Before jumping into any particular set of solutions, however,
> policy makers need to be more realistic about what can be done
> to improve the education of students in a heterogeneous,
> non-totalitarian country. Specifically, critics of American educa-
> tion must come to terms with the reality that *in a universal education
> system, many students will not reach the level of education that most
> people view as basic.* Consider again the example of functional
> illiteracy mentioned earlier: that over 20 percent of 17-year-olds
> are below the intermediate reading level on the NAEP, meaning
> that they are marginal readers or worse. This is usually consid-
> ered a failure of American Education, and perhaps it is. But most
> of these non-readers come from the bottom of the cognitive
> ability distribution. How well *should* they be able to read after a

44

proper education given the economic, technological, and political constraints on any system of mass education?[11]

People are not equal athletically, goes the argument—or musically, or intellectually. Some are preordained to serve, others to be served; sorting and selecting of students is, indeed, a proper role of public schools. Bolstered by those who believe so strongly in inherent inequality in learning potential, the purpose of public schooling becomes inordinately simple. High schools should be comprehensive; students need to be sifted and offered learning experiences correlated with intellectual ability. High-level academic classes should be only for gifted pupils, aimed at preparing them for the finest of colleges and a life of leadership. Other pupils need to be groomed for lesser status institutions and professional life. The remainder need only vocational training, life skills, and survival skills as workers and consumers, and to be taught to lead healthy lifestyles and make responsible consumer choices. Only those selected to succeed should participate in national testing programs; educators cannot be held accountable for their low-performing pupils who should not be tested and not be expected to succeed academically.

Equality in educational performance has always been outside the paradigm. The alarming statement of the National Commission on Excellence in Education that "the educational foundations of our society are presently being eroded by a rising tide of mediocrity that threatens our very future as a Nation and a people" rings hollow.[12] The rising tide of mediocrity, many believe, is inherent in people, not the system.

This issue is the crux, the most important confronting America and public education. Can we break out of the paradigm and come to believe that we can educate every student at a high level, except those with physiological disabilities that prevent learning? If the answer is yes, boards of education must demand that the antiquated paradigm no longer be protected by unions, associations, politicians, tenure, administrators, and school systems.

School board members should ensure effective pedagogical practices are learned, and practiced, by educators; and they should provide meaningful staff development programs to continually improve teacher knowledge and skills. Board members must be courageous enough to announce that spending taxpayer dollars for staff development is necessary and probably their most important expenditure. They must ensure that every administrator is an expert in these practices and that they supervise and evaluate teaching around effective practices.

School board members must demand that teachers and administrators zealously believe that all children can and must learn. Those who do not must be separated from the system. Boards must demand the right, and accept the responsibility, of employing only educators dedicated to the fulfillment of this mission.

The struggle to provide a basic education for each child is analogous to swimming upstream. It is hard and exhausting; the way is strewn with rocks and traps. Considering the exigencies of late-twentieth-century global economy, the reality is that the system must succeed. Every child must learn the required outcomes of schooling.

The Paradigm in Action: Why Don't All Children Learn?

Greek mythology tells us of the cruel robber Procrustes (the stretcher). When travelers sought his house for shelter, they were tied onto an iron bedstead. If the traveler was shorter than the bed, Procrustes stretched him out until he was the same length as the bed. If he was longer, his limbs were chopped off to make him fit. Procrustes shaped both short and tall until they were equally long and equally dead.[1]

Kindergarten is a time of tears and excitement, new clothes and freshly washed faces, a milieu of lunch boxes with logos from favorite television programs, colorful backpacks, a few sacks emitting odors of peanut butter and bananas, and an assortment of supplies laden with the pungent aroma of glue. A great new adventure has begun. We send our children off to school to be cared for, kept safe, and taught the things that young children should know.

Little children want to go to school; they cannot wait for that magical first day. Playing school, practicing the roles of teacher and pupil, is an important early childhood activity. Becoming one of the big kids, being old enough for school is one of life's important milestones. Mothers and fathers cry as they walk to the classroom hand-in-hand with the anxious young scholar on the first day of kindergarten, for they are turning the well-being of their children over to someone else.

Not all former kindergartners are eager to return to school for the first grade. As the years go by fewer and fewer retain a sense of excitement about either school or learning. For many there is a growing sense

47

of frustration as they begin to doubt their own ability. They feel dumb and start to believe that school is too hard; their self-esteem is slowly shattered until the excitement and natural love of learning is finally replaced by fear and anger. For many American children schools and schooling become repugnant.

It is easy to blame teachers. When children do not thrive in elementary schools, it is logical to assume the reasons rest with the adults who are paid to teach them. Skillful teachers, we believe, should be able to sustain interest while keeping alive the excitement of learning and protecting the esteem of each child. The failure of innocent children, it seems, can only mean that they were placed with incompetent mentors. Operating under the theory that a close and bonded relationship needs to occur, most elementary schools provide one teacher as a significant other for children. If we believe children can learn and know they are not learning, then it would appear teachers are at fault.

The fault with our educational system is much greater than the pedagogical skills of teachers and much harder to correct than merely weeding out incompetence. Ills plaguing education are systemic, a result of structure and form created by the paradigm and based on the belief that all students cannot learn the required outcomes of schooling. Many of the adults working in schools have been victimized as relentlessly as their students. They fail, grow embittered, and burn out because of the unwritten rules of schooling. Yet these structural deficiencies are not esoteric, discoverable only through years of research; the light of common sense provides enough illumination for anyone to see if they take off the paradigm's blinders.

As economies transformed from craftsmen working alone in cottages to laborers on assembly lines in huge, smoke-belching plants, the academic study of management became a legitimate pursuit. Management's job was to create tasks for the workers, assess competence, and hire and fire them. Workers needed to know only one task to help produce a finished project. Managers managed and workers worked. As automobiles rolled down the line, one workman attached a wheel while another bolted on a fender. Workers did not need to know each other or how to drive the finished product.

Public education copied the system, taking the wheat and chaff, all of the strengths and flaws of the factory system and transferred them to schooling. Children are not raw material for industrial processes; they do not roll down assembly lines at the same stage of completion. The same learning cannot be bolted onto different children just because they are the same chronological age. Parents know that children do not walk, talk, run, or read at the same age; any middle-school girl can describe the wide range of maturational levels of the boys in her class. Everybody knows that children do not reach developmental stages of maturity at the same age—everyone, that is, except the people we pay to operate our schools who continue to insist that all students of the same age belong in the same grade.

Schools continue a structure predicated on uniform physical and intellectual maturation that was modeled after automobile assembly lines. The first workman puts in kindergarten stuff; another bolts on skills to be learned in the first grade. The second grade teacher, assuming (as does the entire system) that all kindergarten and first-grade components will stay attached, welds on second-grade essentials. When the students get to the end of the line, it does not matter if they are "completed," they are sent to middle school.

Many children who do not thrive in elementary schools simply are not prepared for assembly when the factory is ready for them. Common sense should prevail: It is folly to cling to a strategy founded on outmoded industrial procedures inferring that children develop on a rigid time schedule. Those whose physical or mental time clocks are slower than their friends' are placed into a cycle of failure from which few escape. "Kids who aren't reading at grade level by the end of first grade face 8–1 odds against ever catching up."[2]

Children who begin kindergarten not ready for the standard curricula taught to all children fall farther behind as they grow older. Without adjustment of teacher expectations, these children may expect years of frustration. If they do not learn in one grade, they are probably not going to do very well in the next. Self-esteem is crushed as pre-adolescents begin to believe that they are not as smart as other kids. Because no one really enjoys being a failure, many children decide school is not the place for them. They find success someplace else, usually with a group of peers who have also started to think of themselves as scholastic failures.

Americans have known for a long time that all children of the same age are not developmentally equal. Quick-fix (and nonsensical) solutions to the problem of elementary students who do not learn are readily available and easily rationalized within the paradigm. "All we need to do," according to a refrain heard around America, "is fail those kids—hold them back until they can pass." It would be more correct to say, "Retain them at the same place on the assembly line until advanced components can be attached." People who operate in the paradigm are sure that the ultimate problem in public education is social promotion, the practice of advancing students to the next grade when they have not earned passing marks.

Holding them back does not work! Retention in grade level is not only a simplistic answer, it is a practice research has shown to be harmful to children. Studies have found that forced retention does not improve academic skills. Instead, it is a significant causal factor in increasing dropout rates. Retaining students for one year places them at definite risk of dropping out; holding them back for two years practically guarantees they will.

A significant number of longitudinal studies comparing well matched retained and non-retained students show that retained children are worse off in terms of both personal adjustment and academic outcomes than non-retained children.... We know the practice of retention does not work. In controlled studies of the effect of non-promotion on both achievement and personal adjustment, children who repeat a grade are consistently worse off than comparable children who are promoted with their age-mates.[3]

Taken as a whole, the experimental data collected over the past 70 years fails to indicate any significant benefits of grade retention for the majority of students with academic or adjustment problems.[4]

These research findings are overwhelming and have been known for years. It is a subject that is no longer arguable through research. Retention of young children is the educational equivalent of the old medical practice of blood-letting for those who were sick—doctors believed that draining diseased blood would cure the patient, so they drained it out; if the patients did not die from the illnesses, they bled to death. The same kind of myth-driven practice that killed our first president is destroying educational opportunities for many of our children. Through the use of retention, adults have decided not to support the schooling of children who are not at the maturational level demanded by the assembly line. Unfortunately, this system of mass production was designed by people with educational knowledge equivalent to the medical wisdom of a seventeenth-century colonial physician.

> Retention is harmful. It is the coup de grace to scholastic self-esteem, it is the boogie man finally coming to a child's house. After anxiety about going blind, one notch higher than worry about the death of parents, fear of retention in school has been found to be the second most major cause of stress in elementary children. It also does not work. Socially promoted students usually outscore their retained counterparts within three years of the promotion.[5]

Support for retention is a product of the paradigm. Many polls and surveys of the 1980s and 1990s report that most Americans favored ending social promotion. Many teachers, especially those who have never followed the school careers of retained children, endlessly lobby for the right to hold their students back.

Like retention, the practice of ability grouping to teach slow, average, or advanced students only with academically similar peers is one of the most supported traditions in American education. It has been also been found to be equally noneffective.

> For more than 70 years, ability grouping has been one of the most controversial issues in education. Its effects, particularly on student achievement, have been extensively studied over that time period, and many reviews of the literature have been written.

> Although there are limitations to the scope of this review and to studies on which it is based, there are several conclusions that can be advanced with some confidence. These are as follows:

> 1. Comprehensive between-class ability grouping plans have little or no effect on the achievement of secondary students, at least as measured by standardized tests....

> 2. Different forms of ability grouping are equally ineffective.

> 3. Ability grouping is equally ineffective in all subjects, except that there may be a negative effect of ability grouping in social studies.

4. Assigning students to different levels of the same course has no consistent positive or negative effects on students of high, average, or low ability. I also found no differential effects of between-class ability grouping in an earlier synthesis of elementary studies on this topic.[6]

The paradox is inherent in the paradigm. Evidence collected against grouping is overwhelming; there is certainly enough to cause any school district to end the practice. However, teachers and parents strongly support and request grouping without realizing it is an anachronism that harms many students. Ability grouping is especially damaging because it creates a system of tracking students into certain groups. We know that young people live up or down to expectations, especially if they are surrounded by peers doing the same thing.

Jeannie Oakes debunked the assumptions behind tracking and grouping. It is time public educators listened.

Despite the fact that the first assumption—that students learn more or better in homogenous groups—is almost universally held, it is simply not true.... No group of students has been found to benefit consistently from being in a homogeneous group.... However, many studies have found the learning of average and slow students to be negatively affected by homogeneous placements.

Rather than help students to feel more comfortable about themselves, the tracking process seems to foster *lowered* self-esteem among these teenagers. Further exacerbating these negative self-perceptions are the attitudes of many teachers and other students toward those in lower tracks. Once placed in low classes, students are usually seen by others in the school as dumb. What information we do have about the process of teacher and counselor guidance (into tracks) leads us to believe that these judgments are certainly no more accurate or fair than test scores.... We know that these kinds of recommendations often result in more disproportionate placements of students from various racial groups and social classes than do placements by test scores alone.

I also suggested that the widespread belief that tracking is in the best interests of students rests on at least four unexamined assumptions that underpin school culture: (1) students learn better in groups of those who are academically similar, (2) slower students develop more positive attitudes about themselves and school when they are not in day-to-day classroom contact with those who are much brighter, (3) track placements are part of a meritocratic system with assignments "earned" by students and accorded through fair and accurate means, and (4) teaching is easier when students are grouped homogeneously, and teaching is better when there are no slower students to lower the common denominator. We looked at these assumptions in light of the research evidence about them and found them to be unwarranted.

But as we know from research about it, tracking is not in the best interests of most students. It does not appear to be related to either increasing academic achievement or promoting positive attitudes and behaviors.[7]

There may be a benefit to ability grouping for the extremely gifted.[8] Grouping, to the dismay of many practitioners, however, does not make a difference for merely high-achieving students in public schools.

Is ability grouping beneficial for high ability students? My reviews of research on between-class ability grouping (tracking) found it was not. In elementary studies I found a median effect size for high achievers of +.04 which is trivially different from zero.[9]

There is more than a little truth in the belief that children are not grouped for learning in a desire to help slower children, but to feed the egos of parents who believe their children are better than others. Having the brightest children in the community has become a status symbol, a matter of bragging rights. Grouping is also practiced in schools because classes of eager children ready to learn and all consistently on the honor role are a joy to teach; the others are just hard work. Teachers, of course, prefer to teach successful pupils. As a result lower groups are usually given to first-year teachers; children who need the best teachers often get the least experienced. In many districts, being awarded the top groups is a benefit of seniority.

Ability grouping and retention are easily seen as harmful if viewed from outside the paradigm. Practices that sort and select students into successes and failures assail the self-respect of children in a system predicated on uniformity. With bewilderment a child might ask, "If I am eight years old, did God plan for me to be in the second grade?" American schools certainly act as if He did. Unfortunately, children not ready for the second grade at the age of eight will probably never attain higher levels of academic success.

Therefore, the questions that educators in each district must answer, led by board members in search of truth, are of the gravest importance. If some eight-year-old children are not ready to learn what schools expect them to, and those who are not continue to fall farther behind until they lose their love of learning and either drop out or become barely literate underachievers, who is at fault? Is it God, parents, environment, or the structured grade-level programs that schools continue to insist on? If the answers, in any part, can be found in schooling, then the practice must be stopped and board members must look far enough outside the paradigm to make the decision. One could hardly imagine voluntarily opting for a medical procedure that was worse than the illness.

Retention and grouping are efforts to enhance learning while preserving a flawed structure. At best, they create a negative environment for a significant portion of the population. We have learned enough about humans to know that behavior is predicated on expectation. People respond in the way that they are treated. Expect the best of people and you are usually rewarded; expect the worst and you will generally get it.

Teacher expectations and perceptions of student ability are directly linked to achievement. High expectations produce more and better instruction; low expectations result in less instruction and attention. This is simply the Pygmalion effect: the self-fulfilling prophecy. If adults believe in them, children succeed. The natural proclivity of children for acceptance is an extremely powerful force on human behavior.

Does the level of teacher expectations influence the level of student achievement, i.e., do high expectations produce high achievement and low expectations produce low achievement? The answer, based on extensive research, is a clear-cut "yes."[10]

Studies to determine why American youth compare poorly on tests in relation to children from other countries found low personal perceptions of ability to be a leading cause. When students in China, Japan, and Korea fail an examination, low scores are explained as a lack of

54

effort. American children, supported by their parents, believe they are not smart enough to do any better.[11] The land of equality has created an educational system that denies opportunity based on perception of ability. Schools sort and select by causing children to believe they are not smart.

Solutions that enable educators to meet the increasingly difficult burden of teaching all students will not be found within the traditional structure of public schools. Only by stepping out of the paradigm and looking at school systems without the blinders of familiarity will we find the answers and break the cycle of failure. Schools must end the practice of age-level grade placement. No longer should children be considered first-, second-, third-, fourth-, or fifth-grade students; they should just be considered children learning.

A much better practice would have four or five teachers and eighty to one hundred first graders organized into a family of learners. Students and teachers from this closely knit unit would remain together from the first to the fifth or sixth grade. Daily, monthly, and yearly scheduling of learning experiences would be made by the teachers with a goal of preparing their students for middle school. Teachers and students remaining together throughout elementary school would nurture supportive relationships and eliminate the urgency of content coverage on a yearly schedule. A five-year teaching period is long enough to permit diagnosis of the learning requirements of each student and allow for the creation of individual learning plans.

As physicians treat each patient individually and not as a part of a generally ill population, educators should treat learners. The timing of the introduction of subject matter and appropriate learning experiences should be made for individual students and not as a general plan based on assembly-line time schedules. There should be little reason for retention because children progress as they develop—especially if they are allowed to learn without the overwhelming fear of failure.

Transforming traditional schools into nongraded ones is not a guarantee that all students will learn; nor does it mean that poor pedagogy will disappear. However, consistent and persistent implementation of such a plan would breach the walls of the paradigm. Lock-step elementary grade-oriented practices are the handmaidens of the ultimate evil—the nefarious sorting and selecting of children into those who can learn and those who are not allowed to.

Secondary schools are no different; comprehensive high schools are intensely controlled by the paradigm. Most high schools are the illogical but natural extension of the manufacturing process that was adopted as the production model for public education. From the ninth to the twelfth grade the assembly line continues to haul students from one grade level to the next for the attachment of new learning. But the assembly line speeds up, jumping quickly from station to station, not because the work is complete, but because the allotted time has expired.

Secondary schools are ruthlessly dominated by class schedules. Tremendous energy is invested in making changes and creating new schedules. Scheduling problems are well known to teachers.

1. The time of the day influences student learning. By definition some periods will be more productive than others.

2. Any scheduled time is too short if the students are actively engaged and learning.

3. Any scheduled time is too long if students are not engaged and learning.

4. Passing from class to class is a waste of time and promotes truancy and absenteeism.

5. Learning experiences are a product of the schedule; they take place because of clocks and not student readiness.

6. Students who take seven classes each day cannot and will not complete an hour of homework for each.

7. Students will do math homework first, science second—and social studies infrequently.

The time allotted is only sufficient for teachers to talk and make general explanations while students who must sit and listen in class are expected to study and to learn at home. This design is the assembly line at its worst; not only do adolescents have to be in the ninth grade because of their age, they have little time in class to acquire new learning. All over America, energetic adolescents sit and listen to teachers talk. Traditional secondary classes taught by teachers lecturing in front of the room are examples of the "sit and get" method of learning. Perhaps a better exam than a test of subject matter at the end of such a class would be a measurement of patience.

Many high school students complain that teachers and school are boring. Most adults understand this complaint because they remember boring classes. Not many people, including adults at conferences, profit from listening to speakers with little probability of interaction; fewer still enjoy the experience. Almost no one emerges refreshed and invigorated from days of sitting and listening in silence. Yet the sit and get routine endures as the most commonly used teaching method. Students arrive for class, sit, listen, and take notes while all the time their predominate motivation is to find ways to make classes speed along.

Teacher talk cannot compete with the marvels of today's technology. Modern students are accustomed to viewing polished televised monologues delivered by professionals. Teachers are not entertainers; they do not have time to perfect performances. Continual talk will never again, if it ever did, stimulate high-level learning in post-adolescent Americans. Life is too exciting, too fast, and too interactive. Experiences that can be created, not the voice of the teacher, enable children of technology to learn.

The system is maintained because from the time they were first created, American high schools have never been intended to educate all students academically. Constructed as giant centrifuges, these schools continually spin, separating students on the basis of perceived ability and each child's reaction to those adult perceptions. The sorting and selecting of students into learners and nonlearners has always been the first priority. High schools offer nonacademic, often anti-intellectual classes to students who have been convinced they cannot learn.

Different levels of achievement are accepted and even encouraged because most schools do not require evidence of learning for graduation. A student only needs to prove that he or she has successfully completed an array of classes and earned the required number of Carnegie units. The same credits are given for a D- as for an A+. Homework, which does not even have to be completed by the student, often counts as a portion of a grade. Extra credit points are awarded for anything from taking attendance to acting politely. As a result, a Carnegie unit simply means that through some method of assessment—of something— the student received a grade above an F in a course.

The structure, the schedule, the talking of teachers, the low expectations for some students, the failure of schools to insist on graduation based on performance, has created a system that for most students (except those special few whose innate nature compels them to excel) becomes a compromise.[12] Teachers forge compromises with students on standards of behavior, work ethic, and expectations of accomplishment. Demanding high standards of excellence is often a violation of the compromise. The compromise goes on all of the time; it is an unspoken agreement that almost everyone in a high school understands. "Okay, come into my class; if you want to learn, fine. If you don't, just don't bother me, don't give me any problems, and you can get out of here with a passing grade."

Students graduate through compromise. Formal assessments of standards are not part of the process. High school diplomas certify only that a student has earned grades of D or better in a requisite number of classes—to infer that earning one certifies learning is a grave error. Diplomas signify only that a student has spent time sitting in class. Pupils are marking time and so are teachers.

> "No one really cares if you work or not," a Texas senior told me. At a California high school I visited, it was *school policy* to allow students with good disciplinary records to go home early one day a week. In many classrooms, nothing more is expected of students than that they aren't disruptive. Keeping their classrooms free of hassles, rather than educating students, seems to be the first priority of many teachers.[13]

There is little impetus for students to learn and small reward for teachers who maintain high standards. Teachers are neither evaluated nor rewarded through student learning. Those who maintain safe and well-disciplined classrooms, especially if they are popular, have reached the pinnacle of their profession.

Perhaps, the high burnout rate of teachers is a direct result of the compromise. Lowering professional standards, reducing once-eager aspirations to teach in order to survive, extracts a high price. Each day teachers face students they know they are not teaching, children who can learn but will not. The emotional struggle between teaching and surviving creates enormous stress. In other professions the assistance of a provider is sought; in public education one's services are often shunned.

School? It's just a getting out of the house thing. Kids don't come to learn, they just come, a junior at a California high school told me. At a Virginia high school I asked a senior if his four years at the school had been meaningful. He laughed, saying, "I'm just doing my time." Unfortunately, such attitudes are widespread among the nation's students; they pervade affluent suburban schools as well as their urban and rural counterparts. By one estimate as many as two-thirds of the nation's public secondary students are "disengaged" from their studies.[14]

American schools have done a wonderful job teaching children whose environment provides them with a predisposition for schooling. For the rest, it is a day-to-day struggle. There are no standards to meet, only years to endure. Most teachers, administrators, and parents do not accept systemic change willingly. Guardians of the paradigm and living under its spell, they toil against change, refusing to accept research and the knowledge on which effective practices are founded. Change in structure will have to be led stoically and resolutely by those willing to face the pressures of bureaucracy, democracy, and organized educator groups.

Board members who hold high standards and expect to create the changes necessary to produce a system where all students learn face certain challenges. Knowledge workers in a conflict situation are capable of using all of their wisdom and intelligence to greatly disrupt the lives of board members and administrators. Many people elected to boards find their businesses and lives subject to organized obstruction. Boycotts of business, floods of critical letters, phone calls at all hours, and critical publicity in the local media can become commonplace. Losing friends, feeling isolated, and being shunned is a very real occurrence for many board members who demand high standards. Many find that the sacrifices are too great, especially when they see those who curry favor so respected.

The paradigm maintains the system. Knowledgeable school board members who make courageous and enlightened decisions are the only possible instruments of change. Otherwise, our locally controlled system of schooling will continue to falter, and the voices of opposition will become louder until the system withers away, providing educational services only for those children whose parents cannot afford to send them to private schools or cannot allocate the time for home schooling. Public education will fail, not because we cannot do better but because we believe that we are currently doing enough. Wrapped in the paradigm, most believe that educating a few and sorting out the rest is not only good enough, but the way it is supposed to be.

CHAPTER SIX

The Pyramid Cannot Stand Upside Down

*The constant temptation of every organization is safe medioc-
rity. The first requirement of organizational health is a high
demand on performance. Indeed, one of the major reasons for
demanding that management be by objectives and that it focus
on the objective requirements of the task is the need to have
managers set high standards of performance for themselves.*[1]

Watching children play school can be disheartening to teachers
because they see themselves generally portrayed with exaggerated anger; administrators suffer much worse at the hands of adults. Bosses in
general have become fall guys for comedians and comic strips.
Stereotypically, school administrators are represented as political bosses
who prove the adage that people climb to their level of incompetence.
Almost every teacher, parent, student, or taxpayer at one time or another has charged that the school district has too many overpaid and
underproductive administrators.

Unfortunately, administrators have fared little better with scholars. "Effective schools are far less subject to external superintendent and
central office control than are ineffective institutions on every issue."[2] "Far
too many of our school systems are top-heavy with administration; they
are administered to within an inch of their lives."[3] "Strangely, many
administrators seem to relish their role as disciplinarians; they seem
much more interested in controlling students than educating them. They
speak proudly of 'sweeps' to clear halls of students late to class and are
quick to share their latest discipline statistics."[4]

When education began adopting the industrial revolution's philosophy of top-down management, scientific studies of the subject were first being conducted. Based on concepts of turn-of-the-century theoreticians, management's responsibility was to establish carefully structured tasks for workers to complete under close supervision. Management was to know what should be done and make sure that it was. Management knew better than workers, according to managers, and would make correct supervisory decisions resulting in effective production.

The present system of educational management does not work and never will if the objective is to create an organization that successfully teaches all children as efficiently as possible. Better managed traditional hierarchical organizations may be more efficient, but they will never help us carry out the mission of educating all students. The managerial philosophy of public schooling embraced by the prevailing paradigm, copied from traditional big business and labor and antithetical to professionalism, has shaped a system as harmful to educational professionals as to their clients; the system has bestowed a tradition of unions and strikes, and disillusioned and militant teachers.

Top-down management, which originated with Roman legions that set out to conquer the world, was "based on a fundamentally military approach that centered power, authority, and decision making at the top of a descending pyramid of command-demand."[5] The generals (bosses) at the top did the thinking (strategizing); soldiers (workers) at the bottom did the fighting and dying, and levels of officers (managers) were positioned between the top and the bottom. The organization was, and is, pyramidal in shape because of the far fewer number of personnel who occupy each higher level (see Figure 1).

Figure 6.1. Conceptual pyramidal organizational chart from Patrick Dolan, *Restructuring Our Schools: A Primer on Systemic Change*, Lilot Moorman, ed. (Kansas City: Systems and Organization, 1994) 13.

This model worked well for the Romans and has been implemented in governments, armies, churches, businesses, and societal institutions since that time. In the corresponding educational system, teachers far outnumber the principals (or other middle managers) who completely outnumber the superintendent.

When decision-making ability is invested only at the top, an organization will be slow to change and adapt. Frequently, such systems change (if they finally do) in the wrong direction because leaders do not understand what is going on at the lower levels, especially when a middle manager is hesitant to describe the situation honestly for fear she or he will be held responsible.

Innately, the pyramidal organization is almost incapable of meaningful communication, either from the top down or the bottom up. School district trustees know that the most common complaint by both employees and citizens is that communication is poor. Systems large enough to have more than one, and sometimes many, middle managers (such as principals and department heads) work through segmented channels with a guaranteed lack of accurate communication built into the system. If communication from the school board could be traced through the district like blood in a circulatory system, one would see that it is filtered through the perceptions of the superintendent and the principals (at the least) before it is passed through separate channels to each school. With each school, the culture serves as yet another filter. It should not be a surprise that teachers in different schools have different interpretations of the same message.

Communication from the bottom to the apex must pass through the same filters. If any person at any point in the system is loathe to speak honestly or directly, communication will cease. As a result, leaders in the top echelon rarely have an accurate view of what is happening at the point of production and employees seldom have a clear picture of where the organization is going. "It's enormously risky to move tough data up the hierarchy, especially in a blaming environment…Bureaucratic layers increase, and each layer tends to filter out what it considers unnecessary or troubling data as it moves up the organization."[6]

Principals are caught in the middle. They are charged with delivering directives from the board and superintendent to their teachers and parents, communicating it correctly, and convincing employees to carry out mandated instructions and programs. Principals also have to take problems from teachers to superintendents and board members—who do not want to hear the bad news if it reflects on them. Managers who deliver the news from the top in a fashion loyal to the superintendent are often despised by teachers. Those who deliver it in a fashion disloyal to the boss may suffer a worse fate.

In 1973, Peter Drucker, recognized as the father of modern management, warned America about the difficulties inherent in educational management. Using the term knowledge workers to describe the staff of service industries, including teachers, computer programmers, engineers, medical technologists, administrators, and accountants, he predicted that traditional models of supervision and management would no longer work in those fields:

> Managing knowledge work and knowledge worker will require exceptional imagination, exceptional courage, and leadership of a high order. In some ways it will be a far more demanding task than managing the manual worker was until very recently. For the weapon of fear—fear of economic suffering, fear of job security, physical fear of company guards or of the state's police power—which for so long substituted for managing manual work and the manual worker, is simply not operative at all in the context of knowledge work and knowledge worker. The knowledge worker, except on the very lowest levels of knowledge work, is not productive under the spur of fear; only self-motivation and self-direction can make him productive. He has to be achieving in order to produce at all.[7]

His prophecy came true long ago. Teachers have successfully lobbied legislatures for tenure laws, which protect their members from private employment job insecurities. Tenure, one of the most criticized features of public education, is the issue that detractors condemn most loudly. There have been calls for limiting its influence in state after state; yet the concept remains firmly entrenched. Teachers consider it an unalienable right to work in an environment free of externally imposed job anxiety.

Most teachers begin their careers eager and enthusiastic, determined to make a difference, volunteering for a life of low pay, long hours, and personal sacrifice. When they accepted their first position, few considered the demoralizing effects of trying to work as a professional in a factory system of management. The repressed wish of many teachers is to truly be treated as professionals; the failure of society and management to do so, in their collective opinion, has created the wars of education. The stereotype of an embittered, nonperforming, job-guaranteed, unaccountable, union-joining, door-shutting, picket-line-walking American teacher is a legacy of our system of management. We get what we deserve: Educators live down to our expectations.

A management structure ill-suited to the social and political realities of a knowledge organization in a democracy is, unfortunately, not the only problem plaguing the profession of school administration. Too many public school administrators have little understanding of management or teaching and learning; they simply do not know what a successful learning organization is and thus they don't know how to create one, as a compilation of deficiencies in school administrators indicates.

> (1) a lack of concern for organizational outcomes—"the tendency to neglect the careful tracing of connections between organizational variables and student outcomes" (Erickson 1979, 12); (2) the neglect of the moral and ethical dimensions of the knowledge base (Beck and Murphy, (Farquhar 1981); (3) an absence of attention to educational issues (Murphy and Hallinger 1987), what Bates (1984) labels "a deafening silence concerning the fundamental message systems of school: curriculum, pedagogy, and evaluation" (261); (4) gaps in the intellectual scaffolding of the profession due to the failure to adequately consider issues of diversity (Shakeshaft 1988; Valverde and Brown 1988); and (5) inattention to the craft dimensions of leadership, resulting in a knowledge base that "does not provide the kind of experiences or knowledge that practitioners feel they need" (Muth 1988, 5). All in all, the picture is one in which there is considerable room for improvement in the cognitive foundations of the profession. (Murphy 1990; 1992 a)[8]

Michael Imber asked a group of educational administrators and trainees what they knew about managing schools and being educational leaders that the average person did not know.

> While some of my subjects, even after considerable prodding, were unable to respond or could offer only vague generalities, such as "I know how to run a school," most did claim to possess

special knowledge that qualified them for the administrative jobs they held or desired. Many of them...suggested that they knew the things that had been taught in their courses.[9]

He found that some of the more intuitive theories of the respondents contradicted current research and that many answers to his questions were generalizations. "Finally, some respondents offered intensely practical theories of administration: 'The most important thing I do is to keep the parents and school board happy.'"[10] For these administrators education is pragmatically political. What keeps jobs gets done. No waves and no change keep jobs. Stagnation gets rewarded; nothing gets done. As long as many leaders and managers of public education are inexpert in their tasks little will improve. Board members must learn enough to recognize educators who are educationally and pedagogically literate, should hire them, and be sure they recruit equally qualified staff. Keeping teachers and communities happy at the expense of student learning is not good enough.

The democratic nature of school district elections is largely responsible for an administrative profession that lacks highly trained, productive members. In public education, politics prevails over productivity. This year's best intentions of administrators and trustees are issues for next year's elections. Boards and superintendents know their decisions must be capable of surviving the next election. Successful principals know that every district action will be judged by popular vote; it is little wonder that when teachers are on strike, principals can be found pouring coffee for them as they walk picket lines. In a time of conflict, district employees can put more workers and dollars into elections than board members and superintendents.

Democracy adversely affects administrators first. They are most under the influence of school board members who are under pressure from patrons and special interest groups. Administrators, especially superintendents, are expendable. Job security is hinged to pragmatic decision making that may enhance learning but ensures survival first. As long as unchecked democratic processes operate schools, many educational leaders will always do what is politically correct—at that particular moment.

As discussed earlier in this chapter, school districts are managed through a top-down, highly centralized structure. However, school boards are subject to the ballot box; employee organizations have the ability to change management and the structure. From this perspective, school districts are pyramidal organizations turned upside down. Teachers, through students and parents, can influence elections; few superintendents and boards of education can stand against them. The formula is simple: The most votes, the greatest ability to rouse the emotions of the citizenry, wins. A teacher with 25 or 125 students communicates directly with as many voters.

In elections, the teachers and staff of educational organizations can be at the top of the inverted pyramid if they convince the voters to stand with them. Principals, again, are caught squarely in the middle. The people can overthrow a superintendent and board. Principals who have been loyal to the board and superintendent may get thrown out when they are. Those loyal to the teachers and community may get thrown out by the administration before the election is held. Many principals work both ends against the middle in order to survive professionally. They tell superintendents what they want to hear and teachers what they want to hear.

Democracy, therefore, works against systemic improvement. Many principals, along with some superintendents, work hard to stay loyal to—and take direction from—teachers because any change for improvement in an organization predicated on harmony and stability causes a clamor about lack of morale. Often the smallest modification brings loud outcries; if people are creatures of habit, school districts are their most protected reserves. Few administrators ever lost a job because they did not enhance the education of children. In fact, a case may be made that far more have been dismissed for trying to improve the condition of instruction in their district or school than others have for protecting status quo mediocrity.

Change in a public school district is as difficult, it has been said, as moving a cemetery because even the dead have friends. The paradigm and its supporters have plenty of friends. Studies have shown that successful educational change takes as long as seven years to permeate a district. Board members may be sure that each of these years will be turbulent. Many administrators reject change for improvement because low morale and angry staff—the stuff of turmoil that is heard inside the community—often leads to difficult times for leaders.

In some school districts, employees do not pay enough attention to the calls for change (other than to complain) because they know that change will not affect them. Teachers know they can outlast any administrator who attempts to create change. Most teachers know the phrase: "I can shut my door and still be here when that principal is gone." Stay out of trouble, maintain good discipline, turn in lesson plans (if they are requested), keep the kids happy, and you will outlast any administrator is common advice given to aspiring young educators. Teachers have seen principals come and go. Changes one principal brings are gone the day the next one walks into the school. Teachers do not need to change; they just need to shut their door—and wait.

Unfortunately, many administrators do not work for improvement because they are also pragmatically focused against change, even change that will improve learning. Often they worked as teachers in the same school or district before becoming administrators and have grown comfortable with established routines; they are part of the culture. The district in which they work as managers may be the only one they have ever been employed in and the only system of management they know. Probably selected in part by staff members, they are trusted to maintain stability and peace.

Those in the system and the community who want education to remain as they remember it—as it has never been—take refuge in the knowledge that there is no agreed on purpose of education and that there is little quality control. There is no way, except in the most outrageous situations to judge if daily pedagogical activities are unsuccessful. Therefore, the most politically correct course for administrators to take is to leave faculty alone to do what they have always done. Theoreticians propose that principals spend most of their time improving instruction in a supervisory capacity by helping teachers refine their performances. But that is not what the current system usually rewards them for doing. In American public education, success depends on good discipline and keeping the buildings clean, the president of the support group happy, and the teachers feeling they are appreciated.

Since the opening of the first common school, there have been many attempts to reform public education. Most have failed. Little has changed; reforms are remembered merely as someone else's bad idea. A primary reason for the failure of educational reform to take root is the alliance of educators who cannot envision a better future and their community supporters, with untrained school board members. When some in a school system try to introduce improvements, a reactionary movement often arises. As a result, progressive educators find themselves with the task of trying to maintain their own jobs while protecting the traditional district culture.

It is not difficult to understand why leaders of public education have been ineffective in top-down organizations. They are expected to be competent in institutions that do not have an agreed on purpose and to maintain a system of management that works against the best interests of their clients while stifling the professionalism of employees. They are to be strong in organizations where everyone else has virtually life-time guaranteed jobs. Every decision they make has the potential to play to a packed house at the next board meeting—or be subject to popular vote at the next election. We wonder why administrators whose salaries are far below those usually awarded in private enterprise accepted their positions in the first place.

We must expect more from those we consider professionals than just performing pedagogical functions behind closed classroom or schoolhouse doors—with others allowing them to do so. We need to begin considering schools and school districts as we think of the association of partners in a professional firm. Educators need to be bonded to the entire organization, including its mission and underlying belief system. As professionals, they all must embrace personal and institutional accountability for the attainment of goals and the fulfillment of the mission. In particular, we should no longer think of educators as skilled labor in a top-down management system because such a system will never bond professionals. It is also little wonder that the loyalty of teachers and administrators goes to their associations rather than the district in which they work. In their professional organizations at least, they are treated as professionals.

The management structure must change to one in which educators are accountable for the efforts of the entire organization. But changing structure and broadening the scope of responsibility is not enough. Administrators must become educational leaders and managers skilled in the creation and nurturing of effective, accountable, successful teaching organizations that are adaptable to the changing needs of society. School administrators must be experts in educational theory and practice, teaching and learning, management, and organizational behavior, development, and change. They must be motivated to remain continually up to date in the research and implementation of each of these areas. They must understand and know how to create in their organizations the desire and ability to use data to drive improvement.

Board members are the legal authority over American public education. It is time they demanded the creation of a system that works. They need to realize that their role is to represent the people in an enlightened manner and to understand that their job is to create a system that effectively teaches all children. Their role is not to create an organizational democracy of employees and/or noninformed community members. If the public education cradle continues to swing in the political wind, the branch will soon break—brought down by the combined weight of school choice, private schools, vouchers, and uninformed politicians.

CHAPTER SEVEN

The Cycle

There is nothing new in the field of education. Everything has been done before.[1]

In many, perhaps most, school districts, there is a cycle of effectiveness and dysfunction that prevents them from sustaining a level of excellence. They break out of ineffectiveness only to be slowly pulled back in by a force as powerful as the tides. It could be that any attempt at systemic change in a democratically controlled institution is destined for futility. The stories that follow sound hypothetical, but they are true.

The first district is located on the outskirts of a large city. The area has a wonderful reputation, lying in the shade of mountains springing up from the plains almost in the middle of the city. All sorts of recreational areas are nearby. The culture is vibrant. Technology firms, environmentally friendly industries, and service organizations seek to locate in the area because of the lifestyle available to employees.

At the end of the Great Depression and the beginning of World War II, the federal government found the area suitable for the establishment of major military reservations. After the war, more federal facilities were built. Jobs were easy to find, government pay was good, and the mountains were close. By the end of the Vietnam War, the city had become the center of the federal government's aerospace program; the combination of geographic beauty, affluent lifestyle, and technological leadership earned it a reputation as one of the greatest places to live in America.

The hamlet of Paradise, settled as a small railroad junction that at its zenith had no more than ten buildings (including a hotel doubling as a house of ill repute) and thirty people, lies across the city from the mountains. An area of rolling plains and tall forests, the countryside around Paradise was originally divided into large ranches by cowboys who pushed the Native Americans off the land and who, in turn, gave way to a steady onslaught of pioneer farmers.

The little town eventually became the center of the Paradise school system that was gerrymandered into existence by aggregating small school districts started by the settlers. Eight to ten miles on horseback or in a wagon was far enough for pioneer children to travel. In the winter and late spring, blizzards could blow out of nowhere, obscuring clear skies as snow, blown by powerful winds, outraced its own clouds. When school buses became the preferred mode of travel, the small districts congealed into one large system that spread thirty miles in length and ten miles in width.

As the years passed, the city grew larger and developed some of the ills of urban living such as traffic congestion and smog. More and more of its inhabitants imagined living a country life—in Paradise. They wanted to live on their own land and thought it would feel great to go back to the wide-open spaces when their workday in the city was over. These new pioneers each bought several acres of prairie land under clear skies illuminated by millions of stars and a golden moon just a few miles out of the city. On a quiet night, they could still hear the coyotes howl. And so they came: blue-collar workers from the city's labor force and eight-hour-a-day workers from business and government.

They became known as hobby ranchers and farmers. Wages earned in town supported their obsession of owning five or ten acres of prairie. It did not matter if they had electricity or plumbing; they could heat with wood stoves, carry water, and hear the wind blow. Many drove cars back and forth from the city until they wore out and then they lined them up in rows on the back of the property line. Most built wood frames around their trailers and settled in for life.

The wide-open spaces among the areas of tall pines with cool summer temperatures in the northern part of the district became home to another class of residents. Professionals and others with high incomes moved in; they built big houses and ranch-style outbuildings and participated in the burgeoning urban horse culture. Paradise began to attract an upscale segment of dwellers who did not always get along with the proprietors of hobby farms. The congealing of all the small districts created an artificial political structure among groups of people who had nothing in common. Although diversity is usually accommodated in large districts, in Paradise with few inhabitants, feuds, dislikes, and territoriality became a way of life. As the population began to surge, the inhabitants became unable to form a community. The only thing they had in common was the school district, and they did not agree on how it should operate.

Even if the hobby farmers in the south could arrange a compromise with the wealthier families in the north, neither group could abide the folks to the west who were moving into an urban development along the edge of the encroaching city. Bargain-priced homes and apartments attracted many of the city's lower socioeconomic classes. Even more diversity was on its way as personnel from the army and air force bases found the area to be a place where they could afford housing.

Adding flame to a volatile mix, realtors told most of the urbanites they sold houses to that they were in the city school district, which had an abundance of new schools and sophisticated programs supported by the wealth of the urban center. The inhabitants of the prairies and forests wanted these people to be in the city. Unfortunately, they all lived in Paradise and could not even agree to break up the district and allow residents the opportunity to attend the schools they desired. They were stuck with each other.

The Paradise school board fired the first salvo in what was to become a long-running struggle. They established bus stops for urban children three miles across snake-infested and wind-blown prairie. There were no roads and no trails to the bus stops—nothing but wind, yucca plants, and grass tall enough to hide slithering perils. In winter there was no danger from reptiles, but the windchill and sudden blizzards were much deadlier. Was this an innocent but stupid act by a school board who did not understand the danger to children? No! In fact, Paradise had lost two elementary school siblings several years earlier. Bussed home in a blizzard, they discovered the door locked and no one home. The children set off for the neighbors less than one mile away but never made it. Everyone was aware of the volatility of weather in Paradise.

District leaders intended to force urban homeowners to enroll their children in the city's district where they would have to pay tuition. It was an absolutely crafty idea. Paradise would benefit from taxes paid by the developers and urban dwellers but not be responsible for educating their children. All of the tax money for the education of children would go to the rural ranchers and hobby farmers. They would be able to provide more for their children at the expense of others.

The urbanites could not afford the cost of tuition; they lived in some of the least expensive housing in the county. They petitioned to have their part of the district removed from Paradise and annexed to the city's district, but such an action required a vote by both boards. The Paradise board would not agree—it meant giving the golden goose away. Everyone could see the potential for industry, shopping centers, and other businesses that would increase the tax base. The people who lived in the urban areas had no choice but to drive their children (angrily) to school.

The district hired a superintendent in the early 1950s who stayed through most of the Vietnam War. After he retired, this revered man was replaced by several superintendents, each of whom lasted only a year or two. During the 1970s, a man who was hired to be a junior high school math teacher switched to teaching high school business when that teacher resigned; he then spent most of the year as superintendent after the one that they had just hired left—all in one year. Superintendents weren't the only ones to leave frequently (there were no other administrators in the district); so did teachers. Paradise reportedly fired all certified staff members after completion of their third year of teaching so that no one ever earned tenure and consequent higher salaries. Paradise did not build a great reputation.

After a sophisticated search by the state school board's association (it was rumored the district was such an embarrassment the association did the search for free), an educator with an excellent reputation was hired from a neighboring state. The new leader started his career as an administrator in the same state as Paradise, left to serve as an assistant superintendent in a large urban school district, and worked as a community college president in another state where he had also been employed as a superintendent of a reputable district. Known as a fiscal genius, he needed to work only a few more years in Paradise's state before he was eligible for full retirement. He came to Paradise thankful, ready to work, and excited by the challenge of creating a modern and progressive district from the ruins he had been handed.

74

What he discovered and lived through during the next six years left him cynical, angry, and full of despair. He heard his name ridiculed and his work derided. Turmoil, fights, hostility, polarization, and community politics finally claimed him as a victim. He was not in the district more than a few weeks before discovering that many of the past school boards had established accounts for district funds in different banks in the city, hiding money so that the "tax-and-spend liberal" board members that were sure to follow them could not get their hands on the funds previous school boards were protecting. He found all the money (actually totaling very little), but past board members despised him for discovering their hidden reserves.

Christmas of his first year yielded an unpleasant gift: He had to accept and inventory $200,000 worth of desks and equipment the board purchased the day before he started work and had not mentioned to him. This expense, almost 10 percent of the total budget, had not been included in the records. Resourcefully, he was able to borrow money and cut enough out of planned expenditures to make the payment.

He discovered a way to entice the federal government, as a part of impact funding, to pay $1,100,000 for a new high school and enough more to begin building core areas of an elementary school in the urban area. Since funds for the high school were barely enough to build four walls around some classrooms and a gymnasium, the enterprising educator accepted an offer of forty acres of property three miles north of what remained of the town on top of a hill and miles from the developing urban center. The land was free because a local developer, who cared about education and planning, predicted continuing growth of the area and thought the school should serve as the center of what was to be a new city of 50,000 people.

By 1978, the school district served more than seven hundred students. Because the state's finance act was configured so that there was a direct correlation between total assessed value and income per student, Paradise received the lowest funding per pupil in the state. There was not a store in the district or a place to buy a cup of coffee; there were no sites of production other than pastures. Paradise was a bedroom community. People in the developing urban areas were still being told by realtors that they were buying their houses in other school districts; they were still getting extremely angry when they discovered where and under what conditions their children would attend school. Except for the new high school, buildings were overcrowded. There were now three schools: the elementary school core, surrounded by modulars, in the urban area; Paradise elementary and junior high, occupying the original buildings and surrounded by many more modulars; and the high school.

The contentious citizens still did not like each other and started getting the better of the new superintendent. Although he labored to turn the district into a modern educational institution, because of the unfair finance act, he could pay teachers very little. Even the superintendent was a victim of the poor funding; his salary was only half as much as his peers in the urban districts. Unfair state financing ravaged the district: Teachers were the lowest paid, had the largest classes, and the lowest levels of supplies and materials of any in the area. Staff morale and parental regard plummeted to new lows.

In poorly funded school districts (as a result of unfair state finance systems), community anger and frustration are always directed toward the board and superintendent and seldom at the real culprits: state legislators. Even among teachers and principals, who should know better, the belief seems to be that if district leaders were more astute they would not be in this situation. Problems caused by a lack of funding, which usually include large class sizes, insufficient supplies of textbooks, library materials, computers, and poorly funded activities, almost always bring a public outcry to school board meetings and almost never to the legislative session. In states with unfair systems, rich districts often border poor ones, and reputation usually correlates highly with wealth. Residents of poor districts see what others have that they do not, believe what they hear about wealthier districts being better, and take their anger out on the board and superintendent. People will run for the board because they believe the lack of funds is the result of a budgeting mess caused by previous officials; the candidates usually target waste, bloat, and inefficiency—certain that they can solve the financial problems. Often campaigning to cut administrative salaries, numbers of employees, and other nonteaching personnel, they are elected only to discover that they can do little about the problem.

During the summer of 1979, all of the problems of financial disequity could be found in Paradise. Schools opened in the fall severely overcrowded, class sizes were the largest in the metropolitan area, teachers were poorly paid, and morale continued to spiral downward. The superintendent did not listen to anyone. The state's system of school finance did not give him the funds to be successful; he tried to maintain high expectations and high standards without staff input or participation. He believed that he could lift the struggling school system to a higher level by the force of his command. Teachers were so angry they openly wore pins, bracelets, and tie tacks ostentatiously displaying the letters FYTIMO. Supposedly a secret, but known by everyone in the district including most parents and community members, the acronym stood for, "F____ You, T____ (his name), I'm Moving On!" Most of the district's sixty teachers proudly wore their pins and tie tacks to class.

The teachers' fury was only partly because of poor pay. They were more upset by their exclusion from the very traditional and strict top-down management structure. On a scale of dissatisfaction, a higher salary may make a teacher less dissatisfied but will not create job satisfaction. Respect, input, participation, and an opportunity to share in their own and the organization's destiny create job satisfaction. Knowledge workers want to achieve and without the opportunity to do so, they only go through the motions of work.[2]

There was no building control of budgets, no opportunity for teachers or parents to participate in governance, and as a consequence, no understanding of the district's financial condition. Most thought that poor salaries, inadequate supplies, and large classes resulted from the miserliness of the administration. There was no explanation from the superintendent and the board. As in most other districts managed in this fashion, the fiscal frustration of the teachers and parents grew out of ignorance. Few parents and teachers understood the state funding mechanism; they knew nothing about educational finance. When it was finally explained to them, they were beyond the point of listening. Uninformed perceptions people develop inside the paradigm are always stronger than the truth.

There was yet one other reason for the district's poor reputation with its staff. The superintendent insisted on not renewing the contracts of teachers he felt were not up to his standards. Even in the 1970s this was a risky proposition in educational leadership. In 1976, he did not renew the contract of a second-year high school social studies teacher. Whether or not it was the right decision, the superintendent guessed wrong on two counts. He thought that the principal would testify for the district and that the local branch of the state university the teacher had attended would stay out of the fray. However, the principal was no longer in that position and supposedly disclaimed any responsibility. In fact, there were rumors that he thought the fellow was a good teacher. Faculty members at the university sided with the teacher, believing that the termination was for reasons other than performance. Finally, the state education association filed a wrongful termination lawsuit.

Even without support from the principal, the superintendent prevailed; the jury found in favor of the district. Instead of reducing emotions, the verdict exacerbated the situation. Teachers and their parent supporters were now certain there was a conspiracy against them; association lawyers pledged to get back at Paradise and the superintendent. They were going to make sure he was brought back to court. More than just expressing their anger, they were making a promise to the angry teachers and parents.

The following year the district did not renew two first-year teachers. The association, which quickly filed civil rights litigation charging denial of free speech and right of assembly, claimed the teachers were released because of union activities. Although termination of teachers should always be a task of the building principals, and district supporters believed this was the situation, the litigation centered around the superintendent. He was supposedly behind the firings. The state association and local teacher members believed the dismissal had nothing to do with pedagogical competence.

The district lost. The insurance company paid each teacher, association lawyers pocketed district funds, and the hatred on both sides grew more intense. Parents still wanted their children to attend city schools and most of them lobbied the board to fire the superintendent, who became more bitter. He even used his inflexible, centralized fiscal control to prevent the purchase of learning materials simply because such resources would have made the work of teachers easier.

The five-member board began to operate under the cloak of small town politics. The members started talking to and listening to everyone, forgetting that they were also responsible for the superintendent's management system. What then happened to the board members occurs frequently in such situations: Five volunteers who had opted to serve children, read about themselves in newspapers, had scorn heaped on them by employees and parents, and were shunned by the community. They then, in turn, began to make exaggerated responses to issues. As a result of the tension, stress, and invasion of privacy, they lost direction and focus.

One of the members, a transplant from an industrial area, was a virulent anti-unionist. He became the superintendent's most outspoken supporter, seeing the conflict as an attempt by the National Education Association to force a master agreement stipulating a formal negotiations procedure onto the district. He made his points with anger, threats, and hostility. During one meeting, he made a motion to delete reference to any employee association from board policies and procedures; he recommended that the association not be recognized as existing. The motion passed and the war of words became louder.

Another member assumed the dual role that is so damaging to districts: He agreed with the board during meetings, but worked closely with the teachers' group the rest of the time. He sabotaged any effort by the superintendent or other board members to improve the situation. Resolution by anyone other than him, when he fired the chief executive, would have robbed him of his importance.

The superintendent was still a dedicated educator, but his concern for learning was sublimated to an obsessive belief that he could break the local education association and its national organization. He thought that all America would recognize his plight, rush to his defense, and crush the union. Paradise would be the place that future teachers and administrators studied as a model, enshrined as the district where the triumph of one man over unions gave control of education back to superintendents and school boards. He waited anxiously for the arrival of the 60 *Minutes* television crew whose factual reporting would herald the demise of education's organized labor. The organizational structure established by board members and the superintendent did not work. The model they used never has and never will work in public education. They made three critical errors.

1. *The superintendent installed such a system of management based on his word as law that principals were emasculated.* None of the classified departments even had a supervisor or foreman. Control was vested completely with the superintendent. He picked wax for floors and instructed custodians how to clean rooms. He coordinated recipes for the food service program and told cooks how to prepare meals. He devised bus routes and set stops. Even in a district of only

seven hundred students, it was impossible for him to know everything and be able to tell each employee what to do and how to do it. It was equally impossible for him to have the time to supervise each person and evaluate the completion of each task—so there was no supervision. Each employee did what he or she thought best.

Thus, several axioms of management were in place: (a) Employees who are told what to do through orders but never supervised or held accountable will act in the way they think is best; they will find their own way to accomplish what they believe they were hired to do. Often, they do different things than what they were hired for and the entire system loses focus. (b) These employees become very comfortable with what they are doing and how they are doing it. When they are finally told that they have not accomplished the organization's goals, they may be counted on to react with anger and recrimination. Great personal loyalties are formed to self-created jobs. Change becomes very difficult. (c) Any job, no matter how long it takes, can become full time if worked at by people who are creating their own schedule. It is difficult to reduce any full-time position to part-time; when the job was created by an employee who is still working in the position, the task is almost impossible.

2. *The superintendent alienated the three principals.* They often sided with employees and parents against the superintendent who never left his unkempt second-story office in the fifty-seven-year-old, mostly vacated school building that should have been torn down years earlier. He spent as little time as possible in the district and never attended an activity or athletic event. He often said that the district paid him to run the schools, not to live in their community.

There is another axiom of school district governance that can often be found in districts operated by superintendents who centralize all authority to themselves. They either hire weak and ineffective principals who serve as "yes" people or place them in such a conflict-laden environment that they begin to act as if they were. This inherently denies their ability to be supportive of the superintendent, because "yes" people say "yes" to the person or group they perceive has the most power. During such times, some principals worry more about their own employment than doing what is right. Others begin to tell teachers what they want to hear, the superintendent and board members what they want to hear, and everybody else what they want to hear. In private as well as public enterprise, middle managers in strife-filled systems often join into a grand conspiracy to outlive everyone else. Desiring to assume power, they may encourage the chief executive to assume intractable stances, believing such will hasten the fall from grace. Some may work clandestinely with organizations battling leadership; their motivation is to survive or to assume power.

3. *The superintendent trusted the school board to back him completely as he broke the yoke of unionism in America.* His battle was an ideological quest for control of American education. This position was too extreme for most. Even the board members who disliked unions were not agreeable to a battle that would consume their lives. Most of them wanted to be liked more than they wanted to break the National Education Association.

The year went from bad to worse. Anger was omnipresent. Sensing that an explosion was imminent, city newspaper and television reporters camped in the district. The superintendent still refused to change, reacting with anger to any suggestions that a different management style would produce healthier results.

The local education association, supported by petitions signed by almost 1,000 parents, urged the State Education Association to investigate the district in November. If the school system was found as bad as claimed, the association was ready to issue sanctions in lieu of calling a strike. Paradise was so bad, the teachers claimed, it was not worth striking over; they did not wish to suffer through the struggle a strike would bring. The investigation was conducted; state leaders interviewed parents, teachers, and principals; they found reasons for sanctions (as they knew they would) and called for a forty-five-day cooling-off period— time for the superintendent and the board to understand the dysfunction of the system and restructure its operation.

Still believing that national news crews and public pressure would support him, the superintendent ignored the association and parents. Sanctions, which in many ways are more damaging to a district than a strike (they incur more citizen support since teachers remain at their duties), were imposed. In Paradise, it looked like the only people hindering education were the district leaders.

Everyone in the state was notified of the sanctions imposition through a well-planned press release; so was every teacher-training college in America. Prospective educators from coast to coast were urged not to accept a position in a district officially labeled substandard.

The sanctions and the skillfully developed report, supposedly written after an intensive study of the district, were to generate positive press for teachers and negative publicity for district officials. The report contained statistics showing that 80 to 90 percent of the teachers believed their morale was low and that the depressed level was caused by a lack of supplies and equipment, poor working conditions, unfair treatment, favoritism, reprisals, and little respect for their opinions. The two central administrators were accused of harassing teachers and pushing morale down to an all-time low.

> The Committee recommends that [Superintendent] and [Assistant Superintendent] be fired immediately. Paradise School District has outgrown [Superintendent.] He definitely assisted the School District in its early stages of being financially strapped, but in the committee's opinion, he has no management skills in terms of dealing with people. [Superintendent] has not provided positive leadership, and he continues to be the major problem relative to the District. [Assistant Superintendent] is not accepted by the bulk of the building administrators or teachers either as a leader or as a public relations person.
>
> [Assistant Superintendent] is allied too closely with [Superintendent] and has, therefore, lost any effectiveness. Both [Superintendent] and [Assistant Superintendent] have demonstrated they cannot or will not change.[3]

Teachers were urged not to leave the district and to stay and fight for their rights and the education of their students. Everyone in the region was constantly reminded how bad things were as they passed huge billboards erected by the association on every highway and road into the district that declared Paradise a place of substandard education. No one could escape the struggle.

The board chose to go on as before, ignoring the sanctions and not allowing any reference to the education association in board policy. Teachers began a strategy of guerrilla warfare: attending workshops to learn tactics such as interrupting board meetings, taking charge of the board, and preventing trustees from making decisions. Meetings were soon attended by armed sheriff's deputies hired by the board to maintain order and to throw hecklers and combatants off the premises. Trench warfare developed. Neither side moved.

Oblivious to the political disaster, the board ordered a bond issue election to build a new elementary school in the rural area, to transform the existing elementary/junior high into a middle school, and to build classroom wings onto the urban elementary. It passed by two votes: 217 in favor, 215 against. In this outcome there is a tremendous lesson. Most parents want only what is best for their children, according to their perceptions. Except for the most conservative members, communities will always side with the teachers in a time of polarization with the board. The teacher's association came out in support of the bond issue. The community did not vote positively because the board wanted them to; they did it because the teachers asked them for support. Parents usually believe that teachers will do more for their children than board members and central office administrators. In times of turmoil, teachers are seen as self-sacrificing professionals driven by a desire to help children; board members and administrators are perceived as reactionaries bent on preventing teachers from being successful.

Conservative and old-fashioned in his values, the superintendent let anger and bitterness drive him into a totally noncompromising position. Allegedly, the board was finally moved to terminate his contract when he exclaimed that he would not start construction on the new schools because teachers would work in them. He appeared to have forgotten that children also spent their days in the schools.

Under a new superintendent, the ensuing eight years constituted a time of peace and relative prosperity, even though the district remained the poorest per student in the state. Two more bond issues passed as enrollment increased from seven hundred to twenty-seven hundred students. Every facility was remodeled, buildings from the original bond issue were constructed, along with yet another middle school. A third elementary school was financed through a building authority (a group of private citizen volunteers sold bonds and lease-purchased the structure to the district). Even the athletic facilities were rebuilt. Teachers became some of the highest paid in the area; Paradise began to play a state leadership role in site-based decision making and curriculum. Test scores climbed to the highest levels ever achieved. Three years after the firing of the superintendent, the State Education Association formally removed the sanctions.

But school districts are cyclical in nature. What goes around comes around and goes around again. Those who have been vanquished struggle to reach supremacy again. The ultraconservative, anti-teacher board members from the time of the previous superintendent slowly began to resurface. Although they had either left or were voted out of office, as years passed, their longing to return to power increased.

A new conspiracy began. Some employees and residents who remembered the old days as better started working clandestinely with a board leader from the days of the sanctions. He wanted to be a board member once again. Every Saturday a group met for breakfast to develop takeover strategies. Any member of the district with an ax to grind was invited to join. The pendulum was swinging back. The board member was reelected; he arranged a coalition with two of the other three board members, and top-down management was installed once again. During the next nine years the district went though seven different superintendents. The revolution to reinstate the paradigm was led by a coalition of old paradigm board members and old-line administrators who wished to reinstate the past.

The Paradise school district epitomized the problems in a politically driven system of K–12 education. A combination of administrators and teachers with traditional views of management joined with a group of board members who struggled continuously to keep the district—and education—as it had always been. Even if the times they wished to return to were troubled, they represented what was no longer and had always seemed better. People in the paradigm usually remember better times—not the reality. Perhaps, this district will change only when enough new people move in to overwhelm the traditional culture.

Another district, Flagstone, is not Paradise, but most of the people who live there think it is. Flagstone is the home of the frontier spirit; belief in the self-made man and that hard work is the key to prosperity pervades the community. There is little ethnic or racial diversity; some people may have moved there for just that reason. It is a city of independent-minded folks who believe that they have found the perfect place to live.

The school system had never had student test scores resemble a bell-shaped curve; results usually had been bimodal. Many students earned As and Bs, while many others received only Ds and Fs. Many residents of this community, as in so many others across the nation, believe that this is how it is supposed to be. As in the rest of America, even the parents of those earning lower grades agreed. Many of the people of Flagstone, replicating the prevailing American paradigm, do not believe that all children can learn.

For a stretch of five years in a row the district had been outspending income; no one in the community seemed to know this or to care because in the past the district had, on the basis of its oil economy, built up $5,000,000 in reserves (at one time it was one of the richest school districts in the United States). It was so rich that teachers got everything they wanted. Any annual income left over and all of the reserves were just added to all line items, effectively padding each. Unfortunately, changes in the state finance act drastically altered the wealth of the district.

During the years of over expenditure, led by conservatives on the board, the district had frozen all salaries with no movement on salary schedules for three years. The employees' salaries were not just frozen at the base; they were not even given yearly experience or additional education pay. Not only was this a conscious decision to reduce costs; reportedly the trustees also did not believe anyone deserved a yearly raise just because they survived the previous nine months.

Flagstone schools had few computers until the board and superintendent purchased IBM clones for a high school lab. Teachers were furious; most were sure that these new contraptions were paid for with their raises. Faculty members who were not angry about the purchase of computers in general, were infuriated about the brand that was purchased.

Relations between teachers, the board, and the superintendent were strained, to put it mildly. Hateful would be a more accurate term; the hatred knew no boundaries. All pretense of civility was gone. One board member who voted against staff raises was reported to have lost more than 40 percent of his business. In a loud yelling match with the superintendent, a high school teacher was surprised when the administrator grabbed his chest and fell to the floor with an apparent heart attack. As the superintendent was transported to the hospital, high school faculty members were reported to have snake-danced through hallways.

The board became an object of distrust and the subject of great rumors in connection with a land purchase that seemed suspicious to many residents. The school board had purchased forty acres for a new high school site. They paid more than $800,000 for property assessed at less than $200,000. No one knew why. Many alleged that personal wealth was improperly gained by all the participants in the deal. The community was furious; residents trusted neither school board members nor superintendents.

The heat of conflict broke out into open conflagration. The chief executive was reported in the local newspaper as saying that teachers work only for three reasons: June, July, and August. The teachers retorted that administrators do not work at all. They called each other names and made terrible accusations. Board decisions, the rumors went, were made when the five male members met in the restroom during breaks; votes were held in public only as a show of legality. Teachers were ridiculed; so were administrators and board members. Finally, the community, aided by a strong teacher vote, elected a new slate of citizens to run the schools.

The lessons for school board members should be obvious.

1. In a fight for control of a school district, the board almost always loses. Teachers control the hearts and minds of the community because they work with children. For a board to win, the issues have to be clear and extremely serious—and the board members have to become excellent communicators.

2. When board members, administrators, and teachers enter into public fight, everyone loses because people listen to both sides. Many residents believed that teachers were lazy and only taught for summer vacations; they also believed that administrators were lazier and did no work at all and were not interested in education. The public always listens and believes the worst.

3. Above all, community members want peace and harmony in their school district. They may not know the difference between good and poor education, but they can recognize fighting. As long as there is peace, most people accept the school system as doing well.

Flagstone was a school district in which many residents believed that only students from the best and brightest families were expected to succeed in school. The wealthiest children went off to private boarding schools in the East. The next echelon, based on wealth, graduated from the local high school and attended colleges all around the country. Bright students passed because they were smart. The rest failed. Often the yearly drop-out rate was 18 to 20 percent.

During a year-long planning session Flagstone's problems became evident. Employee morale was recognized as terrible. There was no written curriculum. Facilities were in terrible condition because there never had been an effective preventative maintenance program. Most textbooks were more than ten years old. The school system seemed to have rejected technology.

Through the leadership of the board, change came quickly to Flagstone. The district began to concentrate on maintaining high levels of work by top students while raising those on the bottom to the same pinnacles. Administrators and board members worked with teachers relentlessly to adopt a belief system that would allow all students to learn. New administrators were hired to help install that belief across the district and community.

Within seven years all buildings had been rebuilt on the strength of a bond issue and a state grant; three had been torn down and reconstructed from the ground up. Curriculum and assessments were written. A computer and technology system that networked all buildings was installed. Test scores climbed higher than ever, and the war between the board, the administrators, and the teachers ended. Strife was replaced with respect and professionalism.

Yet storm clouds gathered. Some members of the community prepared to reinstate the paradigm. They would not listen to the voices for education of all children; they heard only the dissidents and those who believed the old ways were better. They rallied around the belief that all students should not learn. Their efforts were unflagging in denigrating any practice based on holding high standards of learning for all. Harbingers of the paradigm's return were the pleadings from old-line teachers, a few administrators, and some townspeople for a return to the practices of retaining primary students, holding transitional first-grade classes for children not ready to enter the assembly line, and grouping secondary students by ability.

In this, and most other districts, many of the older teachers who began their careers when it was accepted that only some could learn are a force continually working to bring back the old days. They do not wish to change; they do not want to believe that all of those children they failed in the past could learn. Many of these teachers desperately wish to return to the days when they were at war with the superintendent and school board. Decision making was easy then: They were against anything the administration supported. Now they were expected to participate in decisions and this was a great deal more stressful.

An important lesson to be learned from Flagstone was aptly described by an old rancher as he talked about change. "People who try to change this place are about as successful as a one-legged man in a butt kicking contest." Many people in the community determined to fight against the changes, even if schooling had improved. School boards cannot promote positive change toward the improvement of education without upsetting many of their constituents. This is probably the major dissonance of most school board members. Change to improve education is always uncomfortable. Keeping everything the same, even if the system does not work well for children, is more comfortable.

More than anything else, most people want their school districts to be happy places. The business of teaching all with high standards, of creating a system in which all children learn, is fraught with anxiety and strife. Principals who do not have happy and satisfied teachers in their buildings are those most commonly criticized. Administrators who make changes are attacked. Not rewarded for continuing to carry on the struggle, they begin to yearn for peace and less stress. They grow tired and no longer wish to fight. Happiness, satisfaction, and low taxes are the key to great school districts.

So the paradigm's coalition, the one that can always be found working to maintain the status quo, slowly grew. It was a coalition of parents, teachers, administrators, and board members who wanted things to be like they always had been. Attempting to teach students from lower socioeconomic classes causes disequilibrium; telling some parents that poor children can do as well as theirs causes more disequilibrium. Progenitors of change are often driven out, not reelected, terminated, or forced to leave. The system grinds on. Flagstone, like many other districts, was preparing for a change back to the past.

The only group that can fight for progress and for all the children (in any community) is the local board of education. Members must take on the paradigm, fight the good fight, and advocate for the right of every child to be educated. Board members need to analyze their school system to discover the influence of the paradigm. The best way is by asking themselves two simple questions. (1) Is there anyone currently in our district that we would not fire if the superintendent recommended it, even if the only reason is because the person does not do enough to improve learning? (2) Is their anyone in our district that the superintendent would not fire if the situation warranted that action? If the answer to either one of these is yes, chances are good that the district exists to employ adults rather than to educate children.

CHAPTER EIGHT

Money, Equity, and Learning:
Educators' Shame

*For the reasons we have explained in detail, this system
conditions the full entitlement to such interest on wealth,
classifies its recipients on the basis of the collective affluence
and makes the quality of a child's education depend on the
resources of his school district and ultimately on the pocket-
book of his parents. We find that such financing system as
presently constituted is not necessary to the attainment of any
compelling state interest* [1]

I had just become an assistant superintendent. After teaching in
the same state for fifteen years and studying educational finance during
doctoral studies, I knew as much about the subject as most. Or so I
thought. But it was not until I became a central office administrator
that I understood financial inequity and the devastation it can cause.

My new district housed students in extremely poor buildings. Sew-
age was pumped from buildings on one campus into a leach field that
did not work; students played in the overflow as they walked to the
playground. Playground equipment was thirty years old; concrete poured
when the structures were installed was exposed and dangerous where
the covering dirt had eroded. Teeter-totters were full of splinters; swings
were usually useless, hanging only by the chain on one side. School
buildings, equally hot in the spring and fall, were so unevenly heated in
the winter that one side of the hall was so cold you could see your breath
while the other was much too hot. Parents sewed curtains for classrooms out of any material that could be found.

But the physical deficits were only part of the problem. There had never been a written curriculum. Textbook procurement consisted of discovering which other districts were throwing books away and rescuing them from the trash. (Teachers called themselves the Midnight Textbook Company since most acquisitions were made late at night.) We could not afford library books or reading, music, and art classes. Our teachers had the lowest salaries, largest classes, worst buildings, and poorest equipment of any in the area. They were forced to continually spend their own money for teaching supplies—if they were going to have any. Teachers were angry and parents were furious. They did not understand why their children and schools could not have the things that others had.

Across the district's southern, western, and northern boundaries were larger and wealthier school systems. To the east were wide-open spaces replete with small communities and the built-in pride that enables citizens to look beyond matters of funding. My district was a milieu of dwellings that, with a stretch of the imagination, could possibly be called suburbs. There were no stores, businesses, or industry, and it was mostly inhabited by low-income families. You could not buy a cup of coffee or a pair of socks inside the district's boundaries; it was a bedroom community with little assessed value to pay for education.

Although several of the neighboring districts held national reputations for excellence, people continued to move into my district when, for the same price of home, they could have lived in one of the others. They moved in so quickly that the district became the fastest growing in one of the country's fastest growing western states. These people, like most others, wanted the very best for their children, but they did not understand the differences between districts when they bought their house. By the time they borrowed money and mortgaged the property, it was too late to move again.

While searching for the reasons causing our financial situation, I discovered that my district was the lowest funded, per pupil, in the state. Spurred by the anger of teachers and citizens who realized what they did not have, I learned several immutable rules of school finance.

1. Parents do not care about funding or educational finance; parents want the same things for their children that others have. When educators do not deliver, parents believe it is time to get rid of them.

2. Teachers usually do not care about funding or educational finance; they just want the same things others have. Only incompetent administrators do not deliver.

3. Administrators and board members in wealthy districts do not care about funding in other districts; they define the word equity as stealing—from them.

4. Most teachers, administrators, board members, and legislators do not understand educational finance.

5. There is no commitment to equity.

When I became the superintendent of the district, I took the job of leading the poorest school system in the state. I had the task of building a quality school system that was competitive with the others around us and I had to do it with a lot less money than the others had. I soon learned that legislators refused to help; they would not consider a new act based on equity. Superintendents in other districts spoke condescendingly while meeting with their representatives to ensure continuation of the unequal allocation formula. This attitude is the shame of education and educators. Perhaps it is an outgrowth of local control, maybe just an extension of capitalism, but the pervasive attitude among school people is one of protection of students in their own district with little concern for students in another. It is more than not caring; it is a vicious and emotionally violent form of protectionism.

I filed a lawsuit that was financed by a nationally known foundation against the State Board of Education during my seventh year as a superintendent. I expected that the legitimacy of the action would be warmly received by educational organizations and parent-teacher groups. Who, I wondered naively, could react negatively to an effort to ensure equal treatment of children? The first such reaction came from the leaders of the administrative association who derisively referred to the suit as the "Son of Lujan," named after failed litigation filed ten years earlier. For my remaining two years in the state, I was looked at suspiciously. Even several administrators in my district were publicly critical of the action because they wished to court the favor of wealthier districts.

Before the case went to trial the legislature adopted a new finance act that made many of the changes we requested. Our suit was no longer relevant since the system we challenged was no longer in place; we joyfully dropped the litigation. However, a great many people were unhappy with this turn of events. Parents, teachers, and administrators from wealthy districts were angry because a leveling system was invoked and some districts would lose funding. Superintendents from districts helped by the new legislation were quick to side with those from wealthier systems; inequity had become so accepted that administrators from poor districts used to try to find jobs in wealthier ones. They believed that financial leveling would ruin their chances of getting a higher paying position in a wealthy district.

The adverse reputation I earned from leading the struggle to change the state's finance act stayed around for a long time. Six years after the suit was filed, and after I had been a superintendent in another state for four years, a school board from yet another state more than a thousand miles away dropped me from consideration for employment partly because administrators in my first state told them of the damage I caused with the suit. This board, in a wealthy district in a state with rumblings about fiscal disparity and litigation, did not want to hire a superintendent who was notorious for advocating equity.

America has created a system of public education that functions very much like our economy. Those who have money are able to use their resources to gain more. Rich districts accumulate wealth and use it to defend an unequal system. Wealthy districts can afford lawyers to protect the status quo. Having campaigned to help children, school board members live a lie every day they serve in a state with inequitable funding and use tax funds to defend an unfair state finance system. Equity will never occur until school board members make it a priority of their service.

Two years after filing the suit, I accepted a new position. My new district had a great reputation in a state known for generously funding education. After being there one week, I found only the reputation remaining. Teachers were angry and depressed; the district was polarized between staff and the superintendent and board. Most textbooks were twenty years old, equipment purchased ten years earlier was in an acute state of disrepair and the district could not afford its operation.

I was overwhelmed when I learned at a state department work session my second day on the job that by every measure, my new district was the state's lowest funded in terms of operational dollars per pupil even though it remained one of the wealthiest in terms of assessed value. Most people in the system still believed the district was well endowed with funds. They had always heard it was because the growing district was home to the state's largest oil fields and a fairly diverse economy. A decade earlier when the state had a reputation for funding education per pupil at a very high level, this district spent the most. At that time funding for each district was based almost entirely on local taxes but that system was declared unconstitutional by the State Supreme Court in the Washakie Case ten years earlier. State leaders were mandated to institute an equitable system. As a result, each district's ability to generate income had been limited.

The search to discover why the district was the lowest funded revealed ten years of intrigue, legislative naiveté, and power-brokering. On the surface—and at best—it appears that some board members and superintendents took advantage of a citizen legislature and an overworked state department of education. At worst, it was the inevitability of politics in education. Local district officials became determined to provide adequate educational funding for their districts at the expense of other children—and begged their legislators for protection. In either scenario, the story is one of manipulation of the state funding mechanism with interwoven themes of disequity defended by wealthy districts and legislative action taken in complete ignorance of the principles of educational finance. It ends with a decision written by the justices of the Supreme Court who knew less than anyone else.

The state's finance formula was based on a Class Room Unit (CRU). Trying to use diseconomy of scale—the axiom in education that it takes more money to educate a smaller group of students than a larger number—legislators had established a series of divisors to be divided into the total number of students attending a district's schools, the Average Daily Membership (ADM), and then multiplying the quotient by a set amount. Districts were allocated $92,333 for each class room unit in 1996. Therefore, a school district counting ten units would be funded at a total of $920,333 while a school system with one hundred units would get $9,203,330. Diseconomy of scale was factored into the formula by allocating smaller divisors to smaller districts. For instance, a district with ten to twenty-seven elementary students used a divisor of eight. Thus, a school district with sixteen elementary pupils using a divisor of eight would divide the number of students (16) by the divisor (8) and multiple the quotient (2) by $92,333 and receive funding of $184,666. The divisor system is shown in Table 8.1.

Added to the amount received for class room units, the state reimbursed 85 percent of all special education costs and 75 percent of all transportation expenses incurred while carrying students to and from school. Calculations showed that district funding ranged from a high of almost $18,000 per pupil to just over $4,000 per student where I was superintendent. In theory, the smallest districts should have received the most per student while the largest received the least, and there should have been an almost straight-line progression from the largest to the smallest.

Why was my district the lowest funded? We were certainly not the largest. Using a statistical analysis, I found a significant negative correlation between district size and income per pupil; smaller districts did receive more. I could not identify a significant relationship between income per pupil and per pupil assessed wealth or total district assessed wealth. It did not seem that districts that had high assessed value spent more.

Table 8.1: State Divisor System for School Funding

Number of Students (ADM)	Divisor
Elementary Schools	
Less than 10	8
10 but less than 27	8
27 but less than 44	12
44 but less than 76	14
76 but less than 151	16
151 but less than 301	19
301 but less than 501	22
501 and over	23
Middle Schools	
Less than 51	13
51 but less than 151	15
151 but less than 301	18
301 but less than 501	21
501 and over	23

Number of Students (ADM)	Divisor
High Schools	
Less than 76	10
76 but less than 151	14
151 but less than 301	17
301 but less than 501	20
501 and over	23

Source: Wyoming State Department of Education, School Finance Department, 1996.

I asked educators and legislators around the state why my district was the lowest funded district per pupil. Each person had a different answer. Many legislators and some school officials believed the cause to be the unfair distribution of vocational education funds, which, in itself, is a tale of legislative bumbling and school district avarice. When the school finance act was passed as a reaction to the earlier litigation, legislators funded vocational education categorically: Districts were to receive a 75 percent reimbursement for every dollar spent on vocational education. Some district officials recognized immediately that anything could be justified as vocational—attach a vocational label and the state paid.

Manipulation of vocational funding almost became a science. Some districts received five to six times the amount of vocational funding as like-sized school districts operating the same programs but not labeling them vocational. Finally state legislators, not wanting to be taken advantage of any longer, froze the amount funded annually—at the amount each district had been receiving and removed the funds from a categorical account. This meant that vocational funds could be spent on anything; manipulation was no longer necessary.

Now school systems that had called programs vocational and received more could legally keep and spend the funds. Inequity was caused by manipulation of the system; legislators merely formalized the deal. Several years later, even these patient politicians had enough and rolled vocational dollars into the general fund on a CRU basis. Districts that had been receiving less received a windfall; those spending more took a loss.

However, the correlation of total income per pupil and per pupil vocational funding was not significant. It was a cause of inequity, but not a primary cause. Perhaps, I thought, this was because two other parts of the plan, special education and transportation, were as easy to manipulate. The legislature had tried to help districts with potential dissimilar expenses by reimbursing special education at 85 percent and transportation at 75 percent. Experts from around the country believed the state's finance act, especially the special education and transportation components, to be one of the nation's best. This state, it appeared, was generously repaying major percentages of what was spent on these programs and financing schools through need.

Actually, special education refunded all expenses by position with no limitation on number of personnel. Some school districts implemented their own peculiar model of inclusion by placing a special educator in every classroom and reducing class size by one-half since both teachers taught the same subject. The state paid 85 percent of the salary of one of the teachers. In essence, the act funded positions with no accountability of how they were used.

Transportation was the same. Districts could pay bus drivers $40 an hour to drive three hours a day as long as they volunteered to clean schools for five hours. Drivers made $120 per day, and custodial expenses were reimbursed by transportation.

Vocational education, special education, and transportation funds certainly created variances in district income per pupil. But none of them correlated significantly with per pupil income and neither did the aggregate. Special education and transportation lumped together after the vocational funding roll-in also did not. I still had not learned why my district was the lowest funded. No one knew why, and no one really cared because most districts just wanted more—equity was not considered important as long as everyone had enough.

Unrelated to my search, and after threatening for several years, four of the largest districts filed suit over the issue of disparate funding. The state education association quickly joined. Plaintiffs believed the spread between large and small districts was too great. Officials in those four districts expressed a need to be funded on a level more nearly equaling smaller systems. Within a month, a majority of the smaller districts filed as friends of the state, fighting to retain their funding and maintain the differences.

The suit was, in many ways, a joint district effort against the state. Concerned with equality, plaintiff and defendant districts, along with educator groups, began searching for a level of funding high enough to meet everyone's needs. Superintendents from large districts believed they should have class sizes as small as the smallest districts whose board members replied that they should have the same number of course offerings as the largest.

The case was against diseconomy of scale as it was practiced. The new proposal was to fund schools-not districts-on the basis of size. This plan would allow districts to operate as many small, inefficient schools as they and their community wished with little regard for fiscal responsibility. Economy of scale only works if it is applied to entire school districts. School systems have the ability to create larger and more efficient schools, individual schools do not. People confused equality with equity; actually equity means unequal funding because the needs of children are not equal. Funding children equally is disequitable.

School finance is complex and confusing. Analogous to reading a Russian novel, it is a long, slow, and boring process and everyone gets killed in the end. School finance is different in each state; each has invented its own version of the wheel. Lessons learned in one state seem almost purposefully ignored in the next. "It is fifty separate stories of controversy, of fumbling, of false starts, of long periods of inaction, and of application of various forms and degrees of informal local and state action."[2] There has never been a time of equity within states, between states the gap is often just as wide, as Table 8.2 shows.

It is possible for a state to achieve equity because framers of most state constitutions included a clause that calls for a thorough and uniform system of education. School board members and administrators should have the same passion for equity as those early statesmen did. Financial equity, based on four axioms, should be a priority of anyone who runs for a seat on a school board.

1. Quality of education, as measured by spending, should not be a function of the wealth of the parents. Wealthy communities in one part of the state should not be able to spend more on the education of their children than is spent on the education of children in other districts.

2. The cost of education statewide should, on a ratio basis, be the same for each taxpayer. People in poorer communities should not have to allocate a higher percentage of their income for the support of education.

3. Equitable school finance is a state burden.

4. States and local school boards must hold administrators to the highest levels of fiduciary responsibility.

Table 8.2: Allocations Per Pupil Spending Adjusted for Regional Cost Differences (1996)

State	Allocation	State	Allocation
New Jersey	8,176	Ohio	5,729
Indiana	8,059	Alaska	5,677
Connecticut	7,802	Washington	5,643
New York	7,416	Texas	5,546
Vermont	6,764	Florida	5,497
Delaware	6,741	North Dakota	5,412
Pennsylvania	6,708	North Carolina	5,349
Wisconsin	6,519	Oklahoma	5,259
Michigan	6,438	Tennessee	5,255
Rhode Island	6,417	Hawaii	5,145
Nebraska	6,380	Wyoming	5,123
Georgia	6,342	Nevada	5,084
West Virginia	6,340	Colorado	5,051
Montana	6,297	South Carolina	5,015
Iowa	6,105	South Dakota	4,943
Illinois	6,067	Missouri	4,926
Maine	6,066	Louisiana	4,804
Maryland	5,989	Alabama	4,764
Kansas	5,953	Idaho	4,629
Oregon	5,930	Arizona	4,515
Minnesota	5,929	Mississippi	4,455
New Mexico	5,925	California	4,448
Massachusetts	5,899	Utah	3,810
New Hampshire	5,805	Arkansas	3,728
Kentucky	5,801		
Virginia	5,787	**U.S. Average**	**5,787**

Source: "Quality Counts: The Urban Challenge, Public Education in the 50 States," *Education Week*, January 1998, p. 86. See Appendix A for a breakdown of average per-pupil expenditures by category in nine represented school districts in 1967, 1991, and 1996.

Educational inequity is governmental child abuse, which harms its victims as surely as any other type of mistreatment. No matter how rich or poor parents in a community are, states owe children financial equity. Children of wealthy families already have a head start; there is little reason for a state to formalize the differences. Board members and educators who protect what they have at the expense of quality schooling for all children fail a test of ethical behavior. The struggle should be for equity, never for defense of unfairness. Finance litigation occurs only because educators and board members from wealthy districts who have a primary interest in retaining privileges for their children actively attempt to deny educational opportunity for others. Courtrooms in which educational equity is litigated are the arena of America's continuing class struggle.

As learning is increasingly the path to well-being, those who are committed to inequity in funding are committed to societal classes. Education litigation is tobacco litigation in reverse; instead of protecting the people from an unsafe commodity, states advocate for an unsafe system, failing to realize that ills from educational unfairness are more harmful than the carcinogens in tobacco.

In the state where I was a superintendent, the battle raged over money, not equity. The wolf was wearing the lamb's equity clothing. The suit was supposedly over the difference between large and small district funding. The smallest district, with only thirty-nine students, received five times the amount per pupil as the largest. Lawyers representing the complainant districts and the education association argued that the gap was too large; various-sized districts they claimed, needed to be funded equally or at least less unequally. Legislators were asked to spend more on the larger districts to narrow the gap.

Equity could have been achieved by leveling down (reducing the funding of all districts equal to the amount per pupil received by the poorest). The struggle for equity does not have to mean more money; it can merely entail a fair allocation of funds based on logical and justifiable reasons. A finance act must be rational and explainable; equity means inequality based on rational reasons. If the struggle had been over equity, the gap could have been closed by reallocating funds already spent on education. However, after listening to the testimony, the Supreme Court found that all children needed smaller class sizes, more technology, nicer buildings, diseconomy of scale based on school size, and, in general, more money. The justices listened to lawyers when they should have been reading educational research.

After the decision was announced, state legislators began meeting to create a new act designed on the Court's guidelines. Educators packed the gatherings, issuing impassioned pleas for more of everything. Teachers, administrators, and board members quoting nonspecific research, relying primarily on tearful teacher testimony, demanded fewer than twenty students per class, elementary schools of no more than three hundred students, and high schools with only six hundred pupils. Legislators heard that students in the smallest high schools deserved to take as many classes as those in the largest, and those in the largest needed the same kind of small community care as those in the smallest.

There was real disequity in the state, but the Supreme Court failed to recognize it. What everyone missed was that in the state's eighteen largest school districts (about one-half of the total number of districts), no correlation could be identified between funding and pupils. Yet the student enrollment differential of these eighteen districts was great. The largest was almost seven times the smallest and at least four times larger than my district, which was the twelfth largest and funded at the lowest amount. Actually, the districts that filed the suit were some of the state's wealthiest in terms of assessed value and bonding capacity per student and three of the wealthiest in terms of operating funds per pupil of the eighteen largest districts.

There really was disequitable funding, but no one could explain why. Supreme Court justices who should have been thorough enough to find the truth never did. Disequity was allowed to exist because neither the state legislature nor the department of education had ever established a review of the system to analyze how it worked. But even if they had, nobody would have looked for overt manipulation. My district was the lowest funded simply because its educators and board members had never taken advantage of the finance act—and the state's taxpayers.

In 1980 after an earlier suit that resulted in the Washakie decision, the legislature adopted the Class Room Unit funding mechanism, the 85 percent special education and 75 percent transportation plans, and the vocational education plan later rolled in. They established a plan and expected school boards to work within the guidelines.

Perhaps the legislators were overly trusting. Certainly, they had no idea how their special education and transportation accounts were being used. But the real problem was that they left the entire system of divisors open to manipulation. They had created a finance system through which school districts could establish the amount of income they received. The plan required districts to aggregate students of the same age levels within city or town limits for the purpose of figuring class room units. This brought diseconomy of scale into play; if a district had more than five hundred elementary school students in town it was funded at the largest divisor of twenty-three to one; the same divisor was used if they had more than five hundred middle school and high school students.

Because the state is rural, legislators decreed that schools five miles out of town were exempt from the municipal divisor. It did not take long for some educators to figure out that educating fifteen hundred elementary students in town would yield 65.2 class room units. If those units are multiplied by a factor of $93,000, elementary general education would be funded at $6,063,600; but if they operated five schools of three hundred more than five miles from town (transportation was funded at 75 percent of any cost), the divisor dropped to nineteen and funding climbed to $7,337,000, almost $1,300,000 more.

When the lawsuit was filed, the only number that correlated significantly among the eighteen largest districts with funding per pupil was the number of students in the divisor—negatively. The lower the divisor, the larger the amount of per pupil funding. Yet most of these districts had more than five hundred students in elementary, junior, and senior high schools inside city limits. The only way the divisor could be reduced was to build schools (or have old ones) five miles outside the city limits, which is why the state's second largest district advertised yearly for students to attend a school fifty miles away from town. If their students went to school in town, twenty-three of them made one divisor; if they rode on a bus financed at 75 percent, the divisor for the same pupils was reduced to eight or nine. School districts could open a school in a house that was more than five miles from town, educate two middle school students in it, and be guaranteed more than $180,000 per year in state funding without raising district mill levies.

103

There were many ways to manipulate the act, and most were tried. One of the cleverest was to put two teachers into a small rural school instead of one. The operation of a one-teacher school, for any reason, was funded completely by the legislature; state funds paid all of the costs of the school. With five students, supplies, and one teacher, the total cost might have been $35,000, but placing another one-sixth teacher in the school, even with no more students, made it a multiple-teacher school and total income climbed to at least $92,333. There was a need in this state for some small schools, but not nearly as many as were operated. The finance act rewarded inefficiency, and districts took advantage of it.

The role money plays in educational productivity is one of America's most esoteric discussions. Much of the talk about money and its promise for education is just that—talk. The rhetoric is extremely loud; the facts are silent. Nationwide expenditures per pupil grew by 30 percent during the 1980s, 35 percent in the 1970s, 69 percent in the 1960s and 44 percent during the 1950s.[3] Although we spend more on education every year, test scores from a variety of measurements remain uncomfortably low. So far, infusing more dollars has not seemed to help.

Annually, educators harangue legislators to increase funding and school board members to find and spend more money. Declarations are issued that if this country really wants to improve education, schools are going to have to spend a lot more money. Yet these arguments have always been countered by researchers who have never found a relationship between total district income per pupil and student learning—between funding and achievement. No one has been able to prove that any amount of funding more than any other amount will cause test scores to rise.

When all else fails, spokesmen and apologists for the education establishment blame a lack of money—often expressed as a lack of "commitment" by the public or the government—for their problems. The issue is posed as how "serious" the public or its political leaders, are about "investing" in the education of the next generation. This cleverly turns the tables on critics and loads guilt onto the tax-paying public for the failures of American schools and colleges. Implicit in all this is the wholly unsupported assumption that more money means better education. Neither comparisons among states, comparisons over time, nor international comparisons, lend any credence to this arbitrary (and self-serving) assumption.[4]

Certainly, funding between states is not equal. Lower funded per pupil states have students that outperform those in more generous states. As shown in Table 8.3, during the academic year of 1987–1988, the difference between state per pupil expenditures seemed extreme, but neither total expenditure nor funds allocated for teacher salaries seemed to make an appreciable difference in performance on SAT scores—or in the percent of students who took the test.

Wyoming, the state that funded education at the highest amount per student, had neither the highest scores on the test nor the largest percentage of students taking the exam. Colorado, with the highest total spent on average teacher salaries, had neither the highest scores on the test nor the largest percentage of students taking the test.

The voices of people who study educational achievement related to funding are seldom heard in the clamor for more, but they have always been clear. "Contrary to conventional wisdom, little systematic relationship has been found between school resources and student performance."[5] Chubb and Moe, who studied education for the Brookings Institute, agree: "Countless studies have concluded that economic resources of various kinds are unrelated to school performance."[6] "In past decades, funding increases have been spent on overall increases in teacher salaries and reductions in class size, but student performance—and thus education productivity—have not improved that much."[7]

States that spend more per pupil in the public schools do not generally have any better educational performance to show for it. The correlation between financial inputs and educational outputs is very weak and shaky. Connecticut, for example, spent more than $4,000 per pupil in 1984 but student test scores were lower than those in Vermont, which Spent just under $3,000 per pupil.[8]

Table 8.3: Relationship Between Expenditures and SAT Scores in Ten States, 1987–1988

State	Expenditure per Student	Average Teacher Salary	SAT Average (Verbal)	SAT Average (Math)	Percent Taking Test
Arizona	3,744	29,859	443	480	23
Colorado	4,462	30,968	458	508	29
Kansas	4,076	28,666	495	545	10
Nebraska	3,943	24,983	469	523	10
Missouri	3,786	27,247	471	518	13
Montana	4,248	25,586	469	523	20
S. Dakota	3,249	21,510	498	543	6
Utah	2,454	23,942	499	537	5
Washington	4,164	30,169	430	472	59
Wyoming	5,051	29,006	462	516	14

Source: United States Department of Education. National Center for Education Statistics. *Digest of Education Statistics: 1990.* Office of Educational Research and Improvement, 1991, 85–157.

The lack of relationship between school expenditures and learning, as measured by test scores, has been known for quite some time. In his 1966 study, Coleman identified a relationship that appeared critical: "For blacks in the South, achievement is appreciably lower in schools with low per pupil expenditure than in schools with high expenditure."[9] However, he diminished the significance of the correlation when he wrote:

> When student body characteristics are taken into account, the variance accounted for by a facilities measure (which includes per pupil expenditure) is very small indeed. In fact, if adjustments had been made to remove student body factors in the present analysis, together with facilities and curriculum measures, the unique contribution of per pupil expenditure for Southern blacks would have nearly vanished.[10]

Every year at budget time board members listen to public testimony about the effects of increased funding on learning. The most impassioned pleas come from teachers and principals for more help, for a reduction in class size by hiring more teachers. Teachers offer testimonials about how much better they and their students can do with smaller classes. They speak glowingly of the amount of time they can give students with smaller classes—and everyone listens. State legislatures listen. Courts listen. A U.S. Supreme Court justice wrote in a dissent from the majority opinion: "[that] a child forced to attend an underfunded school with poorer physical facilities, less experienced teachers, larger classes...may excel is to the credit of the child, not the state."[11]

However, there has been little research to prove that for students in most grades, class size is related to student achievement. Studies indicate just the opposite: "First, according to substantial evidence, variations in student-teacher ratios do not strongly affect student performance."[12] "Studies show that reducing class size usually has no general effect on student performance."[13] Class size has been one of the most studied and debated aspects of modern American schooling. A comprehensive examination of class size research found a mixed bag of results for younger children (50 percent of the studies were positive) and no evidence that class reduction in secondary schools will do anything but provide employment for more teachers.

For grades K–3, Robinson and Wittebols gathered research that showed that smaller classes tended to have a positive effect on pupil learning in the primary grades. Their conclusions were based on an analysis of twenty-two studies.

11 of the 22 studies found that *smaller* classes influence pupil achievement in a positive direction; 2 studies found pupil achievement to be higher in larger classes; and 9 studies found no effects of class size on pupil achievement.

50 percent of all class size studies in this group found pupil achievement to be higher in smaller than larger classes.

40.9 percent of the studies found no significant differences in pupil achievement between smaller and larger classes; 9.1 percent found differences in favor of larger classes.[14]

Although 50 percent of the studies found benefits for smaller classes, a much lower number identified any advantages for grades 4–8.

Studies to date indicate that smaller classes tend to have a slight positive effect on student achievement in the junior grades of 4–8, but the evidence is not nearly as strong as in the early primary grades of K–3.

38.1 percent of all class size studies concerned with grades 4-8 found student achievement to be higher in smaller classes than in larger classes.

47.6 percent of all the class size studies concerned with grades 4-8 found no significant differences between pupil achievement in smaller and larger classes; 14.3 percent found differences in favor of larger classes.[15]

For grade levels 9–12, the senior high years, the researchers succinctly concluded that class size made little difference. "Research to date fails to indicate that in the senior grades of 9–12 smaller classes have positive effects on student achievement in the ranges and under the conditions studied."[16] Many educators believed that a 1978 study by Glass and Smith, *Meta-Analysis of Research on the Relationship of Class-Size and Achievement,* provided such information. It was not original research but a statistical analysis of a large collection of results from other studies. Robinson and Wittebols reported their conclusions.

1. When the data are taken into account, the authors concluded that: "A clear and strong relationship between class-size and achievement has emerged." They added that "there is little doubt that, other things equal, more is learned in smaller classes."

2. Class size and achievement effects were "consistently stronger in the secondary grades than in the elementary grades."[17]

Although this meta-analysis has been used to justify smaller classes, it has been attacked repeatedly by other researchers for methodology as well as for the definition of small classes. "There is nothing in the Glass et al. meta-analysis to contradict an assertion that class size makes no meaningful difference in achievement unless the smaller class has no more than three students."[18] Other scholars have hypothesized that even if the meta-analysis did find a relationship between class size and achievement, the size of classes needed, perhaps less than four to one, made any implementation unreasonable.

It seems that the impacts of small classes in the Glass and Smith study were driven by a small group and one-to-one tutoring, which admittedly produce large effects. If these effects had been eliminated from their analysis of the 14 studies, class size reduction even down to 15 or 20 would have shown essentially little or no impact.[19]

A relationship between total educational funding and student achievement has not been found between most of the things money is used to buy and test scores. But with the publication of two studies, both in the 1990s, there is a growing belief, still disputed by many, that although the total amount spent per student is not relevant, how it is spent is. New data and new methods of statistical analysis reportedly show that reducing class size in early elementary grades may, indeed, create a significant increase in learning.

1. *The* Tennessee Project Star *shows a benefit to smaller classes through the second grade or third grade*. Tennessee randomly assigned kindergarten through third-grade students into schools so that each building that had small classes (thirteen to seventeen students) also had two other class size conditions, one with twenty-two to twenty-five students and an aide and one with the same number of students without an aide. The project was conducted and studied by a consortium of four colleges. The results, found in the *Summary of Recent Class-Size Research with an Emphasis on Tennessee's Project STAR and Its Derivative Research Studies* prepared for Tennessee State University, are extremely important to decisions about the size of classes in schools.

STAR's kindergarten results showed a definite advantage for students in small classes in achievement and no significant advantage for the use of an aide.

Students in small classes in kindergarten had significantly higher self-concept scores. In Grades 1 through 3 being in a small class did not have an impact on student self-concept or motivation.

18 of the top 33 classes in Kindergarten were small.
22 of the top 34 classes in First Grade were small.
23 of the top 34 classes in Second Grade were small.
25 of the top 32 classes in Third Grade were small.

Non-Free Lunch Minorities in suburban small classes performed as well as Non-Free Lunch Whites.[20]

In the years following the experiment, Tennessee researchers found that "students from (S) (small) outperform the other students (R, RA) (regular with an aide and regular without an aide) has already held true for grades 4, 5, 6, 7, and 8."[21] In other words, smaller classes for early elementary children will provide benefits for children throughout their school career.

2. *The Educational Testing Service's Policy Information Center published a 1997 study that also found a relationship between class size and achievement.* Using improved analytical methodologies, the study looked at the relationships between scores on the 1992 National Assessment of Educational Progress mathematics tests and school variables including social environment, teacher-student ratios, average teacher-education level, the socioeconomic status of the pupils; and expenditures for capital outlays, instruction, district-level administration, school administration, and support services such as guidance counseling and transportation.[22]

With data from 203 school districts and 10,000 fourth graders and 182 districts and 10,000 eighth graders, the researchers concluded that expenditures can affect the achievement of fourth graders in two steps and eighth-grade students in three.

Fourth Grade

Step 1: Increased expenditures on instruction and school district administration increase teacher-student ratios.

Step 2: Increased teacher-student ratios raise average achievement in mathematics.

Eighth Grade

Step 1: Increased expenditures on instruction and school district administration increase student-teacher ratios.

Step 2: Increased teacher-student ratios reduce problem behaviors and improve the social environment of the school.

Step 3: A lack of problem behaviors among students and a positive social environment raise average achievement in mathematics.[23]

Fourth-grade students in smaller classes were about a half year ahead of those in larger than average classes.

Increases in school administration expenditures and capital outlays do not appear to raise achievement or any of the intervening characteristics that might themselves raise achievement (teacher-student ratios, teacher's highest degree, school environment). On the other hand, increases in instructional spending and central office administration spending both appear to raise teacher-student ratios. In other words, more spending on instruction does allow school districts to hire more teachers for each student, and more spending on central office administration makes it more likely that they will spend money in this manner.[24]

Significant increases were also found in the eighth grade, but the route was more complex. Achievement, according to the study, did not increase because of smaller classes, but improved social conditions in schools were associated with smaller classes and those conditions were related to achievement levels. "For eighth graders, increased spending in instruction and central office administration raises teacher-student ratios, which improves the school social environment, which in turn raises mathematics achievement."[25] According to the study, difference in class sizes that were related to such increases are very small in some areas and quite large in others.

Now board members, superintendents, and state policy makers seem to have two divergent theories, each supported by research, on the effects of funding on educational achievement. For some, this new evidence may result in easier decision making; for others it may once again resurrect the old adage that educational research may be used to justify anything.

Rather than viewing the quandary as schism between camps of researchers, district leaders may view these findings as finally setting a clear direction for logic in budgeting. It seems unarguable that there are no benefits to increased funding if dollars are merely siphoned off into all of the traditional accounts and programs. But there is strong evidence that using funds to decrease student-teacher ratios for very young children can result in increased learning—especially for poor students.

In the eighth-grade study by the Educational Testing Service (ETS), social environment was measured by indicators of student involvement (including tardiness, absenteeism, cutting class, regard for school property) and of teacher involvement (including absenteeism, control over instruction, and control over course content).[26] Each of these is a condition of schooling that can be easily created by school districts without decreasing the student-teacher ratio. Each of these is related to an improvement in management structure; each is under the control of the board of education.

School districts that spend more on instruction and district-level administration have lower teacher-student ratios, according to the study, and higher scores on a mathematics assessment. If we assume that districts that had higher expenses for instruction also spent more on the training of teachers, we find evidence that supports other research. "Every dollar you spend on improving the quality of teachers has a bigger effect on student achievement than any other dollar you spend."[27]

Indirectly, the results of the ETS study also seem to show that increased district spending per pupil will, in fact, result in increased learning if dollars are used wisely. Logic would dictate that all districts need to maintain buildings in safe order and do some maintenance work. To attract excellent teachers, pay scales need to be commensurate with the area and all schools need a modicum of support services and school level administration. It is logical to conclude that districts that receive more total funding should be able to support all of those functions and still spend more on instruction and additional early elementary teachers. These findings require even greater equity within states; perhaps there is now conclusive proof that students in poor districts do not do as well as those in wealthier systems.

Probably the most significant of all reports emanated from sixteen schools in Austin, Texas, that served minority populations. The study is important because it seems to show that reducing class size alone, without any other changes, may not be an effective procedure. As a resolution to a court case, each of the schools was given an additional $300,000 for five years. In fourteen of the sixteen schools, the extra funds made no difference; in two, however, the money made a large difference. Although all the schools used the funds to reduce class size, only in the two successful schools was it part of a much larger improvement program that included establishing clear goals, structuring incentives, providing high-quality training, and developing measures of progress. "Dollars made a difference when schools specifically adopted the goal of raising student achievement and found ways to engage teachers, parents, and students."[28]

For students of most ages, class size remains a labor-management issue; but when considering class size, board members and school leaders need to remember that the attitude of the teachers is extremely important to the learning of children. As we have seen, attitude may be the primary political battleground of the paradigm. There is little incentive for teachers to produce the extra effort required by larger classes, even though their students would learn just as much as they would in smaller classes. Even worse, if the paradigm has convinced administrators, teachers, and parents that children will not learn in larger classes, they probably will not. When adults in the schools believe they can teach children, children learn; if adults believe that they cannot, for whatever reason, children will not do as well.

> Those who cling to the argument that small classes aren't cost-effective tend to overlook two important points: the economic costs and the education costs that stem from low teacher morale, job dissatisfaction, and increased teacher turnover. Each of these costs is incurred in overcrowded classrooms. One study, in particular points up the hidden costs of not reducing class size. John M. Johnston of Memphis State University found discrepancies in the perceptions and attitudes of those teachers who taught small classes and those who taught regular-size classes. Teachers of small classes said they were more relaxed and less pressured because they were able to complete their daily lesson plans. In addition, they said they felt more satisfied with their jobs because they had more personal and academic interactions with students, fewer classroom control problems, and more opportunities to accommodate individual student needs.[29]

Board members who are belabored with the need to reduce class size should remember it is a labor issue with potentially devastating consequences. Although it cannot be predicted that students will learn more because class size is reduced, one may be able to predict they will learn less if class sizes are not lowered—the important factor is the attitude, even if subconscious, of teachers. In the paradigm, positive teacher perceptions of job satisfaction and a lack of teacher stress are results as important to achieve in school management as are test scores. Certainly, to the politics that controls education, those characteristics are more important than efficient financial management.

Contrary to conventional thinking, variables that may be applied to private enterprise to increase production do not work in education. As with smaller classes, there is no evidence to suggest that the more teachers are paid, the better their students will perform. According to the Tennessee summary one other common request for more workers does not result in higher test scores. There are no benefits to placing aides in elementary classrooms; student learning, as measured by testing, does not improve as a result of providing teachers with assistants.[30]

More money can produce more learning opportunities for students and create more comfortable surroundings, buy the newest and latest technology, place more books in the library, hire more teachers, and pay them higher salaries. But there remains very little evidence to show that dollars alone will provide more student learning. Consider an article from the December 3, 1997, issue of *Education Week* titled "Dollars Don't Mean Success in Calif. District."

> The Bayside/Martin Luther King Elementary School would seem to have it all. It's in California's fourth-highest-spending elementary school district and sits on a 13-acre wooded site in picturesque Sausalito. Its computer lab hums with new equipment. The library resembles a two-story chalet. What's more, in the 1995-96 school year, the tiny, 260-student Sausalito district that includes the school spent $12,100 per student, compared with $4,977 per pupil statewide. And its pupil-teacher ratio was 12-to-1, compared with 29-to-1 across California. But those numbers don't add up to an academic paradise. By most accounts, the K-8 school district could be doing a lot more with its abundant resources to educate its students, as well as attract the hundreds of local children now opting for private schools...the Sausalito system has been plagued by low academic achievement, discipline problems, and an almost-annual turnover in leadership: Bayside has had five principals in six years.[31]

"Money is not what makes some schools more effective than others," Chubb reported, noting that private schools that outperform public schools spend less and offer a superior education for fewer dollars.[32] Coleman came to the same conclusion.

> In our study of high school sophomores and seniors in both public and private schools, we found not only higher achievement in the Catholic and other private schools for students from comparable backgrounds than in the public schools, but also major differences between the functioning of the public schools and the schools of the private sector. The principal differences

were in the greater academic demands made and the disciplinary standards maintained in private schools, even when students from comparable backgrounds were compared. This suggests that achievement increases as the demands, both academic and disciplinary, are greater. The suggestion is confirmed by two comparisons: Among the public schools, those that have academic demands and disciplinary standards at the same level as the average private school have achievement at the level of that in the private sector (all comparisons, of course, involving s t u - dents from comparable backgrounds). And, among the private schools, those with academic demands and disciplinary standards at the level of the average public school showed achievement levels similar to those of the average public school.[33]

The search for relationships between expenditures and student learning will consume great amounts of researcher time and money in the future. What we have learned so far offers little help for school board members as they sit in budget sessions, except that increased spending does not seem to constitute a magic pill that will cause improved student learning in America's schools.

CHAPTER NINE

Be Prepared for
Your Day in Court

*I am a lawyer and so tragedy is my business. Riches lurk for
me in the least likely of places, in that dropped package of
explosives at the railway depot, in that cup of drive-through
coffee that scalds the thighs, in the airplane engine that bursts
into a ball of flame mid-flight. Think of your worst nightmare,
your most dreaded calamity, think of injury and anguish and
death and know that for me it represents only so much profit,
for I am your lawyer, the alchemist of your tragedy.[1]*

A new reality is growing in intensity and gaining dominion over all
other facets of educational governance. When an employee is discharged
(in some cases merely subjected to contrary management action, such
as a written reprimand), the district may be taken to federal court and
charged with transgressing on that person's civil rights. State tenure
laws are only one source of protection provided teachers; state legislatures no longer hold complete control over labor relations in schools.
Federal court juries and the lawyers who argue in that arena continually create new guidelines for the treatment of employees in the
education system.

This development is extremely important for all connected with
school management. If school leaders decide to take action against an
employee in order to maintain high standards, boards and their administrators are likely to find themselves in court. School district insurance
companies have deep pockets, and everyone working in the district has the

ability to tap those funds through litigation. To successfully defend their clients, plaintiff attorneys will put administrators and school board members on trial, accusing them of deliberately violating their clients' civil rights.

Tenure laws were written to protect teachers from the arbitrary and capricious whimsy that may arise in a politically governed organization. These laws provide safeguards that may still be necessary, but even tenure is taking a back seat to the allegedly aggrieved employee's ability to secure a financial nest egg through litigation. Because suits will not be about the employee's job performance, it matters very little if the administrators correctly carried out their duties. Administrator behavior, not employee work, will be the subject of the charges, and administrators and board members can be sued individually as well as agents of the district.

Civil rights lawsuits seek to establish that a supervisor violated the constitutionally guaranteed rights of an employee. Thus if the case goes to court, testimony will not be about whether the employee was a competent teacher, custodian, cook, bus driver, or even principal; but whether the administrator discriminated against him or her on the basis of sex, age, marital status, ethnic origin, race, disability, or any other protected status. The charges will be that an agent of the board attempted to deprive the aggrieved of a right that Americans usually take for granted. In court, you are much more likely to hear that a principal violated an employee's freedom of speech than an employee refused to carry out his or her job assignment.

Publicity resulting merely from the filing of the suit can be devastating. Few administrators can politically survive such accusations if school board members are not prepared to defend them. Such suits are written to smear administrators and to find them guilty in the court of public opinion before a decision is made by a jury. The publicity resulting from the filing paints all the accused, innocent or guilty, with the same brush. Once in the public mind, such charges are not easily forgotten.

During litigation, board members and administrators will be represented by lawyers appointed by the district's insurance company; accused administrators and board members have little recourse other than to help with their own defense. Except for the deductible, districts frequently will not pay any expenses—other than for productive work time lost to many hours of legal research and preparation. When a settlement is reached, often before the trial is held, the plaintiff will receive a sum of money—a good part of which will go to his or her lawyer who is often the attorney for the education association. District officials cannot win in such a situation. Distrustful patrons will read about the case in the newspaper, watch the proceedings on television, and believe the administrators are guilty. If the district loses money because of the suit, people will be angry about the loss of taxpayers dollars—not understanding that the insurance company paid the bill.

Throughout the proceedings, administrators will suffer. Representing the aggrieved ex-employee, opposing attorneys attack the bosses, labeling them as scurrilous human beings who should never have been hired in the first place. To prove their client innocent of the stipulated reasons for termination, they must persuade the jury of the culpability of their client's former supervisors. Board members will be charged with negligent hiring and supervision (meaning that they should never have hired the administrators in the first place) while the ethics, honesty, and integrity of administrators will become the primary thesis of the trial. Plaintiffs will insist that the causes for termination (which emanated from evaluations) are figments of evil minds; the real motivation was because she was a woman or he was a member of the union, or she said something the principal did not like, or he was a thorn in administrative sides, or because they were members of a racial or ethnic minority. Frequently, it will be all of the above. For innocent administrators, the proceedings are nothing more than legal character assassination.

Highlighting the effort to depict administrators as vindictive, scheming miscreants, plaintiffs often claim damages against them as individuals as well as agents of the district, opening them to personal damages not protected by insurance. Inevitably, one of the charges will be willfully causing the plaintiff severe emotional distress resulting in psychotherapy expenses and loss of enjoyment of life.

School districts are insured through errors and omissions (E and O) policies designed to protect boards and their agents from litigation resulting from their actions, faults, and negligence. Unfortunately, this insurance may not pay off on many of the charges found in current lawsuits, although it is possible that a combination of E and O and general liability will cover most situations. Figure 9.1 shows an example of an errors and omissions exclusion page.

It is probably safe to assume that few dismissed employees (or those who believe they have been mistreated) comprehend enough law to specify the wrongs that will be alleged; the aggrieved are angry and want the vengeance and vindication of successful suits. It is their attorney's responsibility to find allegations of wrongdoing that are covered by protected rights. An examination of recent cases might lead one to conclude that allegations are often chosen from a menu of statutes and court determinations by lawyers who then shape their client's employment history to fit selected protected rights.

From reading lawsuits one would think that public schools are one of the last havens of prejudiced America. According to suits filed every day, schools are places in which harassment and deprivation of rights are common, and employees need special protections not found in most other institutions. Inadequate school employees are protected by civil rights legislation and litigation that affords more protection than is offered workers in private industry—because school districts are officially a part of state government.

Chronicles of public education record the slow but persistent intrusion of courts into a realm once considered sacred as a bastion of local control. Based on the concept that the people of a locality should be able to design the educational system for their children, local control remains firmly imbedded in our philosophy. Yet board control over school personnel has become almost nonexistent since laws crafted to thwart tyranny are the nexus between employees and courts. It is not against the law to terminate a teacher's contract and it is still lawful to dismiss a custodian, cook, or bus driver. But it is not acceptable to violate an employee's civil rights in the process, and what seemed legal at the time of evaluation and termination may become illegal when a jury is told by a lawyer that an impropriety occurred—whether it did or not.

EXCLUSIONS

This policy does not apply to any Claim:

1. alleging fraud, dishonesty or criminal acts or omissions; however, the insured shall be reimbursed for the reasonable amount which would have been collectible under this policy if such allegations are not subsequently proven;

2. arising out of (a) false arrest, detention imprisonment, (b) libel, slander or defamation of character, (c) assault or battery, (d) wrongful entry of eviction, or invasion of any right of privacy, including, without limitation, any allegation that the violation of a civil right caused or contributed to such Claim;

3. arising out of bodily injury to, or sickness, disease, emotional distress or death of any person, or damage to or destruction of any property, including the loss of use thereof, including, without limitation, any allegation that the violation of a civil right caused or contributed to such Claim;

4. arising out of alleged sexual molestation, abuse or harassment including any alleged direct sexual activity and any allegation relating thereto that an Insured negligently employed, investigated, supervised or retained a person, or based on an alleged practice, custom or policy and including, without limitation, any allegation that the violation of a civil right caused or contributed to the Claim;

5. arising out of the failure to effect or maintain any insurance or bond; however, the Company will defend such a Claim but without obligation to pay Damages;

6. arising out of the gaining of any profit or advantage to which the Insured is not legally entitled or to any award of salary;

7. for punitive or exemplary Damages, fines or penalties imposed by law, the multiplied portion of multiple Damages or matters which may be deemed uninsurable under the law pursuant to which this policy shall be construed.

Figure 9.1. National Union Fire Insurance Company: School Leaders Errors and Omissions Policy.

When the Constitution was written, the pain of revolution and memory of King George's soldiers were fresh in American minds. The Bill of Rights (Amendment I, in particular) was adopted to protect citizens from governmental abuse. In the same vein the Fourteenth Amendment, passed in 1868 with the Civil War barely over, was intended to provide former slaves with the gifts of freedom. A third piece of legislation, the Reconstruction Era Civil Rights Acts 42 U.S.C.§1983 passed in 1871, is frequently used in employment discrimination cases because it prohibits any person acting under color of state law from depriving any other person of rights protected by the Constitution or by federal laws.

That, any person who, under color of an statute, ordinance, policy, custom or usage, subjects or causes to be subjected, any person to the deprivation of any rights, privileges or immunities secured by the Constitution and laws, shall be liable to the party injured in any action at law, suit in equity, or other proceeding for redress.[2]

Thus, if an employee can convince a jury that the conduct of district officials under color of state law deprived him or her of rights, privileges, and immunities secured by the Constitution of the United States, the district and the administrators are liable. Public employees may also seek punitive damages against public officials acting in their individual capacity; there is no cap on the compensatory damages that may be awarded under this act.

The Civil Rights Act of 1964, Title VII, is a frequently used anti discrimination statute. As amended in 1991, it provides a broad prohibition of discrimination by employers based on race, color, religion, sex, pregnancy, or national origin. Title VII applies to hiring, promotion, benefits, compensation, training, termination, and other terms, conditions, and privileges of employment. Further it provides that plaintiffs are entitled to a jury trial and compensatory and punitive damages in addition to back pay, reinstatement, and attorney fees. Although Title VII is most commonly used by employees in the private sector, it is also applicable to the public sector of employment.

Certified nonsupervisory staff enjoy the dual protection of tenure and federal civil rights legislation, but even noncertified employees are beginning to discover that public school employment may be a secure career—regardless of job performance. Many states continue an employment presumption known as the at-will rule, a holdover from turn-of-the century management. Absent a contract for a specific length of time, the rule assumes employees work at the will of the employer, meaning that classified or support employees may be released at any time. Succinctly, at-will means that employees can be terminated for no reason or for cause; they cannot, however, be dismissed for a reason that violates their civil rights.

But at-will is fading in the private sector and almost gone in the public arena—a victim of courts and juries. Tenure provides certified staff a property right to employment, which means jobs may be eliminated only for certain reasons and only through due process. Classified workers are approaching the same benefits as provided by tenure through court action, seeking every avenue possible to place their employment into the protective embrace of a property right. It is not difficult for nontenured employees to acquire property rights to their employment. For instance, a property right is automatically granted to all employees if one of them ever receives a formal notice of probation. The inductive rationale for this courtroom employment law is simple. If one employee is on probation and the others are not, then what are they? Courts have found them regular or property right employees.

Many school districts have progressive discipline plans for noncertified employees. According to these plans, the first infraction or work problem results in an informal talk with the supervisor; the second infraction or work problem results in a written reprimand; the third infraction or work problem results in suspension with pay. Under such a policy, all classified employees have been granted a property right to their job and may not be terminated without due process. When a noncertified employee is hired, if the supervisor says, "I hope you stay a long time and enjoy working here for many years," that person (and probably all the others) has been granted a property right to that position.

In a recent case, three custodians were able to settle for $10,000 each for claiming among other allegations that the supervisor who hired them told them he was tired of looking for custodians and that he hoped they would stay a long time. The man had been dead for ten years. The district could not disprove their claims; $10,000 compensated each of the custodians and their attorney for thinking up the claim. If their story were true, another twist is added, for court cases limiting at-will employment had not been adjudicated when the custodians were hired. What the administrator was accused of doing was acceptable at the time but not today. Attorneys can use valid employment practices from the past against employers because limitations and restrictions have been attached by subsequent court action.

A school district began restructuring its special education department, which was centered around a little known theory. The department used a model of cognition describing mental processes as bricks laid neatly in a mental wall. If any bricks were out of line or missing, some thought, learning could not take place. If the bricks were far enough out of alignment, mental problems including retardation and/or severe mental illness could result. Some special educators passionately believed that through a series of realignment procedures the mentally ill could be cured and the mentally retarded could graduate from college. When special education department members told this to their students' parents, they believed it all.

Concerned by what he thought were audacious claims, the wary superintendent called in a team of three college professors to study the program. On completion of their study, the team notified board members and the superintendent that the department was probably out of compliance with existing state law and that the curative claims the educators made were impossible to substantiate.

It was decided that a new director of special education should be hired; the director's initial decision was to hire a Ph.D. psychologist, the first ever in the district. Finding the right person was critical because the teachers still believed in the old program; department morale was terrible. Each member not only had to abandon an adored concept, they had to relearn proper identification procedures, paper trails, and documentation.

The candidate the administrators decided to hire, a tenured psychologist from the state's capital city, concurred during the interview with the restructuring tasks outlined, pledging fidelity to state and federal procedures and regulations as well as to the new director. Through a solid partnership that would create a new culture, the psychologist would serve as a bridge to a model special education department. During the first year, positive changes were noted and attitudes improved. The program appeared to be off to a great start. In the second year, it started to crumble. At the end of the third year, for what the administrators thought were sufficient and just reasons, the psychologist's contract was not renewed.

Represented by the state education association's attorney, the psychologist immediately asked for a due process hearing under the continuing contract (tenure) law. Statutes provided tenure after only two years of service if such status had been gained in one district in the state immediately prior to working in another. Supported by the state attorney general's opinion that professionals such as counselors and psychologists were not teachers and ineligible for tenure, however, district policy stipulated that her employment was predicated on a yearly contract. The psychologist had signed some contracts specifically noting that the position would not lead to tenure.

The district filed a motion for a declaratory judgment based on the belief that since psychologists were not tenure eligible employees, the psychologist should be denied a hearing. If the employee had prevailed she would have been offered a new contract; if the district had won in court she would not have been. Suddenly, however, the request was withdrawn as the psychologist left for a new job. But the district had not heard the last of the matter.

One year later, almost to the day of the announcement that a hearing would not be sought, lawyers associated with the state education association mailed a Notice of Governmental Claim letter to the district. It was a devastating blow. Naively, the administrators assumed litigation would center around the psychologist's actions as an employee and would force them to substantiate their dismissal recommendations to the board. When they read the claim, they discovered the charges were directed at them and at their integrity, honesty, and competence; the superintendent and special education director were to be put on trial—and the board was being sued for hiring them in the first place. (See Appendix B for the complete letter with all names and personal identification deleted.)

> Circumstances which constitute a breach of contract, a breach of the implied covenant of good faith and fair dealing, intentional infliction of emotional distress, tortuous interference with the employment contract of Complainant, violation of public policy, negligent hiring, supervision and training of public employees who supervised Complainant, and other violations of the (state) statutory and common law principles.

> The acts of School District and its employees further constitute a violation of Complainant's First Amendment right to be free from discrimination and retaliation based on protected free speech, as well as Complainant's constitutional right to equal protection based on her gender, and her right to substantive and procedural due process, under the Constitution.[3]

Dazed by reading the legal jargon and the accusations that they had violated the psychologist's civil rights, the administrators found that the remainder of the letter stung even worse. They were accused of calling her names, of making threats that anyone could be fired at any time, and of willful and wanton misconduct; they were being charged deliberately indifferent to her rights. The worst blow was in the final paragraph that asked for damages in the maximum amount allowable because of "increased living expenses, expenses for relocation, pain and suffering, past, present, and future mental and emotional harm, loss of enjoyment to life, injury to career and reputation."[4] The psychologist's lawyers charged that school officials did not just make mistakes in the termination but unlawfully conspired to deny this employee's rights that are guaranteed to all Americans.

The two administrators could not fathom the charges brought against them. Incredulous and obsessed with unanswered questions, they waited for the suit to be filed. How could this have been written for a court if it were not true? Had a subliminal dislike for the psychologist possessed them? Were they really guilty? Would these charges be made public? How would they be treated in the press? Would the media and public believe the charges against them? How long did they have to wait to find out?

When the suit was filed two months later, the formal litigation papers cleared up one issue. Charges in the letter were not exaggerated; the real accusations were even worse, consisting almost entirely of federal civil rights violations. Not only was the district being sued, the administrators were being taken to court individually for purposefully afflicting emotional distress—a charge for which punitive damages could be assessed. Now the anxious administrators had another series of questions. If insurance policies do not pay for damages caused by emotional distress, and if a jury found against them, would the district pay or would they have to pay? Could they lose their own financial security for carrying out their duties? (See Appendix C for the complete case as filed in Federal Court.)

The formal notice contained two new charges not previously stipulated: The superintendent was accused of sexual harassment and the special education director, a woman, of sexual discrimination. The stress became almost intolerable. The possibility of losing personal funds and property weighed heavily on the two administrators throughout the eight-month ordeal. The administrators felt victimized by a complaint that seemed to them to be long, obtuse, abusive, and without specifics; to them it seemed they were caught in the big lie technique popularized by Joe McCarthy in his hunt for communists. This case was not about the competence of an employee; it was about their personal ethics and integrity. Where, they wondered, were their civil rights, protection for their families, protection from slander, and where were honesty and truth?

The suit listed three claims for relief; the first was for violation of rights while acting under color of state law, the second for wrongful discharge, and the third for breach of the implied covenant of good faith and fair dealing/breach of contract. The defendants were accused of a number of wrongs. Allegedly they

- Denied the plaintiff right of association and retaliated against her for associating with other people.

- Exercised personality control requiring the defendant to have absolute loyalty and punished her for holding views contrary to their own, in particular her commitment to the needs of students.

- Retaliated against the plaintiff for exercise of constitutionally protected free speech.

- Maintained a work environment that created a supportive and friendly working environment for males, while creating a nonsupportive unfriendly, hostile work environment for females.

- Took action willfully, wantonly and in callous and reckless disregard for the educational and personal needs of students.

- Wrongfully discharged the plaintiff as a result of her commitment and actions as a professional to uphold fundamental ethical principals and complying with her obligations under state and federal public policy.[5]

This genre of court cases shackles administrators. Although many wish to be accountable and to operate effective schools with an efficient and professional staff, they are forced to weigh their ideals against their future. For relatively small salaries, few wish to smash their careers, families, reputation, and retirement on the rocky shores of civil rights lawsuits. As a result, ineffective or nonperforming school district employees will rarely be released; the wheat will never be separated from the chaff. Frequently, failure to evaluate and recommend termination is a product of jurisprudence, not administrative ineptness.

Administrative careers hinge on the favor of elected board members and they are constantly summoned to judgment in the court of public opinion. With nothing to lose and public opinion to be won, plaintiffs often begin a whispering campaign, labeling the administrator(s) as callous, unfair, and cruel; the public will side with the employee early on, especially when the press becomes aware of the suit and begins asking for comments. When a description of supposed mistreatment is dramatically related in the morning paper, the administrators, on the advice of their attorney simply reply, "No comment." As a result, when a suit is filed against an administrator the administrator will lose, even if he or she prevails before a legally selected jury.

Charges may be written with such hyperbole in civil rights litigation that administrative reputations are blackened as soon as the suit is filed. Although the suit is a matter of open record, the district's defense will not be publicized until the trial. The whispering campaign, substantiated by a formal complaint and lack of defense, dooms administrators. Few professionals recover from charges of sexual discrimination and harassment coupled with abrogation of freedoms in civil rights charges. The administrator is seen as the enemy of democracy and fair play. Few administrators, especially those who have been through it before, will place their careers and retirements in such jeopardy.

Does truth protect the innocent in an employee civil rights lawsuit? Truth sometimes has little to do with legal proceedings. Plaintiffs will ask for a jury trial. The logic is simple. Americans, especially employees, generally side with the underdog in an employment dispute. Most have their own stories of terrible bosses. Employment cases are predicated on the labor card, the jerk boss card, and the uncaring system card, all played from the beginning. Suits deflect accountability from the worker to the supervisor. Lawsuits are won because one side is able to convince a small number of people—of something. Say it enough times and it must be true. Make the charges dire enough and they must be true. Who could say such things if they were not the truth?

Lawsuits are often written in such a manner that the proceedings become one person's word against another. Defendants can be placed in the position of defending themselves against accusations of thoughts they did not have. It is more difficult to prove that one did not do something than it is to prove that one did; it is almost impossible to offer evidence that you did not have the notion someone else ascribes to you—three years after the event.

Litigation disrupts school districts. Once a suit is filed, employees quickly choose sides; almost as many scars are created from a bitter lawsuit as a strike. Lawyers for plaintiffs rely on school districts to concede that such emotional division of faculty and staff is too detrimental to pedagogical procedures to allow suits to go to court. School districts pay off, hoping to protect children from the ravages of a split district.

Other teachers and employees not granted tenure will often line up to offer testimony for the plaintiff because they gain the right to be free from retaliation. After adverse testimony is proffered, any job action directed toward the employee will always be seen as retaliation, at least to association attorneys—and juries.

The damage done with lawsuits relegates termination, and even reprimand, to the almost-never-used category. Public rhetoric about educational employee termination is futile as long as there are few, if any, legislators who will carry bills to limit the ability of public employees to litigate complaints against supervisors. There have been few attempts to curtail the right of public employees to use legislation that was originally designed to protect American civil rights from governmental abuse to secure their own employment. Until there is limitation, the concept of ridding public education of deadwood, is just another meaningless political slogan.

Board members who are accustomed to working in the private sector must understand that public employees enjoy rights that people who work for private businesses do not.

1. Public employees enjoy a governmentally protected right of freedom of speech, with the right to discuss and publish anything they consider important to the public. School employees do not give up any rights of citizenship through employment. As any citizen can be critical of school districts—so can employees. Most attempts to prevent freedom of speech are illegal.

2. As public figures, school board members and superintendents have the same rights as other governmental leaders in terms of slander and criticism.

3. Public school employees have all of the safeguards of life in the United States built into their professional rights because they work for a governmental organization.

4. Evaluations written about administrators can become public property during litigation. These documents may be used in court and argued over. Privacy rights granted to evaluations do not extend through court. The employee's lawyers will try to make a case of

negligent supervision saying that boards negligently supervised superintendents who in turn negligently supervised other administrators.

What is the best advice that can be given to school board members and superintendents to defend themselves from lawyers using civil rights legislation to win money for school district employees?

1. Superintendents and other administrators should never talk with an employee alone; another person should be in the room to take notes or make a tape of the meeting. Without witnesses an administrator cannot prove that he or she did not swear, tell jokes, proposition, or threaten someone, especially if the meeting occurred years earlier.

2. An open-door policy and casual management style can be dangerous. Supervisors who fear litigation should end them. Again, without notes, tape recordings, and witnesses, an accused cannot mount a viable defense.

3. A videotape can be used as a visual and verbal record.

4. School district insurance policies should be up to date and broad in scope.

5. Prose evaluations contain words that can be argued in court. In terms of lawsuits, checklists with noted definitions are preferable.

These precautions will help protect the district from suit but make impossible the effective management of an organization. During a suit, district officials will be asked to prove they did not do or say something they did not do or say. Even worse, they will end up defending the intent behind their actions. What they thought, the privacy of their own mental processes, will be argued by lawyers in front of juries.

Board members need to have long conversations about what actions they will take when the lawsuit comes. As visible, public-minded citizens, board members must protect administrators from the fall-out of litigation. If they believe their administrators are guilty of the things said about them, they had better revisit their evaluation system. Litigation is the wrong time to discover such problems.

CHAPTER TEN

Superintendent Employment and First-Year Care

An unconscious conspiracy in contemporary society prevents Leaders—no matter what their original vision—from taking charge and making changes. Within any organization, an entrenched bureaucracy with a commitment to the status quo undermines the unwary leader.[1]

The superintendent is leaving, having decided it is time to move, or maybe the school board decided that it was time the superintendent went someplace else. Most board members will experience the change of the school district's top executive at least once during their term. Few superintendents, especially those who help create change, make a career out of staying in only one place. Board members should recall Paladin's business card about guns and traveling on the 1950s television program about the Old West. They will discover that many superintendents' cards read: Have Resume—Will Travel.

Generally, the departure of a superintendent is a time of mixed feelings in a school district. Some people will view the chance to hire a new leader as a great opportunity to make improvements—others will experience discomfort and worry about cherished traditions and programs. Wherever on the continuum of emotions about the departure and replacement people are, there is always a heightened sense of awareness about the condition of the district when board members set about hiring a new superintendent.

If board members have decided to improve education in the district, the employment of a new superintendent is their opportunity.

Finding someone who believes all children can learn and who is dedicated to that end becomes their most important duty as a member of the board. This is the time when trustees can make their mark on a district. They must decide if they will reform American public education—or not.

Most school boards that need to find a new superintendent employ a consulting firm. After negotiating a contract to do a national search, the consultants design a brochure, meet with groups of employees and citizens to create a list of qualifications and characteristics for the new superintendent, have it approved by the board of education, and send it to university placement services and national publications. The board now faces its first traumatic decision in a superintendent search. Does it allow teachers, community members, and administrators to help in the selection? Does it request participation on committees and hold votes? Do board members merely ask for input and make their own choice? Perhaps the members of a board do not wish anyone else to be involved in any fashion.

A school board must fully debate the issue of participation in the selection process. A school district performing its own search, without professional help, often makes the mistake of inviting input and not listening to it. It is fine to ask for input; it is acceptable to ask for voting participation; and it is okay to do it alone, but board members need to make sure that teachers, administrators, and community groups understand the rules from the beginning.

Selecting a person who was not the choice of the staff after employees have been promised a voice condemns the new superintendent to almost certain failure. Because new leaders must react to preconceptions of staff, it is unfair to allow a superintendent to think he or she was selected through participation and later discover the choice was made only by the members of the board. Denying a superintendent knowledge of all of the facts surrounding an offer of employment is dishonest; it is hiring under false pretenses. It denies the candidate a chance to make a fully rational decision.

There are basic rules for hiring a new superintendent that board members need to remember:

1. If school board members are not going to give staff members input into the decision, they must be totally honest about their decision from the beginning.

2. If school board members wish to change the district because they find fault with what has gone on in the past, they must make those sentiments known and take responsibility for their actions. The fight that will come over the changes belongs to the members, not the new superintendent.

3. A school board should not hire a superintendent to make changes if board members are not united and in complete agreement about the changes to be made.

4. A school board must make sure that the staff and community are aware of its expectations of the new superintendent from the beginning of the selection process.

5. If a school board wishes to set a new direction because it finds fault with past operations, it must make sure that the new superintendent does not have to be the first one to announce that past operations have not met the board's expectations.

6. School board members should not expect a new superintendent to start making changes unless they are ready for a negative reaction and prepared to visibly support the changes being made.

When making change is a factor in the employment of a new superintendent, trustees must remember that change is not well accepted. Most teachers and administrators want what has been to continue; they know what they have had and it seems more comfortable than anything else. Even if the current system has been top-down, hostile, controlling, and intimidating for some, it will have worked for others. Even initiating a plan as enlightened as allowing teachers a voice in a district where they have never had one before will decrease morale. Progenitors of empowerment will incur the wrath of administrators and community members who supported the former system that left teachers out of the process. The known and familiar is more comfortable than change. If board members desire change, they have to be prepared to live with the consequences without using the new superintendent as the fall guy.

Once applications have been received, it is time to begin the selection process. Paper screening is a laborious process; each application must be read by the same people. The task may be assigned to a committee or several committees or individuals, but each applicant must be

133

awarded fair consideration under the same rating scale. Fairness can only be accomplished by having the same people judging all applications.

With the paper screening completed, it is now time to interview the candidates. Interviews often do not work very well and usually reveal little. Do you hire the man with all the answers you want to hear? Do you hire the assertive woman with no experience who sounds tough? Do you hire the person who makes you feel the most comfortable? All of us know people who are wonderful talkers and terrible producers. How do you measure the ability to act against the capacity for talk? During an interview a board member is in the powerful position of measuring a person's entire career in one hour. This is an awesome responsibility based on a procedure that does not always work very well.

After the interviews, board members normally narrow their choices down to two or three and conduct visits of the districts where the candidates have been working—publicly announcing themselves and proclaiming their business. Boards should have these planned very carefully. Strict ground rules to be followed by every member must be established for a board visit. There have been some board members who, when arriving in the visited district, strike out on their own to collect all the available gossip and innuendo. Such behavior is not acceptable. Visiting trustees need to remember that they are guests in the candidate's locale and in another school board's district. Before the visit occurs, board members should clearly outline what they intend to look for and what people they intend to interview.

Trustees must be careful if one of the candidates is a superintendent and the other is not. The person holding the top job always has a more visible presence and a more dramatic reputation. It is impossible to compare the work of a superintendent with someone who has not been one. No other position is the same. Remember, there are some districts where a good superintendent might not have been successful. There are some where peace and harmony might not be the primary characteristics. Sometimes a leader might be in a district in which morale-dampening improvement is under way. Change for improvement is always accompanied by a loss of morale and a loss of morale is always accompanied by accusations and blame. Board members must be extremely cautious to sort out the facts.

There are two kinds of superintendents available for school board members to consider: (1) place superintendents who are bound by where

134

they live, waiting for a chance in the district where they have always worked or in an adjacent one that functions in much the same manner, and (2) position superintendents who, like Old West sheriffs, move from position to position—usually by choice. Place superintendents serve one or several districts in the same area in different positions. Working as an administrator in that area is their career choice. Position superintendents make the superintendency their career; they usually bring change while place administrators try to maintain harmony and the status quo.

Although there are exceptions to my description of superintendents, it specifies the most common occurrences. People who are committed to place live where they do because they like it there. They are invested in the familiar and need to maintain the prevailing political structure. Harmony is a paramount issue because they are going to live there the rest of their life. Most people are unlikely to strive for changes that will cause animosity if they know that the same angry people will always be their neighbors.

Board members are completely in charge of superintendent selection (unless they give the power away), even if they use a process that is based on participation. Trustees make the final decision by casting a vote in an open meeting. No process is infallible; in the end it just comes down to making a decision. Perhaps school boards need to begin acting more like leaders of major corporations. They should recruit, investigate, and seek out professionals who will do the job outlined by the trustees.

In the 1990s, many boards have eschewed multi year contracts for superintendents, placing them on yearly renewable agreements. The argument for doing so seems to be that superintendents will perform better if they know they may be asked to leave during any year. Certainly, paying a superintendent for unworked years when the relationship has not been satisfactory seems a poor utilization of taxpayer funds.

But this practice should be reconsidered. It makes little sense to have the leader be more expendable than the followers. A superintendent who cannot outlive the anger and retribution of friends of an incompetent administrator who must be replaced is doomed. One who cannot count on continued employment for two years after discharging a popular and ineffective employee will be history within that time period. Without security, top administration is severely handicapped;

decisions become based on survival, not on the education of children. You can expect very few people to willingly put their head into a noose; only the board can provide protection. If board members want changes made, they need to provide superintendents with some security.

Choosing a person for any position is difficult; deciding on the correct superintendent is particularly onerous. Problems in selection are exacerbated by the fact that every situation is politically different. Superintendents who were successful in one district may not be in another; those who have careers marked by harmony may seem like the best choice but may leave a district in an ineffective rut. The interview process must become a concerted program of study and analysis. If not enough time is spent on the selection process, and the board is not completely honest in announcing changes it wishes to make, superintendents will continue to fail. They will continue to be paid off with needed tax dollars. No superintendent can survive without board support; legitimate authority in a school district is only derived from the school board. If a superintendent is doing what trustees expect, the members may not waiver in their support.

CHAPTER ELEVEN

The Board Member Primer

I'll tell you now that the best strategy in almost any case is to find a role model, someone who's already getting the results you want, and then tap into their knowledge. Learn what they're doing, what their core beliefs are, and how they think. Not only will this make you more effective, it will also save you a huge amount of time because you won't have to reinvent the wheel. You can fine-tune it, reshape it, and perhaps even make it better.[1]

How do board members create a system of public education that operates efficiently and effectively, provides satisfaction for consumers and taxpayers, and teaches all the students? Without systemic and structural change, including altering the paradigmatic belief system that pervades society and many of our schools, we may never be completely successful. Many Americans still do not believe that all students can excel without a concurrent reduction of academic standards; evidence that shows all students can learn is quickly diluted by charges of dumbing down.

Public education is a child of politics. It is the political institution located nearest the people and one that 99 percent of all citizens have had first-hand experience with. Education is the public institution that most sways in the populace breeze. As long as it does, it may never satisfy all of its consumers.

Board members should not be nearly as concerned about public opinion as about results. They need to decide what they expect, measure productivity (student learning), and use direct democracy very infrequently for important decisions about teaching and learning. In a representative democracy, informed decision making is the purpose for which school board members are elected. America's system of schooling may yet become effective in its present form of governance, but only informed school board members can make it happen. If the public does not agree with the actions of the board, the only thing trustees have to lose is a volunteer position that is the most demanding job in America.

Does this mean that school board members should no longer listen to their constituents? Of course not, but it does mean that board members have a responsibility to become knowledgeable about education and pass that wisdom on to the community. It means that board members must do what is right before they do what is political. It means board members must become disciples of data-based and research-driven educational management. There are no cookbooks with surefire recipes for success. But learning about pedagogical and managerial best practices is a beginning.

1. Organize: Use your collective power and wisdom to take control. Educators, in the final analysis, are like other people. Some are excellent, some are terrible, some really care, others never did, and some are burned out. A few are miscreants; others are saintly. Many work extremely hard with little reward; some do not earn their remuneration. We call them all professionals—but we have no idea how to measure the quality of their work.

Doctors have an outcome: They cure what can be cured; death is fairly visible failure. Lawyers win cases; losing usually deprives them of more clients. Engineers have the project to produce. In business there is a bottom line. Product is what these professionals know. Each can explain why they use the procedures they do, test their practices against a standard, and use results for improvement.

Most teachers do not know why or how their pupils learn. They do not understand how to make schools effective, and they do not even know which methods most expediently teach reading—the most basic skill the system imparts.

True scientific research on literacy only began about twenty-five years ago. What this means is that every "theory" or "model" of

teaching reading, past or present, has been based either on human reason alone, or on empty theorizing or "fads," rather than
on solid scientific research.[2]

Teachers have been teaching reading for a long time, but few really know how. According to Diane McGuinness, American high school students and young adults are six times more likely to be functionally illiterate than those in Sweden and twice as likely as those in Canada. She concludes that our nation's reading problems are caused by our system of public schooling; there is nothing wrong with our children.[3]

School trustees have a responsibility to recognize practices used in our school systems that do not serve our children and abandon them, especially the three that I have explored in earlier chapters. (1) We know the damage done to children by holding them back, yet that practice is still supported by many teachers and principals. Educators who believe, despite the evidence, that this practice is warranted, need to go back to school. (2) Except for the top 2 percent (perhaps) of students, ability grouping does not work. Yet there remains a fervent belief-based attitude in many schools that slower students impede the learning of brighter children. Many schools still operate on the philosophy that some can learn and the rest should not take up the teacher's time. (3) The assembly-line method of age-level grade determination keeps hauling children down the line for the attachment of new learning whether they are ready or not.

School trustees must learn basic principles of schooling and educational management, ensure their place in the district, hold the superintendent responsible for results, and expect that he or she will do the same for everyone else. On the state and national level, board members must make their organizations the strongest in education, forming them into associations to speak for learners instead of the system and the profession.

Education is a tax-supported system. It is not one where professionals thrive on their ability to earn income through their productivity; rather they survive through their ability to levy taxes. Board members control educational resources. They must make sure taxpayer funds are used to produce results and not to perpetuate parts of our system that are counterproductive.

2. All children can learn: Make sure that a pervasive belief system is the heart of your system. There is nothing more important than belief in a child's capacity to learn. Techniques, pedagogy, learning theories, everything else pales when held up to this belief. We have always known that children respond positively to respect and to those who believe in them. Unfortunately, too many school personnel and community members who live under the influence of the paradigm do not believe that all children can be successful learners.

School board members should be aware of the prevalent belief in their school district. If they aren't, they should begin by asking the superintendent about the statement that all our children can learn. If he or she cannot defend the belief or is not leading the parade, it's time to get a new leader. If the superintendent is on board, trustees should ask all administrators how they could be convicted of believing all children can learn (if it was a crime) by the culture and tradition in their buildings or departments. The board should make sure this belief system is the priority of the staff development program by providing inservice after inservice, posting signs and slogans, and constantly talking about it. The board needs to lead the district in this quest. The board should initiate a program to ensure that teachers learn about the research on successful educational practices.

3. A bottom line: Learn from businesses that there is one. School board members should understand that there is a point of diminishing returns at which spending more and more (throwing money at problems) does not help. For instance, if the district has implemented the most expensive reading program in the area and the students are not reading at remarkably high levels, it is time to look at the wisdom of the expenditure—along with all of the variables that might impinge on success. Perhaps the district is just throwing money at a problem instead of implementing a program that works. In order to evaluate programs, the board should know, publish, and talk about the drop-out rate, the attendance rate, the graduation rate, scores on standardized tests, and how many students start and graduate from college. The board must know results and expect the costs and value of programs to be analyzed.

There is a difference between factors that cause learning and the demands of labor. It is interesting that as American class sizes have been reduced, spending for support staff who attend to allegedly nonpedagogical tasks such as hall, lunch, playground, recess, and bus duty has increased. We have smaller classes and fewer outside the classroom duties for teachers than ever before. Yet acquired learning, as measured by test scores, is not increasing at prodigious rates. Why? School boards should question the results of specific expenditures and ask whether a holistic approach to education and child-rearing is not better than fragmentation based on a certified versus noncertified division of labor. Is this an expenditure that a business person would make if it had no or little effect on production? There is a difference between professional needs and labor demands.

4. Evaluate, evaluate, evaluate. If a board has not assessed the evaluation program, chances are good that it is operating an employment club. The school board should demand a continual study of the district's evaluation procedures and establish a formal process to have evaluations read and analyzed. Are evaluations discerning? Can the board tell one certified employee from another through performance evaluations? Does the district value the administrator who takes the strong stand and risks turmoil by writing discerning evaluations and terminating nonperformers? Are principals friends of the staff and enablers or are they organizational leaders? Board members must know the strengths and weaknesses of the district's leaders. They should read books about educational research and best practices and quiz their leaders; if they are not knowledgeable, no one else in the district will be. System leaders who are ignorant should be educated or dismissed.

Board members need to find the answer to a couple of questions about their school district. Does the district expect administrators to meet standards of instructional leadership? Do administrators get to keep their jobs merely by making everyone happy?

5. Policy and administration: Know the difference and learn that there is no black and white, only shades of gray. School board members should not be put off by the generalization that educators are trained and board members are lay people. Board members have a fiduciary responsibility that cannot be given away. Policy and administration are known as the difference between board and superintendent duties. Unfortunately, the boundaries cannot be defined and in many cases they are coterminous. The delineation of policy and administration is often used to back school boards away from what they need to do—and know.

Is insisting on a belief that all students can learn policy or administration? Is demanding a written and planned program for school and district improvement policy or administration? If the high school operates on a seven-period day and the board is interested in learning about the benefits of a four-period day, is it guilty of micro management when it asks for such a study? Is it policy or administration to be concerned about the number of administrators and average size of classes? Each of these has a policy stipulation and an administrative function.

> As has already been noted, many authorities on boards have enunciated a single, fundamental rule by which to define the function of the board as contrasted to the function of the executive. Most frequently they say, often with an air of profundity, that the board should determine policy and the executive should carry it out. Brian O'Connell has responded succinctly "This is just not so" and has called that distinction "the worst illusion ever perpetrated in the nonprofit field." In addition to making policy, boards must perform a number of executive and judicial functions.[4]

6. Educate: Teach board members and staff every year about research centered on the belief that we can teach all children and that teaching and learning is the only purpose for which schools exist. The board should compel every certified staff member in the district to complete formal courses in best practices research and to participate annually in refresher courses; the staff should be paid for these courses. Everyone in the system and on the board should have an in-depth understanding of the research behind the following statements.

1. We can, whenever, and wherever we choose, successfully teach all children whose schooling is of interest to us. We already know more than enough to do that. Whether or not we do it must finally depend on how we feel about the fact that we haven't so far.[5]

2. What any person in the world can learn, almost all persons can learn if provided with appropriate prior and current conditions of learning. At this stage of the work it applies to the middle 95 percent of the population.... The research demonstrates that under appropriate school conditions almost all can learn whatever the

schools have to teach. It indicates that special and very favorable conditions may be needed at some stages of the learning, but that, over time, these may be gradually discarded.[6]

3. Does the level of teacher expectations influence the level of achievement, i.e., do high expectations produce high achievement and low expectations produce low achievement? The answer, based on extensive research, is a clear-cut "yes."[7]

School boards must fight against a system that exists for the purposes of sorting and selecting and providing custodial functions; the school system should be concerned about teaching and learning. Board members need to be strong enough and knowledgeable enough to announce that their schools will not be used to sort and select students and that their schools exist for teaching and learning. This takes courage: courage to close schools for staff development programs, courage to modify schedules so that teachers may work together, and courage to create calendars built for learning instead of activities. A school board may even have to be strong enough to withdraw support from activity programs and use the money to foster student learning.

7. Assess: Assess districts and schools around standards of effectiveness. An effective school is one in which all students, regardless of socioeconomic status, learn at high levels as measured by standardized assessments. In "Effective Schools for the Urban Poor," the following definition of an effective school was offered:

> Specifically, I require that an effective school bring the children of the poor to those minimal masteries of basic school skills that now describe minimally successful pupil performance for the children of the middle class.[8]

Written prior to 1980, those words provided a lofty goal for schools. However, in a world economy fueled by education where citizens of this country compete with citizens of every other nation, these standards are not set high enough. Simply, if we set minimal mastery of the middle class as a goal, we are doing our children a disservice; we are consigning many to a second-class lifestyle. The middle class has not been competing well against the world field.

143

In mathematics, for example, Stevenson found that students in the U.S. fall further behind Japanese and Taiwanese at each grade level, and, by fifth grade, the worst Asian classes in his large sample exceed the best American class.[9]

If we believe that schools have a responsibility to teach, and that family background is only an obstacle to be surmounted, then we must create schools where children of the poor reach the mastery of school skills that now describe our best students. To set a goal any lower is to provide a great disservice. Therefore, schools should be assessed around two criteria:

[A] quality standard assures that the achievement level in a school is high....

[A]n equity standard assures that the high achievement does not vary significantly across a school's student population by socioeconomic status, race, ethnicity or gender.[10]

A school in which socioeconomic status differentiates student success is not effective. Such an institution should not be acceptable to any school board. If middle-class and wealthier children do well in a district's schools and those from lower groups do not, neither the schools nor the school board members are successful.

Shortly after the 1960s pronunciation by James Coleman that schools made little difference in the learning of children, a group of educators began identifying schools that made a difference—they looked for schools in which all students learned. When they found these schools, they identified commonalties among them that ineffective schools did not have. They discovered correlates, or variables, that maintain a significant relationship with effectiveness. The correlates constituted a belief system that characterized the culture of a school, a district and, probably, a community. Correlates cannot be plugged in, they must become the soul of the organization.

From the late 1960s until today, lists of characteristics of schools that effectively teach all children have remained virtually the same. There have been, and are, reasonable and scholarly arguments with the research and the correlates of effective schools. Some argue that the role of the home is so strong that it cannot be surmounted; "educators alone are insufficient to increase learning productivity dramatically, and they need the cooperation of parents and students themselves."[11]

Certainly, school board members and policy makers must begin to provide for early childhood activities that are congruent with schooling and we must find ways to soften the impact of dysfunctional family life. But to fail to accept responsibility for learning by blaming the home is a disservice to children and society. School board members, community leaders, and state and national policy makers must understand thoroughly the conditions of schooling that should characterize our public education institutions.

A list of correlates, or shared characteristics, originally discovered in New York City by a researcher who studied four "effective" elementary schools in poor neighborhoods included (1) strong leadership, (2) high expectations for all students, (3) an orderly, relatively quiet, and pleasant atmosphere, and (4) an emphasis on pupil acquisition of reading skills, reinforced through frequent evaluation of pupil progress.[12]

A 1974 State of New York Office of Education Performance Review of a high-achieving and a low-achieving school identified effective practices and the importance of believing all children can learn.

1. the differences in student performance in these two schools seemed to be attributed to factors under the schools' control;

2. administrative behavior, policies, and practices in the schools appeared to have a significant impact on school effectiveness;

3. the more effective inner-city school was led by an administrative team which provided a good balance between both management and instructional skill;

4. the administrative team in the more effective school had developed a plan for dealing with the reading problem and had implemented the plan throughout the school;

5. classroom reading instruction did not appear to differ between the two schools since classroom teachers in both schools had problems in teaching reading and assessing pupils' reading skills;

6. many professional personnel in the less effective school attributed children's reading problems to nonschool factors and were pessimistic about their ability to have an impact, creating an environment in which children failed because they were not ex-

145

pected to succeed. However, in the more effective school, teachers were less skeptical about their ability to have an impact on children.[13]

Also, during the 1970s, a study of Michigan schools based on the state department's testing program analyzed schools around consistent improvement or decline and found the adult-controlled conditions of schooling and the underlying belief system to be key.

1. The improving schools are clearly different from the declining schools in the emphasis their staff places on the accomplishment of the basic reading and mathematics objectives. The improving schools accept and emphasize the importance of these goals and objectives while declining schools give much less emphasis to such goals and do not specify them as fundamental.

2. There is a clear contrast in the evaluations that teachers and principals make of the students in the improving and declining schools. The staffs of the improving schools tend to believe that all of their students can master the basic objectives; and furthermore, the teachers perceive that the principal shares this belief. They tend to report higher and increasing levels of student ability, while the declining schools project the belief that students' ability levels are low and, therefore, they cannot master even those objectives.

3. The staff of the improving schools hold decidedly higher and apparently increasing levels of expectations with regard to the educational accomplishments of their students. In contrast, staffs of the declining schools are much less likely to believe that their students will complete high school or college.

4. In contrast to the declining schools, the teachers and principals of the improving schools are much more likely to assume responsibility for teaching the basic reading and math skills and are much more committed to doing so. The staffs of the declining schools feel there is not much that teachers can do to influence the achievement of their students. They tend to displace the responsibility for skill learning on the parents or the students themselves.

5. Since the teachers in the declining schools believe that there is little they can do to influence basic skill learning, it follows they spend less time in direct reading instruction than do teachers in

the improving schools. With the greater emphasis on reading and math objectives in the improving schools, the staffs in these schools devote a much greater amount of time toward achieving reading, and math objectives.

6. There seems to be a clear difference in the principal's role in the improving and declining schools. In the improving schools, the principal is more likely to be an instructional leader, be more assertive in his institutional leadership role, is more of a disciplinarian and perhaps most of all, assumes responsibility for the evaluation of the achievement of basic objectives. The principals in the declining schools appear to be permissive and to emphasize informal and collegial relationships with teachers. They put more emphasis on evaluation of the school's effectiveness in providing a basic education for the students.

7. The improving school staffs appear to evidence a greater degree of acceptance of the concept of accountability and are further along in the development of an accountability model. Certainly they accept the MEAP [Michigan Educational Assessment Program] tests as one indication of their effectiveness to a much greater degree than the declining school staffs. The latter tend to reject the relevance of the MEAP tests and make little use of these assessment devices as a reflection of their instruction.

8. Generally, teachers in the improving schools are less satisfied than the teachers in the declining schools. The higher levels of reported staff satisfaction and morale in the declining schools seem to reflect a pattern of complacency and satisfaction with the current levels of educational attainment. On the other hand, the improving schools staff appear more likely to experience some tension and dissatisfaction with the existing condition.

9. Differences in the level of parent involvement in the improving and declining schools are not clear cut. It seems that there is less overall parent involvement in the improving schools; however, the improving schools staffs indicated that their schools have higher levels of parent initiated involvement. This suggests that we need to look more closely at the nature of the involvement exercised by parents. Perhaps parent initiated contact with the schools represents an effective instrument of educational change.

10. The compensatory education program data suggests differences between improving and declining schools, but these differences may be distorted by the fact that one of the declining schools had just initiated a compensatory education program. In general, the improving schools are not characterized by a high emphasis on paraprofessional staff, nor heavy involvement of the regular teachers in the selection of students to be placed in compensatory education programs. The declining schools seem to have a great number of different staff involved in reading instruction and more teacher involvement in identifying students who are to be placed in compensatory education programs. The regular classroom teachers in the declining schools report spending more time planning for noncompensatory education reading activities. The decliners also report greater emphasis on programmed instruction.[10]

Ron Edmonds, a leader in the effective schools movement, identified five correlates of effective schools:

1. Administrative style.

2. Institutional focus or instructional emphasis.

3. A safe, orderly, clean and suitable school.

4. Teacher conveyance of academic expectations. (Teachers must be able to describe the school wide knowledge and skills that constitute minimal mastery and convey the impression that all students are expected to obtain mastery.)

5. School use of achievement data as the basis of program evaluation.[15]

The April 1998 issue of the *American School Board Journal* lists effective policy initiatives as identified by researchers. Although the initiatives do not appear at first to resemble correlates they do fall under the umbrella of the correlates as strategies for implementation.

1. START EARLY

Students' home backgrounds are responsible for half of their school achievement. You can't control who has babies, of course, but you can step in early with initiatives that give a young child a better start.

2. FOCUS ON READING AND MATH

Kids who aren't reading at grade level by the end of the first grade face 8-1 odds against ever catching up.

3. INVEST IN TEACHERS

Every dollar you spend on improving the quality of teachers has a bigger effect on student achievement than any other dollar you spend.

4. BRING IN TRAINED TUTORS

Several dozen studies indicate that early one-on-one intervention with a trained tutor can set kids on the right academic track and can, in the long run, save schools money by drastically reducing the number of students who later need special education and remedial services.

5. SHRINK THE SIZE OF CLASSES—AND SCHOOLS

Smaller schools (fewer than 1,000 students for high schools and fewer than 500 students for elementary schools) have higher test scores, less absenteeism, lower dropout rates, less violence and vandalism, better student attitudes, better student-faculty relationships, and stronger ties to the community.

6. INCREASE THE AMOUNT OF TIME SPENT LEARNING

"The more you study, the more you learn."[16]

Although all of these ideas seem complex, they are not. Hinged on bringing science to the art of teaching and learning, these ideas have consistent threads of commonality. In order to make sure that a district is moving toward effective instruction, a school board should keep primary characteristics and driving ideas in mind.

The following characteristics (descriptors) are not intended to be comprehensive, inclusive, or a cure for all the ills of public education. They are presented to provide a sense of what may help create effective schools. Using these as a guide to create a management system with an instructional focus should enable districts to advance toward the goal of having all students learn.

These attributes, which address core values and beliefs and speak to the purpose of education and the treatment of children, are important because they affect the structure of the school; they are not programs to be added onto what is already being done.

1. Clear and specific school purpose

- Each school has a written mission statement and clearly articulated yearly and long-range goals.

- Mission and goals are known by all teachers. All adults are bonded to the school's mission and goals.

- "Whether or not we teach the children of the poor is probably far more a matter of politics than of social science."[17]

- "School practices at the high-achieving schools reflected the commitment to student learning. All of these schools had a clear sense of what the school mission was. Extracurricular activities also reflected the importance of the mission."[18]

- A core element of effective schooling is goal-focused activities toward clear, attainable and relevant objectives.[19]

- "Not surprisingly, one critical research finding about school-based restructuring is that learning must be its core focus if it is to produce improvements in student achievement."[20]

2. Strong educational leadership

- "Effective principals focus the majority of their energy and those of the staff on solving achievement problems."[21]

- "The primary orientation of effective principals with teachers centers on task rather than human relations."[22]

- [Effective] principals build commitment for specific academic goals and guide the evaluation of progress towards those goals."[23]

- Principals in effective schools were better organized, spend more time out of their offices and classrooms teaching, have high expectations for students, staff and themselves, and place academic achievement above human relations. Principals in effective schools spent more time on instructional and less time on management issues."[24]

- "In schools where the school improvement plan was working, the principal was the key person."[25]

- "Successful principals understand how curriculum is organized and monitor curriculum programs."[26]

- "The principal who displays strong instructional leadership: Places priority on curriculum and instruction issues; is dedicated to goals; creates a climate of high expectations; functions as a leader with direct involvement in instructional policy; continually monitors progress; demonstrates commitment to academic goals; effectively communicates with others; effectively mobilizes resources."[27]

3. High expectations for staff and students

- The faculty is zealously committed to the belief that all students can learn.

- "Not only are the students motivated to achieve, encouraged by high expectations and positive attitudes on the part of the staff, but teachers are also expected to achieve."[28]

- "The staffs in the high-achieving schools verbally and behaviorally express the belief that their students could learn regardless of family background, socioeconomic status, or past performance."[29]

- "Teachers in effective schools stimulate and challenge their students, communicate interest and enthusiasm. Creating a challenge for students suggests that the teacher believes they are capable of responding to it…. That effective teachers have high expectations is further seen in their encouraging students to take responsibility for managing individual pieces of work."[30]

- "Once a teacher decides where a student stands on a continuum of 'smartness,' his or her academic status becomes fixed. We are not just talking about expectations of teachers, but expectations for competence that students hold for each other and for themselves…and the stage is set for self-fulfilling prophecies."[31]

- "Specifically, teachers who treat their students as able and respond to them empathetically promote cognitive and emotional growth…. When students are placed in environments where they begin to doubt their own value, abilities or self-directing powers, it appears that the brain physically represses information that is threatening to the perceived self."[32]

- "It is often believed that home background limits aspirations and ability to learn in school. We did not find home background to limit students' aspirations or parental interests in school—it limited, rather, the school's aspirations for its clients."[33]

- "Educational literature is replete with studies that provide strong evidence of students conforming to the level of expectations set by teachers."[34]

- "Students who believe that their effort will have a positive contribution to success will fare better than those who feel helpless when confronted with a task because they believe they are doomed to failure."[35]

- "Does the level of teacher expectations influence the level of student achievement, i.e., do high expectations produce high achievement and low expectations produce low achievement? The answer, based on extensive research, is a clear-cut 'yes.'"[36]

4. *School partnership with parents and community*

- "The study found that parental involvement in the life of the school had a positive influence on the academic progress of the students. Schools with an informal open-door policy are more effective."[37]

- "Parent involvement in almost any form improves student achievement. Involving parents in their children's formal education improves student achievement."[38]

- "Several studies of family involvement in their children's education have shown that what the family does by way of active involvement is more important to student success than either family income or parent education."[39]

- "Schools with effective organizations nevertheless appear to have certain advantages. One is better students, another may be more supportive parents. Parents who unite behind a school, trust it to do what is best, and support its objectives and programs in the home can be a real asset to a school that wants to build an effective school organization. Parents who regularly challenge school priorities, frequently object to tracking policies or course assignments, and disagree with personnel decisions can cause real problems for the development of a coherent, ambitious, professional organization."[40]

5. *Positive climate for learning*

- Students, teachers, and parents are free from the threat of physical harm.

- There is a safe and orderly environment conducive to teaching and learning. Adults are consistent in enforcing polices and procedures.
- Students, teachers, and parents are all respected.
- The school has a learning atmosphere that is business-like and productive.
- Buildings and grounds are well kept.
- The staff is zealously committed to the belief that all students can learn.
- "Both around the school and within the classroom, results are favorable when there is less emphasis on punishment and critical control and greater attention to praising and rewarding students."[41]

6. *Frequent monitoring of student success*
- Students are checked often for progress and work is used to diagnose and intervene.
- "Frequent monitoring and adjusting of inputs to assure individual pupil progress on essential skills, based on a variety of data, is a common practice in effective schools."[42]
- "In the improving schools, staff placed more emphasis on the assessment results and made adjustments in instruction so as to improve those results."[43]
- "Almost every state has set academic standards for its students, and many districts have added their own goals to the mix, but all of this doesn't mean much if you don't check to see how students are doing in pursuit of those goals."[44]

7. *Emphasis on student attainment of essential and basic skills*
- The district has an articulated, written curriculum that is used by all teachers in all schools. Instructional guides are available for all teachers—and are used.
- Students are properly prepared for learning new skills at each grade level.
- Skills and information to be taught at each grade level are known.

- "Focus on reading and math. 'Kindergarten and first grade should be about getting basic reading and math,' says Bill Honig, California's former state superintendent of public instruction. 'If you can't do that, everything else starts to disintegrate.'"[45]

- "Teachers and principals assume responsibility for teaching basic reading and math skills and are committed to doing so."[46]

- "But researchers say the critical time comes even earlier: Kids who aren't reading at grade level by the end of first grade face 8–1 odds against ever catching up."[47]

- "Improving schools place greater emphasis on the accomplishment of the basic reading and math objectives. They emphasize the importance of these goals and objectives and stressed that their accomplishment was fundamental."[48]

- "Relatedly, several of the recent studies of successful restructuring found that some combination of district and state curriculum content and performance standards...helped focus the work of the school on the curriculum and the instructional program."[49]

As school districts build a pervasive belief system that all children can learn and teachers, administrators, board members, and parents understand research-driven correlates of schooling, a common understanding of what causes learning is extremely important. A successful professional has knowledge of what he or she does that creates results; a professional not only knows what to do but understands why. The Dimensions of Learning program is an instructional framework based on the best of what researchers and theorists know. "Its premise is that five types of thinking, what we call the five dimensions of learning, are essential to successful learning."[50]

Dimension 1: Positive Attitudes and Perceptions About Learning. Attitudes and perceptions affect students' ability to learn.

Dimension 2: Thinking Involved in Acquiring and Integrating Knowledge. When content is new, students must be guided in relating the new knowledge to what they already know.

Dimension 3: Thinking Involved in Extending and Refining Knowledge. Learners extend and refine knowledge by making new distinctions and reaching new conclusions.

Dimension 4: Thinking Using Knowledge Meaningfully. The most effective learning happens when knowledge is used to perform meaningful tasks. The most effective learners have developed habits of mind that enable them to regulate their behavior, think critically, and think creatively.

Dimension 5: Productive Habits of Mind. The most effective learners have developed powerful habits of mind that enable them to regulate their behavior, think critically, and think creatively.[51]

When board members and professionals in a system understand how children learn and know how to create schools and processes that cause learning, they have the basis for a successful district. But they must also know the purpose for the creation of the system and they must institute a program that holds students accountable for learning—and adults responsible to ensure such learning is acquired. This is done through curriculum planning—by designating the product of the system or the learning acquired by each student.

Board members need to ensure that the district has written performance graduation standards and a plan to assess students for graduation. It should be made clear that the end of schooling at the twelfth grade will be based on what students know and not how long they have been sitting in classes. Benchmarked learning standards, by grade level, from kindergarten to the twelfth grade need to be written. All students' progress must continually be assessed as they pass through the system. This system of product identification—the learning acquired by students—is what makes an articulated, district-wide curriculum plan so important.

After adopting performance graduation requirements, the district (led by a plan approved by the board) should gather people from the community and the school district to decide how the requirements are to be assessed. For a couple of years following the initial adoption of the performance graduation requirements, students should be allowed to choose to graduate by meeting performance requirements or by the traditional method of Carnegie credits. The assessments must be based on academic learning. The purpose is to ensure that all students learn academically at high levels. It is not to lower standards so that everyone can meet them.

As a district-wide curriculum is important, so is the ability of individual schools to modify the plan to meet specific needs of students—but for only that reason and those students also need to learn what is expected for graduation. Curriculum written school-by-school is an exercise in impracticality. Teachers and principals have neither the time nor the expertise to allocate for the research and decision making leadership that is required. Of course teachers and principals are used in the construction of curriculum, but they should be led by experts with the time and ability to do the job well.

School board members armed with the power of knowledge based on educational research and an understanding of educational management theory face a very high hurdle as they set out to build effective districts. So far, research has not been able to crack the walls of the paradigm. Most people equate research in education with a compulsion for meaningless change, for jumping from one fad to another. "Change in educational practice more resembles change in fashion; hem lines go up and down according to popular tastes, not evidence. We do give lip service to research in education."[52]

Although not all research heralded to greatly improve schooling is valid (all sciences and social sciences have reacted to widely announced findings that did not live up to early claims), there has been a consistent increase in the knowledge of effective schooling. But it is seldom used; in fact, it is seldom known by most practitioners. The knowledge we have gained rarely reaches the classroom level.

The only research the paradigm allows into schools are programs that educators can plug into their classes and practices that do not incur change in structure or values. Jeannie Oakes, in a study of detracking for high student achievement, conducted years after educators first identified the devastation of ability grouping and tracking, discovered that research means little when compared with tradition and the paradigm.

We found that teachers holding conventional conceptions of ability pose the greatest threat to the implementation of detracking in part because they resist changes within the schools and in part because they seek political support for their cause among parents who want to maintain their children's place of privilege in school structured around inequality. Thus the school-based ideology of intelligence spills over to fuel the cultural politics of racially mixed communities and vice versa. But even when teachers have adopted new views of intelligence (however tentatively) and support detracking reforms, the efforts are shaped by what community elites will tolerate.[53]

There are many programs that school board members will be told will solve problems in their schools. At board meetings, trustees will be presented evidence of what works and be shown data that seems convincing. But until school board members have the courage to demand structural change and to staff their schools only with teachers and administrators who believe all children can learn and are committed to creating schools with equity and excellence, little will change or improve.

There is a vast difference in the work of people in political positions such as city council members or county commissioners and school board members. On most issues, city council members are truly representatives of the people. Zoning issues, problems with signage, where to draw the city's boundaries, and the necessary number of police officers are decisions that largely depend on what the people wish. Do they need another fire truck? It is pretty simple to understand that they will be able to respond to more fires with another truck but that the acquisition will raise their taxes. The right decision is the one the majority of the people want.

But what about an end to grouping, tracking and retention? Many citizens and teachers support these practices even though the harm of such programs has been well documented. Service as a school board member is not always the same as that of an elected or political official; to do the right thing a school board member probably will have to take politically incorrect action. Publicly demanding a critical review of class size research when teachers are negotiating for smaller classes will probably make board members very unpopular. The establishment of empowered organizations when neither the teachers nor the administrators wish to change is fraught with danger and turmoil. School board members who know what must be done to create an effective educational system have a difficult job. No one ever promised them that the task would by easy—or that they would have any friends when they finished.

CHAPTER TWELVE

Rules of Boardsmanship

One error into which Princes, unless very prudent or very fortunate in their choice of friends, are apt to fall, is of so great importance that I must not pass it over. I mean in respect of flatterers. These abound in Courts, because men take such pleasure in their own concerns, and so deceive themselves with regard to them, that they can hardly escape this plague; while even in the effort to escape it there is a risk of incurring contempt.[1]

1. Any district knowledge or information one board member has, all should have. Although the superintendent should be in charge of dissemination of information, it is incumbent on all members to be sure that they are in the loop. All information should be shared with all members and the superintendent.

2. A board should never operate from a committee structure in which different groups of board members have more in-depth knowledge than others on specific topics. Some boards assign members to issue specific committees such as personnel, finance, transportation, and curriculum. Even though this structure sounds efficient, it will eventually cause jealousy and split the board. A board should always meet as a whole group.

3. A board should know how to evaluate the superintendent. Some board members believe that it is their duty to ask every teacher and community member what they think of the chief executive. If popularity and harmony in the district is a primary goal, the superintendent must know what is expected. Otherwise a superintendent's work must be measured by the job done. Evaluation scales that can be obtained from national organizations should be used with caution. The board's priorities must be the same as those of the organization that created the document. It is important to decide if the board is going to measure the product or the process.

4. The board should attend conferences and state and local conventions to learn what is going on in other districts and how its district compares to others. As board members must have the courage to set aside time for teacher training and development, they need to budget time and money for their own.

5. A school board is the power of education in the district; vocal splits on the board soon split the district. Although the superintendent and his or her staff are the educational leaders, the board is the power broker. At the first sign of a combative division, a board should meet to solve the problem. School boards should work more as a team and less as a panel of commissioners.

6. As a general rule, school board member visits to schools and offices are formal events and someone from the district, a knowledgeable employee, should accompany any member. Often there are activities or procedures that need explanation and just as often there are people who will beseech board members for help. This is why a guide through the maze is necessary.

7. There should be a clause in the superintendent's contract that says any communication a board member has with anyone that may reflect poorly on his or her evaluation will be reported to him or her in writing within five days.

8. When the board is not meeting, there is no board. The board only has power when a quorum of the board meets. At any other time, any communication of concerns a member has about the district must be reported to the superintendent and acted on only by the superintendent. Even if he or she has someone else do the actual task, it is still his or her responsibility to make sure the concern is analyzed and evaluated and that any necessary action is taken.

9. A board member should pass information about trouble or criticism of practices to the superintendent and not take it directly to a principal or a teacher. The superintendent should have procedures set up for dealing with problems and provide for fairness and follow-through. It is not in the superintendent's purview to hide problems from the board.

10. Board members must learn how the state finance act works and be able to explain it. They should be able to read and understand the audit and know the fiscal condition of the school district.

11. A board member must know the difference between policy and administration and understand that the line is often blurry. Sometimes the areas overlap. Sometimes educators are too quick to accuse boards of micro management for dealing with issues that really are in the board's purview.

12. A school board must be willing to do the right thing to enable all students to learn. The board should not take a purely political stance when confronted by pressure groups in packed meetings. Board members can only lose a nonpaying job. Learning must be promoted above everything else, even basketball.

13. Board members have more responsibility as employers than to assume a passive-aggressive manner of opposition to the superintendent. If the superintendent does not have the support of the board, members should find a way to end the relationship politely.

14. The board should have a process to examine evaluations to find out if they are meaningful.

15. Board members should not be overly impressed by educators who boast about how much time they spend at school or on the job. Performance counts more than time.

16. A board member should not allow an employee to take complaints directly to them and to bypass procedures. He or she should politely ask the employee to go through the proper channels. It is extremely important that a district have channels for complaints that may not rise to the level of a grievance. Too often employees can only grieve abrogation of board policy. It is the little unfairness that really causes the problems.

17. School board members should know what is and what is not constitutionally protected free speech. Remember, anything that is in the public interest, such as a bond issue, is protected.

18. If a district is spending more than 83 percent of all funds on salaries and benefits it will not have enough left for necessary expenditures.

19. Only a district that is very tiny cannot afford to hire a skilled person to be in charge—full-time—of curriculum and instruction. Districts of three thousand students or less should consider this formula: Multiply two times the hours allocated for activities and athletics administration and hire someone for that amount of time to handle instruction.

20. The board should consider very carefully the use of employee-teacher committees in hiring principals and supervisors, especially if the employees have a vote equal to the supervising administrators. The procedures to be used must be clearly stated—and publicized.

21. Even in states with mandatory bargaining laws, a board should try to end traditional, adversarial bargaining and use interest-based bargaining. Continually move the district toward a more professional relationship with the district's professionals.

22. A board should have a written improvement plan based on a well-structured program for each school and the district. Summaries and results should be published at the end of each year. An honest end-of-the-year evaluation of the district and of each school, based on data and research, should be published. The school study should be completed, objectively, by the staff of the school.

23. A school board should ensure that each school has a site-based team and should attempt to stipulate that the principal's relationship to the team is the same as the superintendent's to the board. This means that the principal should not be allowed to veto the team's decision. At the same time, the superintendent (or someone on his or her staff) should be given the power, answerable to the board, to delay implementation and direct the problem to the board for resolution. The task of this administrator is to ensure that only research-directed solutions are found for educational problems. The task of the board is to recognize research-related solutions.

24. Community leaders and all employees should understand district and school budgets and finance. The district's books should always be open. Never hide reserves. Everyone should know where the dollars are and how they are used. The budget should be a product of community and staff participation based on empowerment—not democracy.

25. Board meetings should be moved from 7:30 P.M. to 5:30 P.M. so that there is enough time to talk in detail about what needs to be discussed. The board should adjourn at 10:00 P.M. and never go past that time; if necessary the board can meet again the next day or the next week. Forty-five minute meetings once a month indicate a board does not know what is going on in the district. Meetings of eight hours' duration twice a month indicate a board is managing the district.

26. The superintendent should send each board member a lengthy and detailed agenda packet before every meeting; board members should read it and know what it contains.

27. Allow every citizen with a complaint or problem to appeal directly to the board, even if it takes a lot of the board's time. Often parents may have concerns about the application of a policy or procedure as it directly affects their child. Only the board may make an exception to policy—and citizens have a right to ask. Administrators cannot make exceptions to board policy.

28. A board member should not allow back-door approaches. If employees want to tell a member what is really going on and what should be done about it, the board member should politely and firmly tell them to go through the appropriate channels. Once a board member is known as someone who can be approached through the back door, everyone will try to use him or her.

29. It is never appropriate for administrators to use the back door.

30. The board should demand professional ethics. Including:

a. No personnel or student information should be released by anyone in the district without following the letter of the law and ensuring legal privacy rights of individuals.

b. No information on any child should be released without parental permission.

c. No public discussions by staff about anyone in the system except on matters of legally protected free speech.

d. No abuse of any kind of students—physical, verbal, or emotional.

e. No person is ever allowed to abuse freedom of speech rules. People who work with students of any age should not influence parental opinion on school issues through the children they are hired to teach.

f. Employees should not be allowed to "unseat" supervisors or administrators through the back door or out-of-channel means.

g. The board should never discuss, or allow any employee of the district to discuss, any employee of the district adversely in public session or in the media. Employee evaluation, discipline, and/or lack of competence are the business of the district. As with students, personnel matters should never be the subject of public discussion. If the board does not recognize the beginning of such a discussion and does not act to ensure privacy rights, the superintendent has the responsibility to stop the meeting and to demand an executive session.

31. Any time any board member or patron wishes to discuss a known and documented administrative problem, error, or fault in a public meeting, the superintendent must never allow any other employee to be criticized openly, especially by the board. Only the superintendent works directly for the board. Everyone else, through channels, works for the superintendent. For the board to discuss anyone else, hold anyone else responsible, or to even imply that they have a problem with anyone else indicates that they have evaluative authority over anyone else. They do not. They evaluate only the superintendent. All personnel matters that necessitate board knowledge occur in executive sessions.

32. A board member should not allow anyone to hire a friend without an open search—even if it is a competent friend. Every applicant for every position must go through the complete process with no jobs having been previously committed to someone.

33. There is a science to the art of teaching and a vocabulary that goes along with it. Common words in the profession have common meanings and allow professionals to communicate accurately. School board members should learn the language. Most of these words are not educationese any more than tort and litigation are lawyerese and suture and stitches are medicalese.

34. School board members who encounter fiscal unfairness in the state should wage war against it. The school board has an obligation to every child in the state, not just those in one district.

35. If student achievement correlates with socioeconomic conditions of the family, the school district is ineffective.

36. School board member should be visionaries who carry one message: We believe all students can learn.

CHAPTER THIRTEEN

Shared Purpose and Not Autocracy: Empowerment and Not Democracy

To the efficacy and permanency of your union a government for the whole is indispensable. No alliances, however strict, between the parts can be an adequate substitute. They must inevitably experience the infractions and interruptions which all alliances in all times have experienced.[1]

It behooves us therefore to be quite clear as to whether there is any inherent reasonableness in this government by the majority. The answer is simple: the dominion of the majority does not give the smallest guarantee for the dominion of reason and law.[2]

Across the globe scholars and practitioners are conducting research to discover what works in education. How to successfully teach all children has become a big business. Organizations, universities, and publishing companies are sponsoring programs and announcing positive results. Strides are being taken; we are learning how to create conditions necessary for all students to learn. There are databases and catalogues to help school districts find, review, understand, and adapt new and best practices. In this age of communication and easy information access, there is no excuse for a district not to be aware of what works—and what does not work.

Most of the new programs deal with methodology and techniques. Most are premised on the invention of a better mousetrap; if we improve pedagogical skills and programs—the notion is—more students will learn. Of course they will. At least some. A skill and/or program will be used until a new better way is discovered. And then schools will change to that method or system. The one thing we have truly learned about education is that improvement has a difficult time taking root. Best practices do not stick very long to the Teflon walls of the paradigm.

Improving pedagogical techniques without making fundamental changes in the organizational structure of schools and school districts will continue to be an endeavor of futility. Indeed, without major structural change, public education will remain characterized by harmful practices such as retention, ability-grouping, and age-determined grade-level placement; the system will continue sorting and selecting students into those who can (are allowed) and those who cannot (are not allowed) to learn. Teaching a new technique to those who do not believe that all children can learn is analogous to putting new tires on a car with no motor; it still will not go anywhere.

Until teachers are professional members of a learning organization, zealously committed to the educational success of each child, new programs and techniques, no matter how effective, will only be window dressing. Until board members, legislators, and community members are convinced that all children can learn and hold educators to the mission of providing a high-level academic education for each child, schooling will continue to create and ignore improved methodology.

The first step in recreating public education is the determination of a clear purpose; the second is to use what is known about the management of knowledge organizations to create an effective organizational structure. School boards should announce that the purpose of schooling is to enable all students, 90 to 95 percent, to learn at high levels of mastery (that enjoyed by our brightest today) the essential outcomes of the curricula. Trustees need to pass a policy stipulating that differences in achievement levels based on demographic and socioeconomic conditions will no longer be acceptable.

When the purpose is clearly established as teaching and learning, everything else in the system needs to be judged by its contribution to the mission. If districts and schools cannot determine the contribution of certain programs and expenditures to the purpose of schooling through annual value-based reports, those programs need to be considered for elimination. School districts may make political decisions to continue cherished traditions and popular programs that do not enhance student learning, but the cost of those must be known and considered.

There will be patrons and employees in districts and communities who will denounce this work as folly. They will insist that not all children will ever learn successfully; some will become angry with trustees and school leaders for setting this purpose. They will accuse them of dumbing down, of taking funds away from programs for the bright who will be America's future leaders, and of wasting dollars on those who cannot learn. These are the people of the paradigm; board members need to try to teach them—but must never exchange optimism for recidivistic despair.

The new organizational structure should become a self-actualizing system capable of change, of adapting to meet the continually changing and divergent needs of the community, society, and the economy. This organization will be predicated on the differences between democracy and empowerment and the difference between doing the right thing and doing what the majority desires without regard to learning. The paradigm has always equated participation in the organization with democracy, with giving those in the system a vote. Ignorant popular decisions are still ignorant; providing democratic participation to those who do not have knowledge is folly. This is why we maintain a system with retention and ability-grouping; we allow people a vote who do not know any better.

> To be sure, there is a substantial body of research that shows that poorly designed education decentralization has little, if any, positive effect.... These research findings need to be taken seriously and indicate that the legacy of past decentralization efforts in education is generally not encouraging...the belief has been that involving teachers in making decisions or democratizing schools will automatically lead to better student performance. The research shows, however, that this type of decentralization has little effect.[3]

The professional educational organization needs to be a system of empowered participatory governance. Decision making must be shared;

however, the key to the system is knowledge. Governance may only be shared with employees who are knowledgeable. The assumption is that as the organization grows, all employees shall become knowledgeable. Whether or not democratic participation in any organization would ever create effectiveness is doubtful, and there is research to suggest that the practice has not been successful in private enterprise.[4] Such practice cannot work in a system based on knowledge until that knowledge is shared throughout all participants. And since organizations are continually changing as employees come and go, empowerment parameters may never be left to popular vote.

The empowered organization should be based on a set of beliefs and expectations that board members and the superintendent must set as the restructuring begins. As the organization develops, these expectations need to become imbued in all its members and herald its culture. Gaining teacher commitment, bonding them, is the most important task because these expectations are the substance of education's mission. There is only one vision; we shall see the time when all of our children learn the essential elements of schooling at high levels of success.

Assumptions

1. All children (90 to 95 percent) can learn.

2. There is a body of knowledge; there are effective practices; there are right ways to set conditions to create effective schools; there is a science to the art of teaching.

3. There are practices of schooling utilized today that are harmful to children; they will never be used again.

4. Educational practices shall be based on research, and results will be continually assessed through data collection and desegregation.

5. Professional educators will be knowledgeable about pedagogy and schooling. Teachers shall share responsibility for school and district results and shall be invested with decision-making ability. The entire staff shall be held accountable for results.

6. There are no excuses for failing to achieve a high-level standard of learning for all children.

7. Empowerment is the ability to make decisions for improvement within best practices parameters.

170

8. All employees will commit to the learning of all children and the efficient educational and fiscal operation of the system.

9. There is a financial bottom line; funding is not infinite.

10. The employees of the district will be bonded to the organization, its mission, and to the successful learning of each student.

11. The district will operate a program of personal and institutional accountability. People shall be expected to produce.

12. Certified and noncertified staff will be concerned about all aspects of the operation and make data-based, results-driven decisions.

The new organization will be far different from those ruled by autocratic administrators and just as distant from democratically governed systems. Teachers will become both pedagogues and organizationalists—committed to and accepting responsibility for the education of all students in the district. Rather than just being bosses, principals will build an organization around these expectations.

Decision making should be sponsored at the lowest possible *knowledgeable* levels. Teachers should be able to make knowledgeable decisions about how to best teach each child in their class—within school and district curricular guidelines. The adults of a specific school should be able to make the most knowledgeable decisions to best meet the needs of students and their community within district curricula and should have the responsibility and the accountability to modify programs for the learning needs of their students. This is the premise of decentralization, the practice (in many forms) referred to as site-based management or site-based decision making.

Site-based management (decision making) in schools is a logical and effective method of correcting systemic flaws in traditional management structure when the philosophy is implemented correctly. The notion is to allow those people closest to the students to make decisions that will enable all students to learn and cause the adults of the school to accept total accountability for the institution's success or lack thereof.

We realize that not all children are the same and that teachers should instruct them individually; we expect them to diagnose and intervene accordingly. Likewise not all schools are the same. Student bodies, parents, and communities around schools differ greatly within the same district. In site-based management, we empower the institution (site) to operate and make decisions within parameters established by the district; decision making is pushed down to the lowest possible levels.

An abbreviated line/command system enhances communication, which allows spontaneity to meet needs. Central office personnel often serve as consultants and evaluators of programs. In a program of effective site-based management, all certified personnel are supervised only through building leaders; there are never two bosses (such as a principal and a department supervisor) to whom to report. It does not work to have some staff report to a central office member while the rest answer to the principal. Such a practice unnecessarily divides schools and impedes decision-making ability.

District parameters controlling the direction of schools are necessary—especially in a site-based system. Site-based is best perceived in terms of concept, design, and planning on the district level and implementation at the site. For instance, curriculum design and writing is a district task; implementing the design is a building task while teaching for learning is a teacher task. Identifying the budgetary amount for each school is a central task while figuring out how to use it to maintain programs and enhance student learning in the building is the job of those assigned to that institution.

The object of site-based decision making is only to allow for the implementation of best practices and improvement on a school-by-school basis. It does not mean that each school will select its own programs. Few teachers and principals have the training or the ability to write their own curriculum. Instructional specialists using teachers for input, participation, and collaboration should formulate the district curriculum. Not having a district curriculum written and supervised by a professional is akin to home builders allowing the laborers on each job to design the floor plan for each house.

Site-based management does not mean that a district becomes a loose confederation of schools acting independently of each other and the district. It means that each school is part of a system held together by common beliefs and working within established parameters. Site-based management should not be equated to principal-based management for that scheme simply replaces one decision maker with another. To be fully implemented, the concept of site governance ensures the decision-making participation of staff, community, and students through a school improvement team. The team must be concerned about the total operation of the school without limitation of the traditional separation of teacher and administrator spheres of influence.

Because of the paradigm and our management tradition, there is a tendency for participatory organizations to return to top-down management. Structures created to ensure knowledgeable participation are often closed to nonmembers; vested groups often interpret their task as making all decisions alone. Thus, many systems of site-based management merely transfer the superintendent's authority to the principal. Some take the principal's authority and give it to the committee.

> Recent studies have also shown that involving *all* teachers in school-based decision-making and restructuring work groups is another key element that makes school decentralization successful.... Councils tended to involve only a few teachers in decision-making roles; if the council became the major locus of decision-making activities, an "us versus them dynamic" often emerged.[5]

In some districts, led by educators who understand neither education nor management, site-based decision making is merely announced, but there is no plan; the system is left to seek its own form. As a result, responsibility and accountability sink so low into the ranks that no one is left in charge. Correctly done, decentralization rests on a clear plan of responsibility, decision making, and funding. Who makes which decisions and who controls which funding streams must be articulated and known throughout the system.

There are three extremely important aspects of site-based decision making (management) that must be addressed if a board wishes to create an efficient and effective system.

1. The role of the principal. Often site-based plans merely leave the principal completely in charge and provide him or her with the power to label any action as site-based. In extreme cases, district programs such as instruction and personnel systems wither as the principal, perhaps with a committee of hand-picked teachers, claims authority.

Properly implemented, site-based decision making is localized within district-designed procedures and parameters and is a responsibility of the collective wisdom of the adults in the building. The principal's role is one of facilitator, researcher, supporter, and leader, who acts with the collective will of the school. The goal is neither democracy nor autocracy, but informed, synergistic decision making. An obstacle in many systems is the veto ability of the principal. The staff does not have to assume accountability if the principal, through the ability to veto or approve a decision, reserves total responsibility. Staff members will not commit to the process if they are given the task of decision making and find that they are overruled by an administrator. On the other hand, unrestricted decision-making power leads to democracy and little accountability.

The solution is to have the principal act in concert with the staff, working with them, in some respects, as the superintendent does with the board of education. Superintendents and their staffs must convince board members who retain complete decision-making authority on the basis of knowledge. Likewise, the power of the principal to veto the decision making of the adults of the school needs to be limited.

A system of checks and balances should be implemented to provide accountability by providing the superintendent with the ability to delay or terminate implementation of building decisions. When necessary, the final determination may rest with the board. Thus, as nearly as possible, the power of the group is invoked. The principal is evaluated more as a leader and less like an old-time boss.

2. Responsibility for finances. People must have the power to use fiscal resources to carry out their responsibilities. Schools should receive their yearly funds in a lump sum and be allowed to set expenditures to meet the needs of their students. There are many designs for funding that districts may use to devise their accounting structure. However, there is one axiom to which they must hold steadfast. The amount schools receive at the beginning of the year is all there is. There are no excuses for overspending. There are no excuses for not being successful within the amount of funds provided. The principal must be held accountable for fiscal responsibility.

3. Making decisions. Decisions must be made by people with knowledge—and all knowledge does not have to be shared. Districts hire specialists for technology, accounting, curriculum, instruction, special education, personnel procedures, and a plethora of other functions that are not affordable building by building. These people, who are employed to create a system and a plan, are hired specifically because of their specialized knowledge. Some decisions should not be site-based.

Properly implemented, site-based management constitutes a program of articulated decision making with each level of the district operation given specific areas of responsibility—all under the influence of the board of education.

The Board of Education

The board has the responsibility to:

- Develop and allocate all resources.
- Develop, evaluate, and approve policy.
- Develop and approve curriculum.
- Establish the educational vision and goals of the district.
- Select and evaluate the superintendent.
- Be visible visionaries in an advocacy role.
- Be the guardians of standards while being catalysts of change.

District

The district has the responsibility for:

- Developing district-wide priorities.
- Developing educational objectives for students at each grade level.
- Developing curriculum to meet educational objectives.
- Determining the district's over-all budget.
- Supervising capital expenditures, new construction, and major repairs.
- Selecting textbooks.
- Selecting principals.
- Maintaining files of applicants for positions.
- Personnel procedures.

School

The school has the responsibility to:

- Develop educational priorities for the building, based on the district's priorities,while taking into account the special needs of students.
- Develop new programs to meet the needs of a school's student populations.
- Develop scheduling to meet instructional objectives.
- Allocate building resources to best meet the needs of the students.
- Determine professional development programs to meet needs.
- Select supplemental instructional materials.
- Select applicants from a pool of files.
- Establish disciplinary procedures.[6]

Site-based management is designed to flatten the hierarchical pyramid of traditional management. However, the organization must remain in the pyramidal hierarchical shape for evaluation and supervision because real accountability is only to one person, never to a team or a group, and it is never found in a democracy. "Individual accountably is more difficult to maintain than group accountability because it leads to conflict and confrontation…. But without a personalized approach, you give people an accountability escape clause."[7]

Some districts, in a rush to flatten the organization, have reduced district leadership to a democracy of principals. These "principarchies" are a management system unique to education, and are most systematically counter to effective management. They are characterized by entrenchment, a lack of accountability, an inability to change, and an extremely charged political climate; the superintendent takes the role as supporter of the ruling group with the primary job of protecting the principals from the board. A skillfully operated principarchy may become a coalition of management and union leaders constituting an almost invincible force. Since members of the community (and many board members) are most often swayed by employees closest to the children, such a group is able to groom, select, and elect members of the board, closing the circle and preventing citizen governance.

These organizations create extremely smooth relations with the community because the flow of information is so consistent. The more peace and harmony that can be created, the more the group is left to rule, without accountability, in peace. The leadership equation is simple; the coalition of teachers and administrators appears to represent most of the district's certified educators. It is a mistake, however, to assume that the group really does have (or want) complete representation; usually only the wishes of a few leaders are heard—other employees know where the real power is and try their best to stay out of sight. In a dispute with board leadership, the public will generally follow the will of the employees. Thus, American representative democracy, which should operate school districts, can become an autocracy of employees.

Two other styles of educational management that characterize education are equally destructive.

1. Cult of the personality is a common form of nonaccountable management; it may exist in a nonregulated, site-based system or in more traditionally operated districts. A manager draws in those employees and followers who succumb to his or her charisma. Those who do not join up are isolated, shunned, and forced out of the organization. This style allows no accountability of the cultist members; it is the epitome of the old boy's style. When the cult is also a principarchy, the superintendent is usually either weak or the head of the cult. Employees in such a structure will always have more loyalty to the cult than to the district.

2. Paternalism is not only ineffective, it can be demeaning to employees; yet it is a form of management that may be found in places in most school districts. Board members and educators across the country should become familiar with Morris Shechtman's identification of the difference between care taking and caring for people in an organization.

> Families, government, and business have disabled people in the name of caring for them. Well-meaning policies have resulted in codependency, unemployment, and bankruptcy. Many apparently good intentions are undone by the confusion between *care taking* and *caring for.*
>
> *Care taking* means that: You do things for people that they're perfectly capable of doing for themselves. The things you do persuade people that they are unable to solve their own problems: that anyone else would be better able to solve them.

Caring for means that: You challenge people to be the best they can be. You tell them what they need to hear, not what they want to hear.[8]

In many districts our system of public education has become the epitome of care taking and paternalism. Many school districts deserve their reputation as places that exist for the employment of adults rather than the education of children. Wrapped in the secure embrace of tenure and protected by the paradigm, educators too often expect someone to take care of them. Administrators may be placed on the hot seat if teachers within their system complain—even if the administrator makes decisions that improve education. Care taking is rewarded; caring enough to help teachers achieve is often punished.

School board members must remember that no matter how they flatten the organization and push decision making down to the shop floor, a hierarchical accountability system must be built into the district. The superintendent works for the board; everyone else works for the superintendent. Evaluation and accountability flow down through the system.

CHAPTER FOURTEEN

End Note: Ethics and School Leadership

fiduciary (fi-doo´shi-eri, -du´-), adj. [< L. < fiducia, trust], 1.
designating or of one who holds something in trust for another:
as, a fiduciary *guardian for a child. 2. held in trust: as,*
fiduciary *property. 3. valuable only because of public confi-*
dence: said of certain paper money. n.[pl. -ies], a trustee.[1]

School board members and the top executives they employ to operate their schools have an almost sacred responsibility to the people
who send them their children and/or hard-earned tax dollars. Administrators and school boards have a responsibility to act only in the best
interests of children and to use funds as efficiently and as effectively as
possible: They also have a responsibility to democracy, to the voters of
the district. Sometimes these responsibilities are incompatible. When
that occurs, it is a difficult task to decide the correct course of action.

Facing a year of inadequate funding, several school boards have
decided to close the district before the required year was over because
they were out of money and used closing as a method of protest and a
declaration of need. Instead of budgeting to operate the year at a reduced amount, they spent according to what they thought they needed
and operated until their funds were gone. In other districts during bond
issue campaigns, some board members and superintendents have been
heard to proclaim that they would not be able to continue academic
improvement programs or even to maintain a level of basics.

People who lead our schools should remember, however, that their
task is to educate the community's children within funding (or any other)

parameters. Choosing not to educate children through the closing of schools or allowing their basic academic education to suffer is not within the bounds of fiduciary responsibility. The obligation of school leaders is to find a way to manage and sometimes this involves making unpopular choices. Frequently there is no choice but to increase class size and exhort professionals to even greater levels of effort and production.

School district management is often about making difficult choices while under siege from groups intent on protecting special programs at the expense of academic schooling. It is about doing what is right for children instead of what is politically expedient. In many districts, it is a frequent practice to pack school board meetings with issue-specific advocates (pressure groups) to convince board members to do things the group's way. Many board members believe that they must always listen to the visible majority. The following situations present typical ethical issues board members will face.

1. *After reading this book, or learning about effective educational practices at a conference, school board members are confronted with the fact that their district has junior and senior high school students separated into five ability groups from bright to slow and retains first and second graders.* They know that it is difficult for secondary students to transfer out of one ability group into another and that retained students are placed back into the same room with the same teacher. Through questioning the board members discover that the practices are supported by many teachers and administrators.

Changing these practices will be traumatic. Under the best circumstances, such a wholesale transition will progress slowly—perhaps over a period of seven to ten years. How do these board members convince themselves that children who may be harmed during the slow process are necessary casualties of the resistant paradigm? They have learned enough to believe that opening these practices up for discussion will cause disruption and a polarizing of the district. Changing too quickly may cause terrible damage to the overall district operation. Changing too slowly will allow another generation of children to be harmed. What should they do?

2. *Unexpectedly an elementary principal dies.* Since school starts in one week the board and superintendent must act quickly to find a replacement. They negotiate a one-year deal with a retired educator to take the position for that year. This person cannot obtain a standard elementary principal's certificate without taking classes because he never had taught or worked in an elementary school before—so the state issued a provisional license. He had worked in the district before for many years and is native of the area; he knows almost everybody in the community.

At the end of the first year, the interim principal for some reason was given one more year in the position. An agreement was reached; board leaders believed the contract was only for one year and a search for the best possible person (keeping with traditional district practice) would be conducted. The interim was supposedly informed that it would be an open search and that he could apply. During the year, the interim became more steadfast in refusing to resign, emboldened by the fact that the personnel department had neglected to write a one-year only contract. A regular contract had been offered and accepted.

The superintendent informed the interim that without a resignation, nonrenewal of the contract would be recommended to the board. This would allow for a search and the best possible person to be located. The interim principal refused to resign.

The night of the school board meeting turned out to be a board's worst nightmare. The board room was overflowing with more than four hundred angry citizens, many of whom were current or retired staff and old friends of the interim. The meeting had been skillfully packed. Tears were flowing; there was a list of designated speakers to plead for the principal's retention in the position. The crowd was angry and the interim denied ever having heard about a one-year deal. The superintendent proceeded with the nonrenewal believing that he had an ethical obligation to do so. What action does the board take when confronted by such a resolute group?

3. A lawsuit is filed against the state, alleging that the education-funding statute is unfair and disseminates funds disequitably. A new member of a board, a retired librarian with grandchildren, decides to learn all she can about the act and its alleged problems. She believes in fairness and learns that one of the districts that filed the suit (the state's poorest) is where her grandchildren live and attend school. During her investigation she makes some startling discoveries. (a) Her district is not only the wealthiest in the state in terms of assessed value and bonding capacity per pupil, but possibly the wealthiest in the country. (b) Her district, relatively large for the state, is funded at $4,000 more per year per student than the slightly smaller one her grandchildren attend. (c) Her district's facilities and equipment are the finest in the region.

She decides to do her own fact-finding and visits her grandchildren for a week so that she can learn all about their district. She talks to board members, teachers, administrators, students, and community members—and tours the facilities. She is shocked to discover the differences between the districts. In her school system, classes are smaller, teachers and administrators are paid more, libraries are better supplied and there is no comparison between the districts in terms of equipment, facilities, and student activities. In her grandchildren's district, teacher moral is lower, teacher turnover is higher, and some of the schools are not cleaned every night because the district cannot hire enough custodians.

Returning to her district, she attends the next board meeting and is surprised when a motion not on the agenda is brought forward to use district funds to have the district join the state as a codefendant. School supporters in her district want to use taxes to defend the system that she believes is unfair. People are rallying around the idea because they believe that a move toward equity may possibly reduce their district's funding. She knows that voting for the motion is condoning unfairness and that voting against it will enrage the voters in her district. What action does she take?

The topic of fiduciary responsibility must become pervasive in public education. For education to be successful, every person who works for, and leads, a school district must live up to the terms of responsibility and trust. Citizens must demand it of board members who must hold superintendents responsible who must hold everyone else responsible. It is the underlying premise of public education and employment—one cannot imagine what schooling would be like without the premise of a fiduciary responsibility. Teachers and schools as institutions must be trusted by the community to keep children safe and to teach them. Districts are trusted to maintain and use tax funds effectively. Employees are trusted to follow policies and procedures. Supervisors are trusted to treat employees well.

Sadly, there are far too many people in America who already believe that educators have dropped the burden of a fiduciary responsibility; there are too many tax protests and statutory limitations, there is too large a movement to take children from public schools, and there are too many tax levies that fail because of a lack of trust. Public leaders, board members, and administrators must always live up to their word. There cannot be a hint of impropriety. People will always make mistakes, but when school leaders for reasons of politics drop the mantle of a fiduciary responsibility, the entire system begins to decay from the inside.

As the superintendent of the lowest funded district in states with courts ultimately deciding that each finance act was unconstitutional, I was often asked why I did not just shut the districts down. Suggestions were made that we should spend all the money we had and close up when we had spent it all. This would certainly, it was presumed, bring the problems of the district to the forefront. But I had a fiduciary responsibility to provide the best education possible within the amount of funding we received. There was no other option. I had the choice of doing that or leaving. I worked through channels to change the system, but to deny the education of children because of state finance acts was not a choice.

What about systems that continue the employment of administrators, teachers, or other workers who are detrimental to the education of children because not taking action is more politically correct—and safer to an administrator's career? What about administrators just ignoring an ineffective teacher who is going to retire in a couple of years anyway? What about an administrator who hires a support employee and sets her pay higher than what the board-adopted schedule calls for and fails to notify the board? Fiduciary responsible or not?

To ensure fiduciary responsibility is the primary task of school board members. It is not always popular, it is not always politically correct, and it may be the reason members are voted out of office. However, the future of public education and, perhaps, our national dream of equal educational opportunity, along with the belief that all students can learn, depends on fiduciary responsibility. There is a science to the art of teaching; there are ways to create effective schools; there is a body of knowledge. There are right ways to operate school districts. There can be no excuses for doing anything else.

Where Do School Dollars Go?

School board members are often asked where education dollars are spent and just as frequently want to know how the spending in their school district compares with other districts across the United States. Table A-1 is a breakdown of average per-pupil spending by category in nine selected districts in 1967, 1991, and 1996. Figures are in percentages.

Average Per-Pupil Expenditures by Category	1967	1991	1996
Program Area			
Regular education	80.1	58.5	56.8
Special education	3.6	17.8	19.0
Food services	1.9	3.3	4.8
Compensatory education	5.0	4.2	3.5
Pupil support (attendance and counseling)	2.1	3.5	3.2
Transportation (regular education)	3.6	3.3	3.1
Vocational education	1.4	2.8	2.7
Bilingual education	.3	1.9	2.5
Desegregation	0	1.9	1.5
Regular health and psychological services	1.4	1.0	1.1
After-school athletics	.4	.7	.6
"At risk" youth education, alternative education	.1	.6	.6
Security and violence prevention	.1	.5	.6
Total	100.0	100.0	100.0

Source: Richard Rothstein, *Where's the Money Going? Changes in the Level and Composition of Education Spending, 1991–96* (Washington: Economic Policy Institute, 1997) 10.

Notice of Governmental Claim Letter

This is an example of a Notice of Governmental Claim letter, which must be mailed to school districts before an actual suit is filed.

Board of Trustees
School District
RE: Governmental Claim of :

NOTICE OF GOVERNMENTAL CLAIM
The following itemized statement is being submitted, pursuant to the (state) Governmental Claims Act procedures, against a local governmental entity as defined in (state) Statutes, School District, and its employees, administrators and agents.

The following individual is a claimant against the above-referenced school district and its public employees:

Claimant
The following attorneys represent the above-referenced claimant:

The time, place and circumstances surrounding the governmental claim are as follows:

Complainant was terminated from her employment with School District [month, day, year] when the Board of Trustees of School District rendered a decision not to renew Complainant's contract for the school year. Dr. (superintendent) of School District notified Complainant in writing on [month, day, year] of the decision to terminate Complainant's employment. Complainant was originally hired as a school psychologist by School District in [month, day, year].

Complainant was terminated from her employment under circumstances which constitute a breach of contract, a breach of the implied covenant of good faith and fair dealing, intentional infliction of emotional distress, tortuous interference with the employment contract of Complainant, violation of public policy, negligent hiring, supervision and training of public employees who supervised Complainant, and other violations of the (state) statutory and common law principles.

Constitution of the (state). The acts of School District and its employees further constitute a violation of Complainant's First Amendment right to be free from discrimination and retaliation based on protected free speech, as well as Complainant's constitutional right to equal protection based on her gender, and her right to substantive and procedure due process, under the Constitution.

During Complainant's initial interview in [month, year] for a position with the School District as a school psychologist, an interview conducted by (superintendent) and (special education director), Complainant was led to believe that both (superintendent) and (special education director) had high expectations for providing needed special education services to identified special needs students. Complainant was led to believe that the philosophy of public schools was that all children can learn, and that the students, teachers, parents and community needed to work together and this was a high priority need in the school district. Complainant accepted the position with School District with the understanding and expectation that additional staff would be hired to assist in the completion of tasks necessary to fulfill the philosophy and goals in identifying and treating special needs students.

At the time Complainant was hired for the position of school psychologist, (superintendent) and (special education director) made assurances to Complainant that additional staff would be hired to assist her in the special education efforts. In [month, year], (superintendent) stated publicly that Complainant would not receive any help and if Complainant didn't like it, she could leave. "It's my way or the highway."

In [month, year] Complainant received a good evaluation concerning her job performance and was offered a new contract of employment which she accepted.

In [month, year] Complainant met with (superintendent). (Superintendent) stated to Complainant that (special education director) thought Complainant wanted (special education director's) job. (superintendent) further indicated that (special education director) believed Complainant's association with other staff members and the advocacy of student rights and employee rights was viewed as an attempt to alienate certain staff members. (superintendent) went on to make veiled threats that anyone could lose their job. Based on the content of the meeting with (superintendent) Complainant contacted the (education association) after that meeting. (superintendent) commented to another staff member that Complainant was an "ambulance chaser."

Ultimately, the retaliation culminated in the administration's recommendation of termination of employment.

School District and its public employees are guilty of willful and wanton misconduct and deliberate indifference to the rights of Complainant. All of the misconduct by employees of School District were done in the course and scope of their duties as public employees of School District.

School District and its public employees, administrators and agents, have engaged in a continuing course of misconduct during the employment of Complainant, all to the harm and detriment of the above-named Complainant, in violation of state and federal law. Although federal based claims are not controlled by the Governmental Claims Act, they are mentioned here so that the district will be aware that both state and federal claims are involved and the availability of attorneys' fees as a remedy exists.

The above-referenced Claimant demands compensatory remuneration for the harm suffered in the maximum amount allowable under the (state) Governmental Claims Act limitations, as well as under applicable federal law. Complainant has suffered damages including, but not limited to, increased living expenses, expenses of relocation, pain and suffering, past, present, and future mental and emotional harm, loss of enjoyment of life, injury to career and reputation.

If you need any further information to act on this claim, or if the district's representatives desire to discuss it, please feel free to contact counsel for Complainant.

Very truly yours,

Litigation Filed in Court

IN THE UNITED STATES DISTRICT COURT
FOR THE DISTRICT OF (STATE)

Plaintiff,	)
vs.	)
COUNTY SCHOOL	) Civil Action No. _____
DISTRICT , DR. (superintendent)	)
in his individual and official capacity	)
as Superintendent of Instruction and	)
Dr. (director of special education), in	)
her individual and official capacity as	)
Special Education Administrator; and	)
JOHN DOES I-V,	)
Defendants	

COMPLAINT

Plaintiff,, for her Complaint against Defendants, states as follows;

JURISDICTIONAL STATEMENT

1. Plaintiff is a citizen of the State of (state).

2. Defendant School District is a local governmental entity situated with the State of (state), and is a "person" for purposes of 42 U.S.C. § 1983.

3. At all times relevant herein, Defendant Dr. (superintendent) was Superintendent of Public Instruction for School District. Defendant (superintendent) is a citizen of the state of (state).

4. At all times relevant herein, Defendant Dr. (director of special education) was Special Education Administrator in the School District. Dr. (director) is a citizen of the State of (state).

5. Defendant John Does I – V are other as yet unidentified employees and/or agents of Defendant School District.

6. This complaint is instituted under the United States Constitution, including, but not limited to, the First Amendment, the Fifth Amendment and the Fourteenth Amendment. This cause of action is further instituted under the remedies provided pursuant to 42 U.S.C. § 1983 et seq., § 1985 and §1988: and statutory and common law of the State of (state).

7. This Court has original jurisdiction over this action pursuant to 28 U.S.C. § 1343 for claims brought under 42 U.S.C. § 1983, 1985 and 1988 and pursuant 28 U.S.C. § 1331 for federal claims generally.

8. Plaintiff duly complied with the requirements of the (state) Governmental Claims Act and submitted a notice of claim to Defendants on [month, day, year], in compliance with (state) Statutes § 1-39-101 et seq.

9. Plaintiff alleges that the Defendants, and each of them in their individual and official capacities, were acting under color of state law at all times relevant to the Complaint stated herein. Plaintiff asserts that the Defendants, and each of them, while acting under color of state law, caused a denial of Plaintiff's rights guaranteed by the laws and Constitution of the United States and laws of the State.

10. Plaintiff alleges that the Defendants, and each of them, have violated clearly established federal constitutional and statutory law of which a reasonable person would have known.

11. Defendant School District, through its employees with final policy making authority, have established a custom or policy which caused a violation of Plaintiff's federal constitutional and statutory rights.

FACTS COMMON TO ALL CLAIM

12. Plaintiff, was terminated from her employment with School District on [month, day, year], when the Board of Trustees of School District rendered a decision not to renew her contract for the school year. Dr. (superintendent) of School District, notified Plaintiff in writing on [month, day, year] of the decision to terminate Plaintiff's employment. Plaintiff was originally hired as a school psychologist by School District in [month, year]

13. Plaintiff was terminated from her employment under circumstances which constitute a breach of contract, a breach of the implied covenant of good faith and fair dealing, intentional infliction of emotional distress, tortuous interference with her employment contract, violation of public policy, negligent supervision and training of public employees who supervised Plaintiff Psychologist, and other violations of (state) statutory and common law principles.

14. During Plaintiff's initial interview in [month, year] for a position with the School District as a school psychologist, an interview conducted by Dr. (superintendent) and (director of special education), Plaintiff was led to believe that both Dr. (superintendent) and (director of special education) had high expectations for providing special education services to identified special needs students. Plaintiff was led to believe that the philosophy of public schools was that all children can learn, and that the students, teachers, parents and community needed to work together and this was a high priority need in the school district. Plaintiff accepted the position with School District with the understanding and expectation that additional staff would be hired to assist in the completion of tasks necessary to fulfill the philosophy and goals in identifying and treating special needs students. Defendant (director) expected plaintiff to fulfill the role of (director's) "best" friend. (director) sought to exercise personal contact over Plaintiff as a part of the job requirements.

15. At the time Plaintiff was hired for the position of school psychologist, Dr. (superintendent) and Dr. (director) made specific assurances to her that additional staff would be hired to assist in special education efforts. However, in [month, day, year], Dr. (superintendent) stated publicly that Plaintiff would not receive any help and if she didn't like it, she could leave. "It's my way or the highway," he stated.

16. In [month, day, year], Plaintiff received a good evaluation concerning her job performance and was offered a new contract of employment which she accepted.

17. When a particular resource room teacher at the local high school did not have her employment contact renewed, Plaintiff advised her to contact the (state) Education Association and gave her the name of the attorney who represents the association. When this information was given to (director) by another teacher, (director) embarked on a course of conduct designed to retaliate against Plaintiff for her employee advocacy efforts through the (state) Education Association and her right to associate with that union.

18. In [month, day, year], based on her ethical duties as a psychologists, Plaintiff made arrangements for a special needs student to be evaluated, primarily for medication, by a psychiatrist. The student was in great need of a psychiatric evaluation which required these reviews of a psychiatrist. On learning of the referral, Dr. (superintendent) embarked on (sic) course of conduct retaliating against Plaintiff for the referral, based on cost considerations and publicly criticized her for seeking to do what was in the best interest of the student. Continuing throughout the school year, changes in policy were continually being made concerning whether or not a student in need would be referred for an evaluation or receive services in spite of ethical considerations. When Plaintiff made statements of public concern advocating treatment and evaluation for students in need, regardless of the attendant cost, employees of School District embarked on a course of conduct designed to retaliate against and intimidate Plaintiff based on her protected speech. Plaintiff was publicly humiliated, embarrassed and criticized unjustly, and treated adversely.

19. During [year] the demeanor of (director) became increasingly hostile and verbally abusive toward Plaintiff in retaliation against her, particularly during special education meetings at (elementary) schools.

20. At (elementary school), when a conflict developed between two employees of the school district, one of the employees confided in Plaintiff concerning his high level of distress because of the conflict. Later, the other employee went to Plaintiff's office and

expressed her feelings of frustration. (director) took the unfounded position that Plaintiff was interfering concerning the conflict between the two employees, and even indicated this in Plaintiff's performance evaluation. At the next special education meeting, (director) stated to the group that no one was allowed to go to Plaintiff to discuss conflicts or "to vent" in a direct effort to chill free speech. (director) continued to escalate her mistreatment of Plaintiff and interfered with Plaintiff's right of association and made comments publicly in derogation of Plaintiff's professional ability. Defendant (superintendent) told Plaintiff she was not allowed to speak to parents of students, during the school year.

21. When neuropsychological assessments and examinations were set up for certain special needs students and Plaintiff informed the parents of the students' rights concerning child treatment and of the existence of Protection and Advocacy, Inc., Superintendent and Special Education Director continued and increased their retaliatory conduct against Plaintiff in the form of hostile, unprofessional statements and threats of adverse employment action, based on her protected speech concerning the needs of special education students.

22. In late Spring of [year], Plaintiff was given a cellular phone to use, apparently because people were finding it difficult to reach her. Additionally three days a week the offices she used did not have a telephone. During the school year, as a part of the pattern of discrimination, Plaintiff was asked to turn in her cellular phone purportedly because of the expense. Nonetheless, the same cellular phone was given to a male employee of the school district two weeks later. It became readily apparent after the male employee who received the cellular phone was hired, that (Director) would provide him with whatever materials he requested while denying Plaintiff, based on the same requests. The male employee received a laptop computer his second day at work, along with a laser printer, while Plaintiff had been promised a laptop computer since the day of her initial employment, but did not receive such a computer for a period of years. Gender based disparate treatment by (director) occurred on a frequent basis. During the course of her employment, Plaintiff and other females were subject to off-color, sexually oriented comments by (superintendent) creating a hostile work environment based on gender, in violation of equal protection.

23. In [month, year], Plaintiff and other employees met to work on a job description and evaluation procedure relative to their work in the school district. Plaintiff wanted to use the NASP ethics as a basis for their job and evaluation procedures, because the NASP ethics principles adhere to the philosophy that the employee's first loyalty is to the student. (director) indicated that (superintendent) would be upset about the use of the NASP ethics, rather than have unqualified loyalty to him and the district. Once again, based on matters of protected speech, (director) embarked on a course of conduct in retaliation for Plaintiff's protected speech. It became readily apparent to Plaintiff that any recommendations she made for student evaluation and treatment would, for unlawful purposes, be blocked by (director) and (superintendent). Therefore, Plaintiff and other staff members were forced to discuss recommendations for students privately and then someone other than Plaintiff would present them to the administration so they would not be blocked, based solely on the suggestion coming from the Plaintiff. The needs of the children, advocated by Plaintiff, were ignored.

24. In [month, year] Plaintiff met with (superintendent). Superintendent stated that (director) thought Plaintiff wanted (director's) job. (superintendent) further indicated that (director) believed Plaintiff's association with other staff members and the advocacy of student rights and employee rights was viewed as unacceptable behavior. (superintendent) went on to make veiled threats that "anyone could lose their job." Based on the content of the meeting with (superintendent), Plaintiff immediately contacted the State Association after that meeting. (superintendent) commented to another staff member that Plaintiff was an "ambulance chaser."

25. Ultimately, the retaliation culminated in the administration's recommendation of termination of Plaintiff's employment, based on impermissible discriminatory purposes.

FIRST CLAIM FOR RELIEF
VIOLATION OF RIGHTS UNDER 42 U.S.C. § 1983

26. Defendants, acting under color of state law, have denied to the Plaintiff rights, privileges and immunities guaranteed by the laws and Constitution of the United States as follows:

a. Defendants have denied the Plaintiff the right of association, as protected by the First and Fourteenth Amendments to the United States Constitution by retaliating against the Plaintiff, both for her association with others, including the State Association, and her preference not to associate with (director) as "friend" outside working relationships.

b. Defendants have violated rights secured by the First and Fourteenth Amendments of the United States Constitution by exercising personality control in that Defendants have required the Plaintiff to provide absolute personal loyalty and conform to molds and patterns of behavior which are entirely personal and subjective to the Defendants. Defendants have punished the Plaintiff for holding views and opinions contrary to their own, in particular for her commitment to the needs of students, rather than personal loyalty to school administrators.

c. Defendants have retaliated for Plaintiff's exercise of constitutionally protected free speech.

d. Defendants have classified its employees on the basis of gender, by maintaining a work environment that creates a supportive and friendly working environment for males, while creating a nonsupportive, unfriendly, hostile work environment for females. In addition, Defendants have treated Plaintiff unequally in the denial of benefits and opportunities based on gender and other arbitrary criteria.

e. Defendant's actions are arbitrary, capricious and violated substantive due process as guaranteed by the Fifth and Fourteenth Amendments to the United States Constitution.

27. As a result of the actions of the Defendants, Plaintiff has suffered injuries and sustained damages including loss of employment and benefits, costs of relocation, damage to reputation and emotional injury.

28. Plaintiff should recover compensatory damages and this Court should enter declaratory and injunctive relief declaring the violation of Plaintiff's constitutional rights and enjoining the Defendants from their practice and pattern in infringing the fundamental constitutional rights of employees.

29. The actions of (superintendent) and (director) were taken willfully, wantonly and in callous and reckless disregard for the clearly established rights of the Plaintiff and in disregard for the

educational and personal needs of students. As a result, this Court should award punitive damages.

30. Plaintiff should recover attorney's fees pursuant to 42 U.S.C. § 1988.

SECOND CLAIM FOR RELIEF
WRONGFUL DISCHARGE IN VIOLATION OF PUBLIC POLICY

31. Plaintiff, as an educational professional, is obligated pursuant to fundamental professional ethics, as well as the laws of the United States and State pertaining to education, to assist in providing a free, appropriate education to all students. As an educational professional, particularly dealing with students who suffer from disability, Plaintiff had an obligation to recommend those treatments and services which were required. As an educational professional, Plaintiff is obligated to recommend and sign off on an educational diagnosis and educational plans to meet the needs of individual students. Both the federal government and the State have a fundamental interest in insuring that students receive the needed services, without having such services denied or delayed on the basis of arbitrary, bureaucratic or financial considerations.

32. Plaintiff was wrongfully discharged as a result of her commitment and actions as a professional psychologist to upholding fundamental ethical principles and to complying with her obligations under federal and state law. Plaintiff's discharge violates fundamental public policy.

33. Plaintiff has suffered loss of employment and benefits, damage to reputation and emotional injury as a result of the wrongful discharge in violation of fundamental public policy.

THIRD CLAIM FOR RELIEF
BREACH OF THE IMPLIED COVENANT OF
GOOD FAITH AND FAIR DEALING/BREACH OF CONTRACT

34. There exists an implied covenant of good faith and fair dealing, which is implicit in the employment contract of the Plaintiff based on the special relationship in existence between Plaintiff and her employer. Plaintiff entered into employment with the District based on the representations and information supplied regarding the District's commitment to the students and willing-

ness to support the providing of professional psychological services.

35. The actions of the Defendants breach the implied covenant of good faith and fair dealing and constitute a breach of her employment contract.

36. As a direct result of Defendants' breach, Plaintiff has suffered injuries including loss of employment and benefits, damage to reputation, and emotional suffering, and is entitled to redress in the form of compensatory damages, declaratory and injunctive relief, punitive damages and costs of litigation.

WHEREFORE, Plaintiff requests this Court grant relief as follows:

1. That Plaintiff recover damages for injury to her good name and reputation, interference with professional career and for embarrassment, humiliation and emotional suffering.

2. That the Defendants be permanently enjoined from interfering from Plaintiff's and other employees' exercise of rights secured under the Constitution of the United States and other federal statutory rights, as well as rights under the laws of the State.
3. That a declaratory judgment issue stating that Plaintiff's federal secured constitutional and statutory rights and State law rights have been violated by the Defendants.
4. That the court award costs and attorney's fees to the Plaintiff pursuant to 42 U.S.C. § 1988.
5.That the Court award punitive damages against (Superintendent) and (Director).

DATED this _____ day of [month, year]
Plaintiff

JURY DEMAND

Plaintiff hereby requests a trial by Jury on all issues so triable.

References

Chapter One

[1]Ron Edmonds, "A Discussion of the Literature and Issues Related to Effective Schooling." Paper prepared for the National Conference on Urban Education, July 1978. St. Louis: CEMREL, 35.

[2]Mike Rosen, "Standard Idiocy in Jeffco." *Denver Post.* May 15, 1998. B11.

Chapter Two

[1]Joel Barker, *Future Edge: Discovering the New Paradigms of Success.* (New York: William Morrow, 1992) 31.

[2]Lester Thurow, *Head to Head: The Coming Economic Battle Among Japan, Europe, and America.* (New York: William Morrow, 1992) 52.

[3]Diane Ravitch, *The Troubled Crusade: American Education, 1945–1980.* (New York: Basic Books, 1983) 371.

[4]National Commission on Excellence in Education, *A Nation at Risk: The Imperative for Educational Reform: A Report to the Nation and the Secretary of Education, United States Department of Education.* (Washington: U.S. Government Printing Office, 1983) 5.

[5]John E. Chubb and Terry M. Moe, *Politics, Markets, and America's Schools.* (Washington: Brookings Institution, 1990) ix.

[6]Chubb and Moe 2.

[7]Chubb and Moe 11–12.

[8]Thomas Toch, *In the Name of Excellence: The Struggle to Reform the Nation's Schools, Why It's Failing and What Should be Done.* (New York: Oxford University Press, 1991) 30.

[9]B. K. Eakman, *Educating for the "New World Order."* (Portland: Halcyon House, 1992) x.

Chapter Three

[1]Reply of Native Americans of the Six Nations to commissioners from Maryland and Virginia who invited them to send boys to William and Mary College, 1774. In T. C. McLuhan, *Touch the Earth: A Self-Portrait of Indian Existence.* (New York: Pocket Books, 1972) 57.

[2] "National News Roundup," *Education Week on the Web.* 5 October 1994.

[3]"National News Roundup."

4National Commission on Excellence in Education, *A Nation at Risk: The Imperative for Educational Reform: A Report to the Nation and the Secretary of Education, United States Department of Education.* (Washington: U.S. Government Printing Office, 1983) 5.

5Allan C. Ornstein and Daniel U. Levine, *An Introduction to the Foundations of Education.* (Boston: Houghton Mifflin, 1981) 108.

6Paul Monroe, *A Brief Course in the History of Education.* (New York: Macmillan, 1916) 60.

7Ornstein and Levine 112.

8Mortimer Jerome Adler, *The Paideia Proposal: An Educational Manifesto.* (New York: Macmillan, 1982) 5–18.

9Phyllis Schlafly, What's Wrong with Outcome-Based Education." *School Administrator.* 51.8 (September 1994) 26.

10Marvin Cetron and Margaret Gayle, *Educational Renaissance: Our Schools at the Turn of the Twenty-First Century.* (New York: St. Martin's Press, 1991) 66–67.

11E. D. Hirsch, Jr., *Cultural Literacy: What Every American Needs to Know.* (Boston: Houghton Mifflin, 1981) 11.

12Charles Leslie Glenn, Jr., *The Myth of the Common School* (Amherst: University of Massachusetts Press, 1988) 236.

13Horace Mann, *Life and Works of Horace Mann,* vol. 3. (Boston: Life and Shepard Publishers, 1891) 402.

14Thomas J. Curran, *Xenophobia and Immigration: 1820–1930.* (Boston: Twayne Publishers, 1975) 40.

15*Common School Journal II.* 2.15 (August 1840) 228.

16Ornstein and Levine 184.

17Diane Ravitch, *The Troubled Crusade: American Education, 1945–1980.* (New York: Basic Books, 1983) 9.

18Ravitch 18.

19National Education Association. *Report of the Committee of Ten on Secondary School Studies.* (New York: American Book Company, 1894) 19.

20National Education Association 20.

21Edgar Wesley, *NEA: The First Hundred Years: The Building of the Teaching Profession.* (New York: Harper and Brothers, 1957) 72.

22Harl Roy Douglass, *Education for Life Adjustment.* (New York: Ronald Press Company, 1950) 23.

23Barbara Z. Presseisen, *Unlearned Lessons: Current and Past Reforms for School Improvement.* (Philadelphia: Falmer Press, 1985) 23.

24Ravitch 44.

25Ravitch 56.

26Douglass 3–4.

27Douglass 42.

28Mary Walton, *Deming Management Method at Work.* (New York: G. P. Putnam's Sons, 1990) 20.

[29]Barbara Tuchman, *The March of Folly: From Troy to Vietnam.* (New York: Alfred Knopf, 1984) 4.

[30]Tuchman 7.

[31]Ravitch 58.

[32]Glenn 84.

Chapter Four

[1]R. W. Emerson, "Essays and English Traits." In Charles W. Eliot, ed., *The Harvard Classics.* vol. 5. (New York: P. F. Collier & Son, 1909) 7.

[2]Benjamin S. Bloom, *All Our Children Learning: A Primer for Parents, Teachers, and Other Educators.* (New York: McGraw Hill, 1981) 132.

[3]Ron Edmonds, "A Discussion of the Literature and Issues Related to Effective Schooling." Paper prepared for the National Conference on Urban Education, July 1978. St. Louis: CEMREL, 35.

[4]Bloom 18.

[5]Bloom 135.

[6]David Perkins, *Outsmarting IQ: The Emerging Science of Learnable Intelligence.* (New York: Free Press, 1995) 29.

[7]Perkins 29.

[8]Daniel Goleman, *Emotional Intelligence.* (New York: Bantam Books, 1995) 81–82.

[9]Jeannie Oakes, *Keeping Track: How Schools Structure Inequality.* (New Haven: Yale University Press, 1985) 21.

[10]James S. Coleman, *Equality and Achievement in Education.* (Boulder: Westview Press, 1990) 119.

[11]Richard J. Herrnstein and Charles Murray, *The Bell Curve: Intelligence and Class Structure in American Life.* (New York: Free Press, 1994) 436.

[12]National Commission on Excellence in Education, *A Nation at Risk: The Imperative for Educational Reform: A Report to the Nation and the Secretary of Education, United States Department of Education.* (Washington: U.S. Government Printing Office, 1983) 5.

Chapter Five

[1]John Goodlad and Robert H. Anderson, *The Nongraded Elementary School.* (New York: Harcourt, Brace and World, 1963) 1.

[2]Rebecca Jones, "What Works." *American School Board Journal.* April 1988: 29.

[3]Mary Lee Smith and Lorrie A. Shepard, "What Doesn't Work: Explaining Policies of Retention in the Early Grades." *Phi Delta Kappan.* October 1987: 130.

[4]Janet S. Rose et al. "A Fresh Look at the Retention-Promotion Controversy." *Journal of School Psychology,* 21 (1983): 206. Center on Evaluation, Development, Research, Hot Topics Series: Student Promotion and Retention. Bloomington: Phi Delta Kappa. 8.

[5]K. Yamamoto, "Children Under Stress: The Causes and Cures." *Family Weekly, Ogden Standard Examiner.* September 1980, 6–8, as quoted in Lucille B. Niklason, "Nonpromotion: A Pseudoscientific Solution," *Psychology in the Schools* 21 1984, 492. Center on Evaluation,

Development, Research, Hot Topics Series: Student Promotion and Retention. (Bloomington: Phi Delta Kappa) 132.

[6]Robert E. Slavin, "Achievement Effects of Ability Grouping in Secondary Schools: A Best-Evidence Synthesis." *Review of Educational Research*. 60.3 (1990) 494–495.

[7]Jeannie Oakes, *Keeping Track: How Schools Structure Inequality*. (New Haven: Yale University Press, 1985) 192.

[8]James A. Kulick and Chen-Lin C. Kulick. "Effects of Ability Grouping on Student Achievement." *Equity and Excellence* 23.1–2. (Spring 1987) 27–30.

[9]Robert E. Slavin, "Are Cooperative Learning and 'Untracking' Harmful to the Gifted?" Response to Allan. *Educational Leadership*. (March 1991) 68–69.

[10]Wilbur Brookover, et al., *Creating Effective Schools: An Inservice Program for Enhancing School Learning Climate and Achievement*. (Holmes Beach: Learning Publications, 1982) 58.

[11]Harold W. Stevenson and James W. Stigler, *The Learning Gap: Why Our Schools Are Failing and What We Can Learn from the Japanese and Chinese*. (New York: William Morrow, 1992).

[12]Theodore Robert Sizer, *Horace's Compromise: The Dilemma of the American High School*. (Boston: Houghton Mifflin, 1992).

[13]Thomas Toch, *In the Name of Excellence: The Struggle to Reform the Nation's Schools: Why It's Failing and What Should Be Done*. (New York: Oxford University Press, 1991) 242.

[14]Toch 235.

Chapter Six

[1]Peter F. Drucker, *Management: Task, Responsibilities, Practices*. (New York: Harper and Row, 1973) 456.

[2]John E. Chubb and Terry M. Moe, *Politics, Markets, and America's Schools*. (Washington: Brookings Institution, 1990) 151.

[3]Ernest L. Boyer, *High School: A Report on Secondary Education in America*. (New York: Harper and Row, 1983) 224.

[4]Thomas Toch, *In the Name of Excellence: The Struggle to Reform the Nation's Schools, Why It's Failing and What Should Be Done*. (New York: Oxford University Press, 1991) 236.

[5]Patrick Dolan, *Restructuring Our Schools: A Primer on Systemic Change*. Lilot Moorman, ed. (Kansas City: Systems and Organization, 1994) 12.

[6]Dolan 32–33.

[7]Drucker 176–177.

[8]Joseph Murphy, "The Knowledge Base in School Administration: Historical Footings and Emerging Trends," as quoted in *The Knowledge Base in Educational Administration: Multiple Perspectives*. Robert Donmoyer, Michael Imber, and James Joseph Scheurich, eds. (New York: State University of New York Press, 1995) 66.

[9]Michael Imber, "Organizational Counterproductivism in Educational Administration," as quoted in *The Knowledge Base in Educational Administration: Multiple Perspectives*. Robert Donmoyer, Michael Imber and James Joseph Scheurich, eds. (New York: State University of New York Press, 1995) 112.

[10]Imber 112.

References

Chapter Seven

[1]Lyle Whiting, an eighty-four-year-old school board member who had been teacher, a principal, a superintendent and who served on MacArthur's staff setting up schools in Japan after World War II.

[2]Peter F. Drucker, *Management: Task, Responsibilities, Practices.* (New York: Harper and Row, 1973) 232.

[3]Colorado Education Association, "Sanctions Report Falcon 49, A Shattered School District" (Denver: Colorado Education Association, 1980) 4.

Chapter Eight

[1]Serrano V. Priest, 5 Cal. 3d 584, 96 Cal. Rptr. 601 (1971) as cited in Percy E. Burrup, *Financing Education in a Climate of Change.* 2nd ed. (Boston: Allyn and Bacon, 1977) 183.

[2]Burrup 119.

[3]Allan Odden, ed., *Rethinking School Finance: An Agenda for the 1990s.* (San Francisco: Jossey-Bass, 1992) 10.

[4]Thomas Sowell, *Inside American Education: The Decline, the Deception, the Dogmas.* (New York: Free Press, 1993) 10.

[5]Erik Alan Hanushek et al., *Making Schools Work: Improving Performance and Controlling Costs.* (Washington: Brookings Institution, 1994) 64.

[6]John E. Chubb and Terry M. Moe, *Politics, Markets, and America's Schools.* (Washington: Brookings Institution, 1990) 102.

[7]Odden 11.

[8]Sowell 96.

[9]James S. Coleman, *Equality and Achievement in Education.* (Boulder: Westview Press, 1990) 98.

[10]Coleman 98.

[11]Wayne Buchanan and Deborah A. Verstegen, "School Finance Litigation in Montana." *West's Education Law Reporter.* vol. 66 (May 1991):32.

[12]Hanushek 10.

[13]Hanushek 11.

[14]Glenn E. Robinson and James H. Wittebols, *Class Size Research: A Related Cluster Analysis for Decision Making.* (Arlington: Educational Research Service, 1986) 31.

[15]Robinson and Wittebols 44.

[16]Robinson and Wittebols 55.

[17]Robinson and Wittebols 12–13.

[18]Robert E. Slavin, "Meta Analysis in Education: How Has It Been Used?" *Educational Researcher.* October 1984: 11.

[19]Allan Odden, "Class Size and Student Achievement: Research-Based Policy Alternatives," *Educational Evaluation and Policy Analysis,* 12 (1990): 217.

[20]C. M. Achilles, *Summary of Recent Class-Size Research with an Emphasis on Tennessee's Project STAR and Its Derivative Research Studies.* (Nashville: Tennessee State University,) 12, 13, 14–15, 18.

203

[21]Achilles 19.

[22]Harold Wenglinsky, *When Money Matters: How Educational Expenditures Improve Student Performance and How They Don't*. (Princeton: Policy Information Center, Educational Testing Service, 1997) 14.

[23]Wenglinsky viii.

[24]Wenglinsky 21.

[25]Wenglinsky 22.

[26]Wenglinsky 20.

[27]Rebecca Jones quoting Linda Darling-Hammond in "What Works." *The American School Board Journal*. April 1988: 30.

[28]Richard J. Murnane and Frank Levy, "Why Money Matters Sometimes." *Education Week on the Web*. September 11, 1996.

[29]Barbara A. Nye, et al., "Smaller Classes Really Are Better." *American School Board Journal*. May 1992: 33.

[30]Achilles 12.

[31]Robert Johnson, "Dollars Don't Mean Success in Calif. District." *Education Week on the Web*. December 3, 1997.

[32]John E. Chubb and Terry M. Moe, *Politics, Markets, and America's Schools*. (Washington: Brookings Institution, 1990) 193.

[33]James S. Coleman, *Equality and Achievement in Education*. (Boulder: Westview Press, 1990) 247.

Chapter Nine

[1]William Lasner, *Veritas*. (Philadelphia: Regan Books, 1997) 78.

[2]Reconstruction Era Civil Rights Act 42 U.S.C. § 1983.

[3]Notice of Governmental Claim Letter.

[4]Notice of Governmental Claim Letter.

[5]Lawsuit Filed in Federal Court.

Chapter Ten

[1]Warren Bennis, *Why Leaders Can't Lead: The Unconscious Conspiracy Continues*. (San Francisco: Jossey-Bass, 1989) xii.

Chapter Eleven

[1]Anthony Robbins, *Awaken the Giant Within*. (New York: Simon & Schuster, 1991) 25.

[2]Diane McGuinness, *Why Our Children Can't Read: And What We Can Do About It*. (New York: Free Press, 1997) xii.

[3]McGuinness 10–12.

[4]Cyril Owen Houle, *Governing Boards: Their Nature and Nurture*. (San Francisco: Jossey-Bass, 1983) 89.

References

[5]Ron Edmonds, "A Discussion of the Literature and Issues Related to Effective Schooling." Paper prepared for the National Conference on Urban Education, July 1978. St. Louis: CEMREL, Inc., 35.

[6]Benjamin S. Bloom, *All Our Children Learning: A Primer for Parents, Teachers, and Other Educators*. (New York: McGraw Hill, 1981) 132.

[7]Wilbur Brookover et al., *Creating Effective Schools: An Inservice Program for Enhancing School Learning Climate and Achievement*. (Holmes Beach: Learning Publications, 1982) 61.

[8]Ron Edmonds, "Effective Schools for the Urban Poor," *Effective Schools and School Improvement*. Ronald S. Brandt, ed. (Alexandria: Association for Supervision and Curriculum Development, 1989) 2.

[9]Herbert J. Walberg, "A Theory of Educational Productivity: Fundamental Substance and Method," in *Fundamental Studies in Educational Research*. Paul Vedder, ed. (Rockmount: Swets and Zeitlinger, 1990) 22.

[10]American Association of School Administrators, *An Effective Schools Primer*. (Arlington: American Association of School Administrators, 1992) 4.

[11]Ralph Scott and Herbert J. Walberg, "Schools Alone Are Insufficient: A Response to Edmonds," *Effective Schools and School Improvement*. Ronald S. Brandt, ed. (Alexandria: Association for Supervision and Curriculum Development, 1989) 12.

[12]American Association of School Administrators 6.

[13]Edmonds *A Discussion of the Literature* 21–22.

[14]Edmonds *A Discussion of the Literature*, 28.

[15]Ronald Edmonds and Larry Lezotte, "The Correlates of School Effectiveness," Distributed at Second Annual School Effectiveness and Organizational Change Workshop. January 1985. Also listed in American Association of School Administrators, *An Effective Schools Primer*.

[16]Rebecca Jones, "What Works." *American School Board Journal*. April 1988: 30, 31.

[17]Ron Edmonds, "Some Schools Work and More Can." *Social Policy*. April 1979: 32.

[18]Maureen McCormack-Larkin, "Change in Urban Schools." *Journal of Negro Education*. 54.3 (1985): 414.

[19]Donald E. Mackenzie, "Research for School Improvement: An Appraisal of Some Recent Trends." *Educational Researcher*. 12.4 (1983): 8.

[20]Allan Odden and Carolyn Busch, *Financing Schools for High Performance: Strategies for Improving the Use of Educational Resources*. (San Francisco: Jossey-Bass, 1998) 26.

[21]K. A. Leithwood and P. J. Montgomery, "The Role of the Elementary School Principal in Program Improvement." *Review of Educational Research*. 52.3 (1982): 320.

[22]Leithwood and Montgomery 321.

[23]Mackenzie 8.

[24]Maryland State Department of Education, "Process Evaluation: A Comprehensive Study of Outliers." *Effective Schools Abstracts* 1.3 (1986–1987).

[25]Terry A. Clark and Dennis P. McCarthy, "School Improvement in New York City: The Evolution of a Project." *Educational Researcher*. 12. 4 (1983): 20.

[26]Edward Pajak and Lewis McAfee, "The Principal as School Leader, Curriculum Leader." *National Association of Secondary School Principals Bulletin*. 76.547 (1992): 23.

[27]Wilma F. Smith and Richard L. Andrews, *Instructional Leadership: How Principals Make a Difference.* (Alexandria: Association for Supervision and Curriculum Development, 1989) 8.

[28]Mary Rhodes Hoover, "Characteristics of Black Schools at Grade Level: A Description." *Reading Teacher.* 31.7 (1978): 761.

[29]McCormack-Larkin 410.

[30]Peter Mortimore and Pam Sammons, "New Evidence on Effective Elementary Schools." *Educational Leadership.* 45.1 (1987): 7.

[31]Elizabeth G. Cohen, Diane Kepner and Patricia Swanson, "Dismantling Status Hierarchies in Heterogeneous Classrooms," in Jeannie Oakes and Karen Hunter Quartz, eds. *Creating New Educational Communities.* Ninety-fourth Yearbook of the National Society for the Study of Education. Part I. (Chicago: University of Chicago Press, 1995) 18.

[32]William W. Purkey and David N. Aspy. "The Mental Health of Students: Nobody Minds? Nobody Cares?" *Person-Centered Review.* 3.1 (1988) 41–49. Abstract. *Effective Schools Research Abstracts.* 3.4 (1988–1989).

[33]Carl A. Grant and Christine E. Sleeter, "Race, Class, and Gender and Abandoned Dreams." *Teachers College Record.* 90.1 (Fall 1988): 39.

[34]Annette Gault and Joseph Murray, "The Implications of High Expectations for Bilingual Students." *Journal of Educational Equity and Leadership* 7.8 (Winter 1987) 301–317. Abstract. *Effective Schools Research Abstracts.* 4.3 (1989–1990).

[35]Barbara Smey-Richman, "Involvement in Learning for Low-Achieving Students." Research for Better Schools, Philadelphia, 1988. Abstract. *Effective Schools Research Abstracts.* 5.9 (1986–1987).

[36]Wilbur Brookover, et al., *Creating Effective Schools: An Inservice Program for Enhancing School Learning Climate and Achievement.* (Holmes Beach: Learning Publications, 1982) 62.

[37]Mortimore and Sammons 8.

[38]Anne Henderson, "The Evidence Continues to Grow: Parent Involvement Improves Student Achievement." Parkway: National Committee for Citizens in Education: Abstract. *Effective Schools Research Abstracts.* 2.4 (1987–1988).

[39]U.S. Department of Education, "Strong Families, Strong Schools: Building Community Partnerships for Learning." U.S. Department of Education, Washington, September 1994. Abstract. *Effective Schools Research Abstracts.* 9.5.

[40]John E. Chubb and Terry M. Moe, *Politics, Markets, and America's Schools.* (Washington: Brookings Institution, 1990) 147.

[41]Mortimore and Sammons 8.

[42]Edmonds,"Some Schools Work" 32.

[43]Wilbur Brookover and Lawrence W. Lezotte, "Changes in School Characteristics Coincident with Changes in Student Achievement" (Occasional Paper No. 17), Institute for Research on Teaching: Michigan State University. Abstract. *Effective Schools Research Abstracts.* 1.1 (1986–1987).

[44]Jones 32.

[45]Jones 29.

[46]Edmonds,"Some Schools Work" 35.

References

[47]Jones 29.

[48]Brookover,"Changes in School Characteristics" [Abstract].

[49]Odden 31.

[50]Robert J. Marzano, et al., *Teacher's Manual: Dimensions of Learning*. (Alexandria: Association for Supervision and Curriculum Development, 1992) 1.

[51]Marzano, et al. 1–2.

[52]Robert E. Slavin, *Show Me the Evidence: Proven and Promising Programs for America's Schools*. (Thousand Oaks: Corwin Press, 1998) 7.

[53]Jeannie Oakes, et al.,"Detracking: The Social Construction of Ability, Cultural Politics and Resistance to Reform." *Teachers College Record*. 98.3 (Spring 1997).

Chapter Twelve
[1]Niccolo Machiavelli, *The Prince*. Charles W. Eliot, ed. The Harvard Classics. vol. 36 (New York: P. F. Collier & Son, 1909) 80.

Chapter Thirteen
[1]Henry Steele Commager, ed., *Documents of American History*. 6th ed. (New York: Appleton-Century-Crofts, 1949) 171.

[2]Heinrich von Treitschke, *Politics*. Hans Kohn, ed. (New York: Harcourt, Brace & World, 1963) 214.

[3]Allan Odden and Carolyn Busch, *Financing Schools for High Performance: Strategies for Improving the Use of Educational Resources*. (San Francisco: Jossey-Bass, 1998) 27.

[4]Odden and Busch 27.

[5]Odden and Busch 32.

[6]American Association of School Administrators, National Association of Elementary School Principals, and National Association of Secondary School Principals. "School Based Management: A Strategy for Better Learning," 1988.

[7]Morris R. Shechtman, *Working Without a Net: How to Survive and Thrive in Today's High Risk Business World*. (New York: Pocket Books, 1995) 158.

[8]Morris R. Shechtman 18.

Chapter Fourteen
[1]*Webster's New World Dictionary of the American Language*. Concise ed. (Cleveland: World Publishing Company, 1966) 279.

Bibliography

Achilles, C. M. *Summary of Recent Class-Size Research with an Emphasis on Tennessee's Project STAR and Its Derivative Research Studies*. Nashville: Tennessee State University.

Adler, Mortimer Jerome. *The Paideia Proposal: An Educational Manifesto*. New York: Macmillan, 1982.

American Association of School Administrators. *An Effective Schools Primer*. Arlington: American Association of School Administrators, 1992.

American Association of School Administrators. *Time on Task: Using Instructional Time More Effectively*. Arlington: American Association of School Administrators, 1982.

American Association of School Administrators. National Association of Elementary School Principals, and National Association of Secondary School Principals. "School Based Management: A Strategy for Better Learning," 1988.

Bailey, William J. *School-Site Management Applied*. Lancaster: Technomic, 1991.

Barker, Joel. *Future Edge: Discovering the New Paradigms of Success*. New York: William Morrow, 1992.

Becham, Joseph C. *School Officials and the Courts: Update 1992*. Arlington: Educational Research Service, 1992.

Belasco, James A. *Teaching the Elephant to Dance: Empowering Change in Your Organization*. New York: Crown, 1990.

Bennis, Warren. *On Becoming a Leader*. Reading: Addison-Wesley, 1989.

Bennis, Warren. *Why Leaders Can't Lead: The Unconscious Conspiracy Continues*. San Francisco: Jossey-Bass, 1989.

Bennis Warren and Burt Nanus. *Leaders: The Strategies for Taking Charge*. New York: Harper and Row, 1985.

Berliner, David C. and Bruce J. Biddle. *The Manufactured Crisis: Myths, Fraud and the Attack on America's Public Schools*. Reading: Addison-Wesley, 1995.

Black, John A. and Fenwick W. English. *What They Don't Tell You in Schools of Education About School Administration*. Lancaster: Technomic, 1986.

Bibliography

Blanchard, Kenneth and Norman Vincent Peale. *The Power of Ethical Management*. New York: William Morrow, 1988.

Bloom, Benjamin S. *All Our Children Learning: A Primer for Parents, Teachers and Other Educators*. New York: McGraw Hill, 1981.

Bloom, Benjamin S. *Human Characteristics and School Learning*. New York: McGraw-Hill, 1982.

Blumberg, Arthur. *School Administration as a Craft: Foundations of Practice*. Boston: Allyn and Bacon,1989.

Bonstingl, John Jay. Schools of Quality: *An Introduction to Total Quality Management in Education*. Alexandria: Association for Supervision and Curriculum Development, 1992.

Borg, Walter R. and Meredith D. Gall. *Educational Research: An Introduction*. 4th edition. New York: Longman, 1983.

Boyer, Ernest L. *High School: A Report on Secondary Education in America*. New York: Harper and Row, 1983.

Bracey, Gerald W. *Transforming America's Schools: An Rx for Getting Past Blame*. Arlington: American Association of School Administrators, 1994.

Brandt, Ronald S. *Coaching and Staff Development*. Alexandria: Association for Supervision and Curriculum Development,1989.

Brandt, Ronald S., ed. *Effective Schools and School Improvement*. Alexandria: Association for Supervision and Curriculum Development, 1989.

Brookover, Wilbur, et al. *Creating Effective Schools: An Inservice Program for Enhancing School Learning Climate and Achievement*. Holmes Beach: Learning Publications, 1982.

Brookover, Wilbur and Lawrence W. Lezotte. "Changes in School Characteristics Coincident with Changes in Student Achievement" (Occasional Paper No. 17), Institute for Research on Teaching: Michigan State University. Abstract. *Effective Schools Research Abstracts*. 1.1 (1986–1987).

Buchanan, Wayne and Deborah A. Verstegen. "School Finance Litigation in Montana," *West's Education Law Reporter*. vol. 66 (1991):19–33.

Burrup, Percy E. *Financing Education in a Climate of Change*. 2nd ed. Boston: Allyn and Bacon, 1977.

Cetron, Marvin and Margaret Gayle. *Educational Renaissance: Our Schools at the Turn of the Twenty-First Century*. New York: St. Martin's Press, 1991.

Chalker, Donald M. and Richard M. Haynes. *World Class Schools: New Standards for Education*. Lancaster: Technomic, 1994.

Chubb, John E. and Terry M. Moe. *Politics, Markets, and America's Schools*. Washington: Brookings Institution, 1990.

Citizens for Quality Schools. *The Power of Collaborative Decision Making: A Handbook for Change in the Denver Public Schools*. Denver: Center for Quality Schools, 1992.

Clark, Terry A. and Dennis P. McCarthy. "School Improvement in New York City: The Evolution of a Project," *Educational Research*. 12. 4 (1983): 17–24.

Coleman, James S. *Equality and Achievement in Education*. Boulder: Westview Press, 1990.

Colorado Education Association. "Sanctions Report Falcon 49, A Shattered School District," Denver: Colorado Education Association, 1980.

Combs, Arthur W. *Myths in Education: Beliefs that Hinder Progress and Their Alternatives*. Boston: Allyn and Bacon, 1979.

Commager, Henry Steele., ed. *Documents of American History*. 6th ed. New York: Appleton-Century-Crofts, 1949.

Common School Journal II. 2.15 (August 1840).

Cook, William J. Jr., *Bill Cook's Strategic Planning for America's Schools*. Arlington: American Association of School Administrators, 1988.

Covey, Stephen R. *Principle-Centered Leadership*. New York: Simon and Schuster, 1992.

Covey, Stephen R. *The 7 Habits of Highly Effective People: Restoring the Character Ethic*. New York: Simon and Schuster, 1989.

Creech, Bill. *The Five Pillars of TQM*. New York: Truman Talley, 1994.

Crocker, Olga L., Cyril Charney, and Johnny Sik Leung Chiu. *Quality Circles: A Guide to Participation and Productivity*. New York: New American Library, 1984.

Curran, Thomas J. *Xenophobia and Immigration: 1820–1930*. Boston: Twayne Publishers, 1975.

Daggett, Willard R. and Bendict Kruse. *Education Is NOT a Spectator Sport*. Schenectady: Leadership Press, 1997.

Data Research, Inc. *1997 Deskbook Encyclopedia of American School Law*. Rosemount: Data Research, 1997.

Data Research Inc. *United States Supreme Court Education Cases*. 4th edition. Rosemount: Data Research, 1996.

Davidson, Jack L. *The Superintendency—Leadership for Effective Schools*. Jackson: Kelwynn Press, 1987.

Dilenschneider, Robert L. *Power and Influence: Mastering the Art of Persuasion*. New York: Prentice Hall, 1990.

Dolan, Patrick. *Restructuring Our Schools: A Primer on Systemic Change*. Lilot Moorman, ed. Kansas City: Systems and Organization, 1994.

Donmoyer, Robert, Michael Imber and James Joseph Scheurich, eds. *The Knowledge Base in Educational Administration: Multiple Perspectives*. New York: State University of New York Press, 1995.

Douglass, Harl Roy. *Education for Life Adjustment*. New York: Ronald Press Company, 1950.

Drucker, Peter F. *Management: Task, Responsibilities, Practices*. New York: Harper and Row, 1973.

Bibliography

Eakman, B. K. *Educating for the "New World Order."* Portland: Halcyon House, 1992.

Edmonds, Ron. "A Discussion of the Literature and Issues Related to Effective Schooling." St. Louis: National Conference on Urban Education, 1978.

Edmonds, Ron. "Effective Schools for the Urban Poor." *Effective Schools and School Improvement.* Ronald S. Brandt, ed. Alexandria: Association for Supervision and Curriculum Development, 1989: 2–9.

Edmonds, Ron. "Some Schools Work and More Can." *Social Policy* April 1979: 28–32.

Edmonds, Ronald and Larry Lezotte. "The Correlates of School Effectiveness." Distributed at Second Annual School Effectiveness and Organizational Change Workshop. January 1985.

Elmore, Richard F. and Associates. *Restructuring Schools: The Next Generation of Educational Reform.* Jossey-Bass Education Series. San Francisco: Jossey-Bass, 1991.

Emerson, R. W. "Essays and English Traits." Charles W. Eliot, ed. *The Harvard Classics.* vol. 5. New York: P. F. Collier & Son, 1909.

Fiske, Edward B. with Sally Reed and R. Craig Sautter. *Smart Schools, Smart Kids: Why Do Some Schools Work?* New York: Simon and Schuster, 1991.

Flinchbaugh, Robert W. The *21st Century Board of Education: Planning, Leading, Transforming.* Lancaster, Technomic, 1993.

Gardner, Howard. *Multiple Intelligences: The Theory in Practice.* New York: Basic Books, 1993.

Gatti, Richard D. and Daniel J. Gatti. *Encyclopedic Dictionary of School Law.* West Nyack: Parker, 1975.

Gault, Annette and Joseph Murray. "The Implications of High Expectations for Bilingual Students." *Journal of Educational Equity and Leadership* 7.8 (Winter 1987): 301–317. Abstract. *Effective Schools Research Abstracts.* 4.3 (1989–1990).

Genck, Fredric H. and Allen J. Klingenberg. *The School Board's Responsibility: Effective Schools Through Effective Management.* Springfield: Illinois Association of School Boards, 1978.

Geneen, Harold with Alvin Moscow. *Managing.* Garden City: Doubleday, 1984.

Glass, Gene V and Mary Lee Smith. *Meta-Analysis of Research on the Relationship of Class-Size and Achievement.* The Class Size and Instruction Project, Leonard S. Cahen, Principal Investigator. San Francisco: Far West Laboratory of Educational Research and Development, September 1978.

Glenn, Charles Leslie, Jr. *The Myth of the Common School.* Amherst: University of Massachusetts Press, 1988.

Goens, George A. and Sharon I.R. Clover. *Mastering School Reform.* Boston: Allyn and Bacon, 1991.

Goleman, Daniel. *Emotional Intelligence.* New York: Bantam Books, 1995.

Goodlad, John and Robert H. Anderson. *The Nongraded Elementary School.* New York: Harcourt, Brace and World, 1963.

Goodlad, John I., Roger Soder, and Kenneth A. Sirotnik, eds. *The Moral Dimensions of Teaching*. San Francisco: Jossey-Bass, 1990.

Goodman, Richard H., Luann Fulbright, and William G. Zimmerman, Jr. *Getting There from Here: School Board Superintendent Collaboration: Creating a School Governance Team Capable of Raising Student Achievement*. Marlborough: New England School Development Council and Educational Research Service, 1997.

Grant, Carl A. and Christine E. Sleeter. "Race, Class, and Gender and Abandoned Dreams." *Teachers College Record*. 90.1 (Fall 1988):19–40.

Hafer, Alan. "The Relationship of Number of Administrators to Central Office Functions in Small-Sized School Districts." Diss. Un. Colorado, 1980.

Hampel, Robert. *The Last Little Citadel: American High Schools Since 1940*. Boston: Houghton Mifflin, 1986.

Hanushek, Erik Alan, et al. *Making Schools Work: Improving Performance and Controlling Costs*. Washington: Brookings Institution, 1994.

Heckscher, Charles C. *The New Unionism: Employee Involvement in the Changing Corporation*. New York: Basic Books, 1988.

Henderson, Anne. "The Evidence Continues to Grow: Parent Involvement Improves Student Achievement." (National Committee for Citizens in Education: Parkway. Abstract. *Effective Schools Research Abstracts*. 2.4 (1987–1988).

Herrnstein, Richard J. and Charles Murray, *The Bell Curve: Intelligence and Class Structure in American Life*. New York: Free Press, 1994.

Hesselbein, Frances, Marshall Goldsmith and Richard Beckhard, eds. *The Leader of the Future*. Drucker Foundation Future Series. San Francisco: Jossey-Bass, 1996.

Hirsch E. D., Jr. *Cultural Literacy: What Every American Needs to Know*. Boston: Houghton Mifflin, 1981.

Hoover, Mary Rhodes. "Characteristics of Black Schools at Grade Level: A Description." *Reading Teacher*. 31.7 (1978): 757–762.

Houle, Cryil Owen. *Governing Boards: Their Nature and Nurture*. San Francisco: Jossey-Bass, 1983.

Johnson, Robert. "Dollars Don't Mean Success in Calif. District." *Education Week on the Web*. December, 3, 1997.

Jones, Rebecca. "What Works." *American School Board Journal*. April 1988: 28–32.

Joyce, Bruce, James Wolf and Emily Calhoun. *The Self-Renewing School*. Alexandria: Association for Supervision and Curriculum Development, 1993.

Kaufman, Roger and Jerry Herman. *Strategic Planning in Education: Rethinking, Restructuring, Revitalizing*. Lancaster: Technomic, 1991.

Kidder, Tracy. *Among School Children*. New York: Avon, 1989.

Kilmann, Ralph H., Mary J. Saxton, Roy Serpa and Associates. *Gaining Control of the Corporate Culture*. San Francisco: Jossey-Bass, 1986.

Bibliography

Konnert, M. William and John J. Augenstein. *The Superintendency in the Nineties: What Superintendents and Board Members Need to Know*. Lancaster: Technomic, 1990.

Kozol, Jonathan. *Savage Inequalities: Children in America's Schools*. New York: Harper, 1992.

Kozol, Jonathan. *The Night Is Dark and I Am Far from Home*. New Revised Edition. New York: Simon and Schuster, 1990.

Kriegel, Robert J. and Louis Patler. *If It Ain't Broke: Break It! And Other Unconventional Wisdom for a Changing Business World*. New York: Warner, 1991.

Kulick, James A. and Chen-Lin C. Kulick. "Effects of Ability Grouping on Student Achievement." *Equity and Excellence* 23.1–2. (Spring 1987) 27–30.

Lasner, William. *Veritas*. Philadelphia: Regan Books, 1997.

Law, Charles J., Jr. *Tech Prep Education: A Total Quality Approach*. Lancaster: Technomic, 1994.

Leithwood, K. A. and P. J. Montgomery. "The Role of the Elementary School Principal in Program Improvement," *Review of Educational Research*. 52.3 (1982): 309–339.

Levine, David, Robert Lowe, Bob Peterson, and Rita Tenorio, eds. *Rethinking Schools: An Agenda for Change*. New York: New Press, 1995.

Lewis, Anne. *Restructuring America's Schools*. Arlington: American Association of School Administrators, 1989.

Lewis, James, Jr. *Achieving Excellence in Our Schools...By Taking Lessons from America's Best-Run Companies*. Westbury: J. L. Wilkerson, 1986.

Lewis, James, Jr. *Excellent Organizations: How to Develop and Manage Them Using Theory Z*. New York: J. L. Wilkerson, 1985.

Machiavelli, Niccolo. "The Prince." Charles W. Eliot, ed. The Harvard Classics. vol. 36. New York: P. F. Collier & Son, 1909.

Mackenzie, Donald E. "Research for School Improvement: An Appraisal of Some Recent Trends," *Educational Researcher*. 12.4 (1983): 5–17.

Mann, Horace. *Life and Works of Horace Mann*. 5 vols. Boston: Life and Shepard Publishers, 1891.

Martin, Reed. *Extraordinary Children, Ordinary Lives: Stories Behind Special Education Case Law*. Champaign: Research Press, 1991.

Maryland State Department of Education. "Process Evaluation: A Comprehensive Study of Outliers." *Effective Schools Abstracts* 1.3 (1986–1987).

Marzano, Robert J. *A Different Kind of Classroom: Teaching with Dimensions of Learning*. Alexandria: Association for Supervision and Curriculum Development, 1992.

Marzano, Robert J., et al. *Teacher's Manual: Dimensions of Learning*. Alexandria: Association for Supervision and Curriculum Development, 1992.

Mauriel, John J. *Strategic Leadership for Schools: Creating and Sustaining Productive Change*. San Francisco: Jossey-Bass, 1989.

McCormack-Larkin, Maureen. "Change in Urban Schools," *Journal of Negro Education*. 54.3 (1985): 409–415.

McEwan, Elaine K. *7 Steps to Effective Instructional Leadership*. New York: Scholastic, 1994.

McGuinness, Diane. *Why Our Children Can't Read: And What We Can Do About It*. New York: Free Press, 1997.

McLuhan, T. C. *Touch the Earth: A Self-Portrait of Indian Existence*. New York: Pocket Books, 1972.

Meyers, Ellen. *Changing Schools, Changing Roles—Redefining the Role of the Principal in a Restructured School*. New York: Teachers Network, 1995.

Monroe, Paul. *A Brief Course in the History of Education*. New York: Macmillan, 1916.

Morgan, Gareth. *Images of Organization*. Beverly Hills: Sage, 1986.

Mortimore, Peter and Pam Sammons. "New Evidence on Effective Elementary Schools," *Educational Leadership*. 45.1 (1987):4–8.

Murnane, Richard J. and Frank Levy. "Why Money Matters Sometimes." *Education Week on the Web*. September 11, 1996.

Murphy, John and Jeffry Schiller. *Transforming America's Schools: An Administrators' Call to Action*. La Salle: Open Court, 1992.

Naisbitt, John and Patricia Aburdene. *Reinventing the Corporation: Transforming Your Job and Your Company for the New Information Society*. New York: Warner, 1985.

National Association of Secondary School Principals. *Breaking Ranks: Changing an American Institution*. Reston: National Association of Secondary School Principals, 1996.

National Commission on Excellence in Education. *A Nation at Risk: The Imperative for Educational Reform: A Report to the Nation and the Secretary of Education, United States Department of Education*. Washington: U.S. Government Printing Office, 1983.

National Education Association. *How Education Spending Matters to Economic Development*. Washington: National Education Association, 1995.

National Education Association. *Report of the Committee of Ten on Secondary School Studies*. New York: American Book Company, 1894.

"National News Roundup." *Education Week on the Web*. October 5, 1994.

National School Boards Association. *Becoming a Better Board Member: A Guide to Effective School Board Service*. Alexandria, 1982.

National Union Fire Insurance Company. School Leaders Errors and Omissions Policy.

Nemko, Marty and Nemko, Barbara. *How to Get Your Child a "Private School Education in a Public School" Without Any Extra Costs or New Taxes*. Washington: Acropolis Books, 1986.

Niklason, Lucille B. "Nonpromotion: A Pseudoscientific Solution," *Psychology in the Schools*. 21 (1984) 485–499. Center on Evaluation, Development, Research, Hot Topics Series: Student Promotion and Retention. Bloomington: Phi Delta Kappa. 125–139.

Noll, James Wm. *Taking Sides: Clashing Views on Controversial Educational Issues*. 2nd. edition. Guilford: Duskin, 1983.

Nolte, Chester. *How to Survive in Teaching: The Legal Dimension*. Chicago: Teach'em, 1978.

Northwest Regional Educational Laboratory. *Effective Schooling Practices: A Research Synthesis 1990 Update*. Onward to Excellence. Portland: Northwest Regional Educational Laboratory, 1990.

Nye, Barbara A., et al. "Smaller Classes Really Are Better." *American School Board Journal*. May 1992: 31–33.

Oakes, Jeannie. *Keeping Track: How Schools Structure Inequality*. New Haven: Yale University Press, 1985.

Bibliography

Oakes, Jeannie, et al. "Detracking: The Social Construction of Ability, Cultural Politics and Resistance to Reform," *Teachers College Record*. 98.3 (Spring 1997): 482–510.

Oakes, Jeannie and Karen Hunter Quartz, eds., *Creating New Educational Communities*, Ninety-fourth Yearbook of the National Society for the Study of Education. Part I. Chicago: University of Chicago Press, 1995.

Odden, Allan. "Class Size and Student Achievement: Research-Based Policy Alternatives," *Educational Evaluation and Policy Analysis*, 12 (1990): 213–227.

Odden, Allan ed. *Rethinking School Finance: An Agenda for the 1990s*. San Francisco: Jossey-Bass, 1992.

Odden, Allan and Carolyn Busch. *Financing Schools for High Performance: Strategies for Improving the Use of Educational Resources*. San Francisco: Jossey-Bass, 1998.

Odom, Guy R. with Leona Rita Osfield. *Mothers, Leadership and Success*. Houston: Polybius Press, 1989.

Ornstein, Allan C. and Daniel U. Levine. *An Introduction to the Foundations of Education*. Boston: Houghton Mifflin, 1981.

Ouchi, William. *Theory Z: How American Business Can Meet the Japanese Challenge*. New York: Avon, 1982.

Pajak, Edward and Lewis McAfee. "The Principal as School Leader, Curriculum Leader," *National Association of Secondary School Principals Bulletin*. 76.547 (1992): 21–30.

Pascale, Richard Tanner and Anthony G. Athos. *The Art of Japanese Management: Applications for American Executives*. New York: Warner, 1981.

Perkins, David. *Outsmarting IQ: The Emerging Science of Learnable Intelligence*. New York: Free Press, 1995.

Peters, Tom. *Thriving on Chaos: Handbook for a Management Revolution*. New York. Alfred A. Knopf, 1987.

Peters, Tom and Nancy Austin. *A Passion for Excellence: The Leadership Difference*. New York: Random House, 1985.

Peters, Thomas J. and Robert H. Waterman, Jr. *In Search of Excellence: Lessons from America's Best-Run Companies*. New York: Harper and Row, 1982.

Pine, Patricia. *Raising Standards in Schools: Problems and Solutions*. Arlington: American Association of School Administrators, 1985.

Powell, Arthur G., Eleanor Farrar, and David K. Cohen. *The Shopping Mall High School: Winners and Losers in the Educational Marketplace*. Boston: Houghton Mifflin, 1985.

Presseisen, Barbara Z. *Unlearned Lessons: Current and Past Reforms for School Improvement*. Philadelphia: Falmer Press, 1985.

Purkey, William W. and David N. Aspy. "The Mental Health of Students: Nobody Minds? Nobody Cares?" *Person-Centered Review*. 3.1 (1988): 41–49. Abstract. *Effective Schools Research Abstracts* 3.4 (1988–1989).

"Quality Counts: The Urban Challenge, Public Education in the 50 States," *Education Week*. January 1998.

Ravitch, Diane. *The Troubled Crusade: American Education, 1945–1980*. New York: Basic Books, 1983.

Reconstruction Era Civil Rights Acts 42 U.S.C. § 1983.

Robbins, Anthony. *Awaken the Giant Within*. New York: Simon & Schuster, 1991.

Robinson, Glenn E. and James H. Wittebols. *Class Size Research: A Related Cluster Analysis for Decision Making*. Arlington: Educational Research Service, 1986.

Rose, Janet S., et al. "A Fresh Look at the Retention-Promotion Controversy." *Journal of School Psychology*, 21 (1983): 201–211. Center on Evaluation, Development, Research, Hot Topics Series: Student Promotion and Retention. Bloomington: Phi Delta Kappa. 3–13.

Rosen, Mike. "Standard Idiocy in Jeffco." *Denver Post*. May 15, 1998. B11.

Rothstein, Richard. *What Do We Know About Declining (or Rising) Student Achievement?* Arlington: Educational Research Service, 1997.

Rothstein, Richard. *Where's the Money Going? Changes in the Level and Composition of Education Spending, 1991–96*. Washington: Economic Policy Institute, 1997.

Schlafly, Phyllis. "What's Wrong with Outcome-Based Education." *School Administrator*. 51.8 (September 1994).

Scott, Ralph and Herbert J. Walberg. "Schools Alone Are Insufficient: A Response to Edmonds." *Effective Schools and School Improvement*. Ronald S. Brandt, ed. Alexandria: Association for Supervision and Curriculum Development, 1989. 10–12.

Senge, Peter M. *The Fifth Discipline: The Art and Practice of the Learning Organization*. New York: Doubleday, 1990.

Sergiovanni, Thomas J. *Moral Leadership: Getting to the Heart of School Improvement*. San Francisco: Jossey-Bass, 1992.

Shechtman, Morris R. *Working Without a Net: How to Survive and Thrive in Today's High Risk Business World*. New York: Pocket Books, 1995.

Shumate, Roger E., Thomas R. Smith and Bruce N. Willougby. *Employment and Labor Law in Wyoming*. Eau Claire: Lorman Education Services, 1996.

Sizer, Theodore Robert. *Horace's Compromise: The Dilemma of the American High School*. Boston: Houghton Mifflin, 1992.

Sizer, Theodore R. *Horace's School: Redesigning the American High School*. Boston: Houghton Mifflin, 1992.

Slavin, Robert E. "Achievement Effects of Ability Grouping in Secondary Schools: A Best-Evidence Synthesis." *Review of Educational Research*. 60.3 (1990): 471–499.

Slavin, Robert E. "Are Cooperative Learning and 'Untracking' Harmful to the Gifted?" Response to Allan. *Educational Leadership*. March 1991: 68–69.

Slavin, Robert E. "Meta Analysis in Education: How Has It Been Used?" *Educational Researcher*. October 1984.

Slavin, Robert E. *Show Me the Evidence: Proven and Promising Programs for America's Schools*. Thousand Oaks: Corwin Press, 1998.

Smey-Richman, Barbara. "Involvement in Learning for Low-Achieving Students." Research for Better Schools, Philadelphia, 1988. Abstract. Abstract. *Effective Schools Research Abstracts*. 5.9 (1986–1987).

Smith, Frank. *Insult to Intelligence: The Bureaucratic Invasion of our Classrooms*. Portsmouth: Heinemann, 1986.

Smith, Mary Lee and Lorrie A. Shepard. "What Doesn't Work: Explaining Policies of Retention in the Early Grades." *Phi Delta Kappan*. October 1987: 129–134.

Smith, Wilma F. and Richard L. Andrews. *Instructional Leadership: How Principals Make a Difference*. Alexandria: Association for Supervision and Curriculum Development, 1989.

Sowell, Thomas. *Inside American Education: The Decline, the Deception, the Dogmas*. New York: Free Press, 1993.

Squires, David A., William G. Juitt, and John K. Segars. *Effective Schools and Classrooms: A Research-Based Perspective*. Alexandria: Association for Supervision and Curriculum Development, 1989.

Stevenson, Harold W. and James W. Stigler. *The Learning Gap: Why Our Schools Are Failing and What We Can Learn from the Japanese and Chinese*. New York: William Morrow, 1992.

Strother, Deborah B., ed. *Student Promotion and Retention*. Hot Topic Series. Bloomington: Phi Delta Kappa.

Taylor, Barbara O., ed. *Case Studies in Effective Schools Research*. Dubuque: Kendall/Hunt, 1990.

Thurow, Lester. *Head to Head: The Coming Economic Battle Among Japan, Europe, and America*. New York: William Morrow, 1992.

Toch, Thomas. *In the Name of Excellence: The Struggle to Reform the Nation's Schools, Why It's Failing and What Should Be Done*. New York: Oxford University Press, 1991.

Tuchman, Barbara. *The March of Folly: From Troy to Vietnam*. New York: Alfred Knopf, 1984.

U.S. Constitution. Amendment X.

U.S. Constitution. Amendment I.

U.S. Constitution. Amendment XIV.

U.S. Department of Education. National Center for Education Statistics. *Digest of Education Statistics: 1990*. Office of Educational Research and Improvement, 1991.

U.S. Department of Education. "Strong Families, Strong Schools: Building Community Partnerships for Learning." U.S. Department of Education, Washington, September 1994. Abstract. *Effective Schools Research Abstracts*. 9.5 (1994–1995).

Vedder, Paul, ed. *Fundamental Studies in Educational Research*. Rockmount: Swets and Zeitlinger, 1990.

Wallace, Betty and William Graves. *Poisoned Apple: The Bell-Curve Crisis and How Our Schools Create Mediocrity and Failure*. New York: St. Martin's Press, 1995.

Walton, Mary. *Deming Management Method at Work*. New York: G. P. Putnam's Sons, 1990.

Waterman, Robert H., Jr. *The Renewal Factor: How the Best Get and Keep the Competitive Edge*. New York: Bantam Books. 1987.

Weldy, Gilbert R. *Principals: What They do and Who They Are*. Reston: National Association of Secondary School Principals, 1979.

Wenglinsky, Harold. *When Money Matters: How Educational Expenditures Improve Student Performance and How They Don't*. Princeton: Policy Information Center, Educational Testing Service, 1997.

Wesley, Edgar. *NEA: The First Hundred Years: The Building of the Teaching Profession*. New York: Harper and Brothers, 1957.

Wheelock, Anne. *Alternatives to Tracking and Ability Grouping*. Arlington: American Association of School Administrators, 1994.

"Where Do School Dollars Go?" *Education Week*. January 14, 1988.

Witcher, Anne and Robert L. Kennedy, eds. *Big Schools, Small Schools: What's Best for Students?* Hot Topic Series. Bloomington: Phi Delta Kappa, 1996.Wyoming Constitution. Art. VII. Section 3.

Wyoming State Department of Education. School Finance Department, 1996.

Index

A

Ability grouping. *See* Tracking
ACT 42
Age-level grade placement 55
  solution for 55
American Eagle Forum 25
American Federation of Teachers
  10
American School Board Journal
  148–149
  effective policy 148–149
Aristotle 24
At-Risk report 41
Austin, Texas, report 112–113
Average Daily Membership
  (ADM) 95–98
Average per-pupil expenditures by
  category 185

B

Bill of Rights, The 121
Binet, Alfred 41–42
Bloom, Benjamin 41
Board members
  challenges of 59
Board of education 88-89, 175
  responsibility to 175

Brookings Institution 16

C

Cardinal Principles 34
Carnegie credits 160
Chubb, John E.
  16, 17, 105, 114
Civil Rights Act of 1964, Title
  VII 43, 122
Civil rights legislation 130
Class Room Unit (CRU) 96–98
Class size 113–114
Coleman, James 43, 106, 115,
  144
Committee of Ten 34
Common school 26
Conceptual pyramidal organiza-
  tion chart 62–64

D

Deming, W. Edwards 31–32
Denver Post 3
  Standard Idiocy in Jeffco 3
District 175
  responsibility for 175
Dolan, Patrick 63
Drucker, Peter 64–65

E

E and O policies 119
Edmonds, Ron 148
Education 22–27
  attributes of 149–154
  definition of 3
  discovering purpose of 22–27
Education Week 21–22, 100, 114
Educational effectiveness 4
  forces controlling 4
Educational funding 109
  relationship with student
    achievement 109
Educational management 177–
    178
  other styles 177–178
Educational paradigm 7–15
  axiom of 8
  definition of 7
  model school district 8–14, 14–
    15
    five goals of 9–10
  survival of 14
Educational reform 69
  failure of 69
Educational Testing Service
    (ETS) 112
  eighth-grade study 112
Effective schools for the urban
    poor 143
Elementary school 48–50
Emotional Intelligence 42
Employee civil rights claims 120–
    121
  exclusions 120–121
Employees 117–118
  treatment of 117–118
Empowerment 167–168
Ethical issues
  of board members 180–183
Ethics 179–183
  fiduciary responsibility 182–
    183

F

Fiduciary 179
Five correlates of effective schools
    148
Five dimensions of learning 154–
    155
Ford Foundation 21
Fourteenth amendment 121

G

Genetics vs. environment 39–46
Gifted pupils 45
Glass, Gene V. 108–109
Goleman, Daniel 42

H

Harshbarger, Attorney General
    Scott 22
History of education
  myths of 15–16
History of education 15–16
Homosexual students 22

I

Imber, Michael 66
Intelligence, Emotional 42
IQ 41–42

K

Kindergarten 47–48

L

Litigation 117–131, 190–198
  avoiding 130
  filed in court 190–198

M

Maclaury, Bruce 16
Mann, Horace 26
Mayor of Boston 27

McCarthy, Joe 127
McGuinness, Diane 139
Michigan schools study 146–148
Moe, Terry M. 16, 17, 105

N

NAEP 44
Nation at Risk 18
National Commission on Excel-
    lence in Education
    16, 22, 45
National Education Association
    28–29, 79
    Cardinal Principles of Second-
    ary Education 29
    Committee of Ten 28–29
National Union Fire Insurance
    Company: School Lead 121
New England Primer 26
New York Office of Education
    Performance Review 145–
    146
1992 National Assessment of
    Educational Progress 110
Noncertified employees 123
Notice of Governmental Claim
    letter 186–189

O

Oakes, Jeannie 52

P

Per pupil spending 100
Plato 24–25
*Politics, Markets, and America's
    Schools* 16
Procrustes 47
Prosser Resolution 30
Public education 1–5, 18–
    19, 26–34, 168–178
    history of 26–34
        contemporary 31

progressive education 29–30
    traditional 29
    in the new century 34
    politics of 18–19
    problems 1–5
    recreating 168–170
Public employee rights 129–130

R

Ravitch, Diane 15
Reconstruction Era Civil Rights
    Acts 121
*Restructuring Our Schools: A
    Primer on Systemic Change* 62
Retention 50–51, 53-54
Robinson, Glenn E. 107–108
Rothstein, Richard 185

S

SAT 42
Schlafly, Phyllis 25
Scholastic Aptitude Test (SAT)
    15
School 176
    responsibility to 176
School administration 65–70
    problems facing 65–68
School board members 137–158
    responsibilities of 139
    rules of 159–165
School boards 5, 16-19, 26, 45–
    46, 59
    as catalysts of change 16–19
    established for 26
    providing staff development
    45–46
    tasks of 5
School districts 71–89
    Flagstone example 84–89
        lessons for school board 86
    Paradise example 71–84

three critical errors 79–81
School expenditures and learning 106–108
School finance 91–106
  equity 99–100, 101–106
  mutable rules of 92–93
School spending and success 114–115
  relationship of 114–115
Schooling 170–171
  essential elements of 170–171
Second World War 28
Secondary schools 42, 56–58
  other problems 57–59
  scheduling problems of 56
Segregation 43–44
Shanker, Albert 10
Site-based management 171–177
  important aspects of 173–175
Smaller classes 108–109, 109–111
Smith, Mary Lee 108–109
Social Darwinists 43
Socrates 24
Sophists 23
Stevenson, Harold W. 144
Superintendents 131–136
  hiring of 132–136

T

Tennessee Project Star 109–111

Tenure 118, 122-123
The March of Folly: From Troy to Vietnam 33
Top-down management 62
Total quality management 31–32
Tracking. *See* Ability grouping
Tuchman, Barbara W. 33
Twain, Mark 3

U

U.S. Supreme Court 107
United States Department of Education 106
  National Center for Education Statistics 106
  Office of Educational Research and Improvement 106

V

Vocational instruction 25

W

Where's the Money Going? Changes in the Level and Composition of Education Spending, 1991-96 185
Wittebols, James H. 107–108
Wyoming 34–38
  eighth grade examinations, November, 1915 34–38